D1475321

LAW'S ABNEGATION

LAW'S ABNEGATION

From Law's Empire to the
Administrative State

ADRIAN VERMEULE

■■■ Harvard University Press

Cambridge, Massachusetts · London, England   2016

Copyright © 2016 by the President and Fellows of Harvard College
All rights reserved
Printed in the United States of America

Second printing

Library of Congress Cataloging-in-Publication Data

Names: Vermeule, Adrian, 1968– author.
Title: Law's abnegation : from law's empire to the administrative state /
Adrian Vermeule.
Description: Cambridge, Massachusetts : Harvard University Press, 2016. |
Includes bibliographical references and index.
Identifiers: LCCN 2016015023 | ISBN 9780674971448 (alk. paper)
Subjects: LCSH: Judicial review of administrative acts—United States. |
Administrative discretion—United States. | Administrative agencies—
United States. | Administrative law—United States. | Administrative
procedure—United States. | Rule of law—United States.
Classification: LCC KF5425 .V47 2016 | DDC 342.73/06—dc23
LC record available at https://lccn.loc.gov/2016015023

For Yun Soo

Contents

There is no question of returning to the pre-1968 situation, if only for the reason that the pre-1968 situation included the conditions that led to 1968.

—Valéry Giscard d'Estaing,
quoted in Jon Elster, *Sour Grapes*

LAW'S ABNEGATION

Introduction

The Abnegation of Law's Empire

Law has voluntarily abandoned its imperial pretensions, for valid lawyerly reasons. Although in earlier eras law claimed (rightly or not) to represent the overarching impartial power that resolved and reconciled local conflicts over the activities of government, the long arc of the law has bent steadily toward deference—a freely chosen deference to the administrative state. Law has abnegated its authority, relegating itself to the margins of governmental arrangements. Although there is still a sense in which law is constitutive of the administrative state, that is so only in a thin sense—the way a picture frame can be constitutive of the picture yet otherwise unimportant, compared to the rich content at the center.

I will attempt to build up this thesis through the sheer weight of example. In area after area, lawyers and judges, working out the logical implications of their principles with a view to rational consistency, have come to the view that administrators should have broad leeway to set policy, to determine facts, to interpret ambiguous statutes, and even—in an intolerable affront to the traditional legal mind—to determine the boundaries of the administrators' own jurisdiction, acting as "judges in their own cause." I hope to show, in area after area, that legal controls crafted by actors who sought to constrain the gradual advance of administration have given way. The Maginot Lines of constraint have all collapsed or been bypassed, not because the state shoved law out of the way, but because the law working itself pure concluded that abnegation was the best course of action, from an internal standpoint. The last and greatest triumph of legalism was that law deposed itself.

That triumph is concealed by a thin fabric, in the form of an argument that judges preserve in its entirety the power to "say what the law is"; however, the argument runs, what the law says happens to be that judges should defer to agencies, within broad boundaries.[1] This form of reasoning reconciles law's abnegation with the administrative state and thereby comforts the traditional legal mind, but the reconciliation is essentially semantic. It leaves judges in possession of a nominal supremacy, reigning without ruling, like a Frankish king who does whatever his own Mayor of the Palace suggests. This overstates things a bit, because we will see that judges retain power to enforce clear statutes and more generally police the outer bounds of law, but it is still true that the locus of effective power to say what the law is hardly corresponds to the judges' nominal supremacy. Judges are the *rois fainéants* of the administrative state, with the difference that they have voluntarily ceded power.

A Self-Reinforcing Process

How did law's abnegation come about? Law works itself pure, here and elsewhere, because judges and lawyers value logical consistency. The main mechanism behind law's abnegation has been a commitment to reasoned consistency on the part of the legal profession. Once law started down the path of deference, for legitimate legal reasons—and we will see that law started down the path long ago, and began to positively run along it no later than 1932—abnegation became ever more difficult to resist, purely from an internal standpoint. Intellectual integrity demands that new problems be resolved in a fashion consistent with old ones. Consistency is never obligatory, and inconsistencies persist in local settings, but the demands of consistency exert a constant steady pressure that tells over time. Courts that start to defer later evolve principles that entail deference on many fronts, such as the principle that agencies enjoy discretion to allocate resources across cases and programs; in turn, those principles themselves become part of law's deep fabric, and increase the impetus for deference in other settings. The result is a self-reinforcing feedback process in which abnegation becomes not a betrayal of law, but the logical consequence of law's own internal commitments.

Given these dynamics, my thesis is embedded, internal, and interpretive, not abstract, external, and top-down. It is carried forward by the broad central tendencies of the caselaw in the areas I will discuss, read in light of the deferential principles generated within and by that caselaw, in a process of reflective equilibrium. I make no claims about what law's role ought to be from the standpoint of eternity. In particular, I make no abstract claims here about the optimal role of law in the administrative state or the optimal allocation of authority between courts and the administrative bureaucracy, except insofar as judges and lawyers have reasoned on the basis of such considerations. This is not a book about law; it is a book *within* law, from a lawyer's own standpoint.

The Curious Silence of Ronald Dworkin

Such are my main claims. To situate and frame them, let me begin with a puzzle about Ronald Dworkin, one of the great legal theorists of the age. The puzzle is that Dworkin essentially ignored the administrative state, so thoroughly that one suspects it had to be a case of willful blindness. Reading Dworkin's corpus one would hardly know that the administrative state existed. When he talks about institutional structure at all, he "generally assume[s] a strict division of powers between legislature, judiciary, and administration, whereby the legislature has a monopoly on making law, the judiciary on interpreting the law, and the administration merely implements the law."[2] But this is bad high-school civics. We have not had such an institutional structure for decades or centuries, if we ever did.[3] At a minimum, well before Dworkin was born, the executive and administrative sector of the state had come to structure citizens' experience of government. Today it often overshadows the classical institutions of the Constitution of 1789 altogether. The administrative state is the inescapable subject of contemporary legal theory. How could Dworkin purport to be a theorist of law, legal theory, and constitutionalism, yet say little or nothing about it?

One possibility is a massive blind spot, a product of an essentially common-law vision that knows only legislatures and courts. This blinkered vision sees the administrative state, if at all, solely in cartoonish terms: legislatures choose "policy"; agencies implement political commands at a technical level, through "utilitarian" methods; while courts are the "forum of principle."[4] As we will see, that vision is cartoonish because utilitarianism is itself a principle, because courts must certainly take the consequences of their decisions into account, and because agencies interpreting law must necessarily choose which of several competing principles to honor, how much weight to attach to principles, and what the rate of trade-off between competing principles will be. Agencies, no less than courts, are, inescapably, forums of principle.

A different possibility is that Dworkin knew a mortal threat to law's empire when he saw one but elected to remain silent, hoping the danger would somehow pass. "Courts are the capitals of law's empire, and judges are its princes," he famously wrote.[5] Dworkin's theory of adjudication—"law as integrity"—requires the idealized judge, whom Dworkin calls Hercules, to find the "right answer" by engaging in a dual process of "fit" and "justification."[6] Hercules rules in a way that both fits with the fabric of the law developed over time and that also justifies the law, putting it in its best possible light from the standpoint of political morality.[7] But the administrative state threatens law's imperial sway. It threatens to relegate courts and judges to a lower status, as marginal officials who are stationed in the outlying provinces and are charged with patrolling the very outermost boundaries of executive authority, but who are no longer central actors—no longer the guardians of principle. As the legal philosopher David Dyzenhaus puts it,

> [Dworkin's] stance of "judicial supremacism" . . . create[s] enormous difficulties for judicial review of administrative action. . . . Dworkin understands legislatures as having a monopoly on making law and judges a monopoly on its interpretation. There is no room in his account for administrative agencies that have an authority to make or interpret the law in the sense that such administrative decisions are ones to which courts have reason to defer. At most, Dworkin can concede to administrative agencies the authority to make decisions

about the policy implications of their constitutive statutes—utilitarian calculations about what decision will best advance the policy—or decisions about what the effects of different arrangements of natural justice might be. But they have no authority over legal principles—the exclusive province of the judiciary.[8]

Here is another way to put the matter, as argued by an Australian law professor, Margaret Allars, in an article that deserves more attention than it has received.[9] The critical problem is the principle of *deference to reasonable administrative decisions*—a principle found in one form or another in many or most Anglo-American legal systems[10] and thus presumably part of the larger legal fabric that Dworkin professed to respect. Allars argues that the deference principle cannot be squared with Dworkin's "law as integrity," which presupposes that judges can find a single right answer even in hard cases. I will quote Allars's summary at length, as I do not think it can be bettered:

> [A test of] unreasonableness allows potentially "incorrect" interpretations (from a Herculean standpoint) to go uncorrected by a court. What then is the correct answer in hard cases such as these? It is the task of the judge to ascertain whether the threshold of fit has been passed, not whether the interpretation would be legally correct had a court had been the primary adjudicator. If a tribunal's [i.e., an agency's] interpretation is patently unreasonable, then a reviewing court may strike it down without proceeding to identify one legally correct answer. However, the very striking down of an interpretation as patently unreasonable also amounts to holding the interpretation legally incorrect. If the tribunal's interpretation is not patently unreasonable, then the court may not interfere. In each case, there is one correct answer to the question, "Is the tribunal's interpretation patently unreasonable?" The proper task of a Herculean judge is to find that correct answer. The judge has no business asking the different question, "Is the tribunal's interpretation legally correct?"
>
> The paradox here is that the correct . . . answer for a Herculean judge . . . may not be the legally correct answer from the standpoint of law as integrity. Had the tribunal chosen another interpretation which was also not patently unreasonable, the judge would have arrived at the same correct answer, i.e. that the interpretation passed the threshold of fit. From the tribunal's perspective, any not patently

unreasonable interpretation is legally correct. The party in whose fa-
vour the tribunal made the decision has a legal right to win. From
the reviewing judge's perspective, the tribunal's interpretation is legally correct because it is not to be quashed on account of patent
unreasonableness. But from the perspective of law as integrity, the
legal correctness of the interpretation is left undecided.[11]

Distilled, Allars is pointing out that Dworkin's right-answerism can
be squared with deference to reasonable agency decision-making only
by the entirely nominal expedient of labeling any reasonable agency
decision as "correct"—an expedient that drains away the substance of
Dworkin's commitment to courts as the forum of principle and the capital of law's empire. The stark choice for Dworkin is then to abandon
either law as integrity or the principle of deference to reasonable agency
decisions. The latter course, although congenial to Dworkin's own idiosyncratic view, would be impossible to square with the settled fabric
of law as it has developed across the Anglo-American world, and would
therefore fail precisely on Dworkinian grounds.

Abnegation, and Its Limits

My thesis generalizes the insights of Dyzenhaus and Allars. Dworkin's
reluctance to face the challenge of the administrative state, his apparently willful self-blinding, was fully justified, for there was no
internal-legal answer he could give that would preserve the dominion of law. From a lawyer's internal point of view, the running
conflict between law's empire and the administrative state is more
or less at an end. The conflict ended not by conquest, not by Richard
Posner's oddly violent fantasy of law being "overcome,"[12] but instead
by a considered, deliberate, voluntary, and unilateral surrender, an
abnegation of authority by the law. The law itself decided to bow to the
administrative state, to leash itself—in Francis Bacon's image—"under
the throne."[13]

The surrender has been only conditional and partial; lawyers play
a role both within the bureaucracy and before courts, and judges have
not closed up shop altogether. They continue to review administrative decision-making for conformity to Constitution and statute where
the legal texts are quite clear, for basic rationality of decision-making,

and for factual plausibility. Yet it *is* an abnegation, relative to any plausible historical benchmark. By and large courts have become marginal actors highly deferential to the administrative state, with occasional exceptions that are more salient than consequential. The judges' crouching posture inevitably affects the status and importance of law outside the courts. The consequence of judicial deference has been to open a larger space, more room to maneuver, for nonlawyers attempting to set the direction of policy choices within the bureaucracy.

Law exists both inside and outside the courts, but the heartland of law's empire has always been judicial decision-making.[14] And today, judicial review of agency action is becoming or has become, in area after area, a highly deferential exercise that attempts only to determine whether administrative agencies have clearly gone beyond the outer bounds of the defensible, whether in a legal sense, a policy sense, or a factual sense. A generation ago, Martin Shapiro already discerned the "root of American judicial review, that judges are to declare unlawful whatever they find to be *very* unreasonable."[15] Today a more accurate version would cast Shapiro's idea in negative terms: judges have decided that they may declare unlawful *only* what they find to be very unreasonable. Shapiro's dictum has been transformed from a sufficient to a necessary condition.

On this view, judges should ensure that agencies stay within the boundaries of the statutes that delegate authority to them, but precisely because the statutes delegate authority to the agencies, the role of judges is to review, not to decide. The question then becomes what judicial review adds to the initial agency decision—a question about the marginal costs and benefits of legalism. Once judicial review is conceived in this way, the marginalist logic of the situation, working itself pure, suggests to courts that agencies with front-line responsibility are better positioned to construe statutory gaps and ambiguities, even when the issue involves the scope of the agency's own power or "jurisdiction." Likewise, judges should monitor the rationality of agency decision-making, but experience has taught the judges (or most of them, most of the time) that rationality is a thin requirement, compatible with a very broad range of justifications at different levels of generality. The caselaw now reflects that experience and the consensus in favor of a thin and undemanding version of rationality review—despite the textbooks that, lagging behind the law, still talk of judges' obligation to take a "hard look" at agency decisions.

Abnegation as Integrity: A Dworkinian Argument

My methodological commitments follow from this framing. I mean to offer an internal lawyer's argument throughout, rather than an argument from economics or political science or political theory. Indeed the argument throughout is itself Dworkinian in the sense that it is neither descriptive nor normative but rather *interpretive*. The aim is to uncover the best constructive interpretation of law's trajectory—"law as integrity." Thus I systematically tack back and forth between fit and justification. Rather than theorize from first principles, I will attempt to show that, conditional on accepting the broad thrust of the extant legal doctrine, abnegation based on good lawyerly reasoning is the best principled justification of that doctrine. Using all the traditional lawyer's tools of precedent, constitutional and statutory text, and mid-level principles of institutional design and operation, I aim to show that the law has leashed itself under the throne of the administrative state; and it has done so because the best internal understanding of the legal arguments, worked pure by virtue of a commitment to reasoned consistency, has indicated that it should.

The principled justifications that I will discuss are therefore very different than the sort of justifications that might be offered on a blank slate. My project is emphatically not to pronounce on the optimal design of legal and administrative institutions or on the optimal allocation of authority between courts and administrators in the modern state. Rather I ask, at a lower level of generality, "What set of principles would one have to hold in order to fit-and-justify the central tendencies of the law's development?" And abnegation, the self-marginalization of law, is the basic answer. Fit does not of course require that every last case be assumed to be correct; a good Dworkinian theory also has critical edge and allows treating some decisions as mistakes or outliers. I will claim that episodically intrusive lower-court decisions are out of step with the very deferential thrust of Supreme Court decisions, for example. But fit does mean that one does not try to recreate legal doctrine or institutional arrangements from scratch.

There is some irony in a Dworkinian argument that, on the best understanding of law's trajectory, law has abdicated its imperial pretensions, and has done so for valid lawyerly reasons. But there is no real methodological puzzle here; good Dworkinians have to follow integrity where it leads. The only thing that makes it surprising is that Dworkin himself and many Dworkinians have romanticized courts and the common law. But all that is idiosyncratic, merely biographical and sociological. I mean to detach Dworkinian integrity from Dworkin's own peculiar proclivities, and the proclivities of his epigones.

Law: In Court and Out

I will focus throughout on judicial review of administrative action, documenting the abnegation of law in that setting. Two related issues then arise: what of law outside of courts? And why focus on judicial review? Courts and judicial review are a slightly unfashionable topic in an era in which every legal academic—in the United States anyway—interested in the administrative state writes on the institutions of the executive branch. Furthermore, it is obvious that the abnegation of law is in part a consequence of decisions by statutory lawmakers—the President and Congress, operating as a joint lawmaking process under Article I, Section 7 of the Constitution—to delegate ever-greater discretion to the President and to agencies by statute. Congress episodically rouses itself to enact framework statutes intended to constrain executive power in a global way; the spate of framework statutes enacted after Watergate, such as the National Emergencies Act and the War Powers Resolution, are classic examples. But these statutes are mostly dead letters, for the spasm of congressional resolve that leads to their enactment is not sustained over time, and the frameworks go unenforced and fall into a kind of quasi-desuetude.[16] Not all of these framework constraints and institutional innovations are ineffectual, by any means; perhaps the most consequential has been the creation of Inspectors General.[17] By and large, however, the scope for executive action has grown steadily, at least since World War II.

Law certainly exists outside of courts as well as within them. Agency lawyers, for example, are important actors in the administrative state; their struggle with other professionals for control of agency decision-making is the major topic of Chapter 6. The major topic of the book as a whole, however, is law within courts. I will focus on courts and judicial review in order to speak directly to the traditional legal mind that Dworkin so perfectly represented, and that is so remarkably persistent, in virtue of the professional substructure and culture that supports it.

The culture of law and lawyering, especially in its common-law guise, has always felt, instinctively and in a sense quite correctly, that "courts are the capitals of law's empire, and judges are its princes."[18] The sense in which this is correct is that law cannot maintain an imperial role if it loses control of its heartland, courts, and judicial review. I will try to show that this is precisely law's strategic situation.

The paradox, however, is that this situation arises because of, not despite, the efforts of the legal profession in general and the judges in particular. The paradox of the traditional legal mind is that law displaces itself over time. The arc of administrative law and judicial review has bent toward deference at least since 1932—my benchmark year, as I will explain shortly. The reasons why it has done so illustrate a larger theme that transcends the divide between law-inside-courts and law-outside-courts.

The tools that lawyers deploy, whether or not those lawyers happen to work in courts, themselves include a suite of arguments and ideas that encourage increased deference to nonlegal modes of decision-making, especially when the function of lawyers comes to be seen not as primary decision-making but as secondary oversight and review. This is particularly true as the questions that confront the administrative state become ever larger, less individualized, and more complex. Under the conditions of complexity, high information costs, and (hence) uncertainty that describe the frontier of agency policy-making—consider health care, climate change, terrorism, and biotechnology—policy-makers in agencies can claim both greater democratic legitimacy and greater technical competence than lawyers can, and the marginal value added that lawyers provide comes to seem questionable. Whatever the external causes, forces, and pressures that have led to the dominance of the administrative state, law also tends to recognize internal legal arguments for allowing itself to be displaced by other approaches. Law thus displaces itself from within.

Constitutional Abnegation and the Scope of Government

My story is about administrative law, not constitutional law. Not directly, anyway. Public law is one whole, both in the sense that all administrative law presumes some background allocation of constitutional authority, and in the sense that "administrative law" as an academic field itself encompasses relevant parts of constitutional law; an example is the law of procedural due process that I will discuss in Chapter 3. So constitutional themes will recur throughout, and we will constantly be glancing at background constitutional allocations— including the judges' ever-more expansive conception of the scope of the national government's legislative powers over time.

This is not at all to say that the story of law's abnegation is confined to administrative law. Far from it. Were constitutional law my topic here, I would be prepared to suggest a parallel story, such that the domain of constitutional judicial review has narrowed over time. This story is partly obscured by the growing visibility of the Supreme Court as a media presence in American life over the course of the twentieth century and into the twenty-first, driven in turn by the dramatic salience of a tiny subset of the issues the Court addresses: abortion, gay marriage, and the like. But as Fred Schauer has demonstrated, convincingly to my mind, the Court's constitutional agenda actually occupies a tiny fraction of the nation's agenda-space.[19] Far from all public issues becoming constitutional issues, the Court has largely retreated from the public sphere, instead policing a subset of free-speech issues and personal liberties, and very occasionally policing government "takings" of property rights.[20] For the most part, however, the Court has abandoned social and economic regulation to the other branches of government, which increasingly means to the administrative state.

Finally, and relatedly, we will have to be alert to a basic but recurring confusion: between the administrative state and the scope of national governmental power. The two questions are sometimes conflated in critiques of the administrative state, with the critic complaining about administrative power, but on grounds that would hold even if all relevant rules were directly enacted by Congress itself—meaning that the complaint is actually addressed to the scope-of-power question. A well-formed critique of the administrative state ought to address the allocation of power *within* the national government, not the scope of power that law affords to the national government as such (including its legislature and, let us remember, its courts).

A Baseline

With these preliminaries cleared away, let us turn to an obvious but indispensable question: what is the benchmark or baseline for measuring the abnegation of the law? Any choice is somewhat arbitrary, in that the process I describe has occurred over an extended period. But a useful baseline and starting point, for reasons I will explain in Chapter 1, is Chief Justice Hughes's colossal effort in 1932, in *Crowell v. Benson*,[21] to achieve a stable accommodation of the claims of law and the imperatives of bureaucratic government, a stable equilibrium between law and state. But the Peace of 1932 has long since collapsed. Every important element of the *Crowell* framework has come unglued; and in every case, the result has been a broadening of administrative discretion—not invariably, and not without occasional setbacks and temporary retrenchments, but steadily, like a stock market rising over time despite occasional dips. Indeed, as I will show with reference to a case decided in 2013, *City of Arlington v. FCC*,[22] views that were unquestioned and indispensable components of the traditional lawyer's framework—such as the view that agencies should never have the power to determine the limits of their own jurisdiction—have now become conceptually incomprehensible to the Justices themselves, even to those Justices who are most anxious about the administrative state.

The Arc of Law Bends toward Deference

Is abnegation already the state of the law, or is it merely the law's current trajectory, to be followed unless and until some force deflects it? The answer hovers between those possibilities; abnegation is an incompletely realized process, a now and not-yet, both the shape of the past and the arc of the future. The abnegation of the law has been well underway for many decades, viewed in the large. I will claim that the fundamental logic of *Crowell v. Benson* is marginalist: the implicit question is whether judicial review, at the margin, adds net value to the process of institutional decision-making that begins with agency decision-making. That marginalist logic, working itself pure, is the driving internal logic that pushes law toward ever-greater abnegation. Abnegation, from the internal point of view, gathers strength when lawyers and judges come to doubt whether law has very much to add to agency decision-making. In the extreme, they may even come to worry that law makes things worse, not better.

Viewed in the small, of course, there are eddies and countercurrents in the broad stream flowing from *Crowell* to the present. Deference to agency interpretations of law has, since 1984, been grounded in the so-called *Chevron* decision,[23] which—roughly speaking—says that unless statutes clearly contradict the agency's interpretation, courts will uphold that interpretation so long as it is reasonable. In Chapter 1, I will examine some of the limitations to *Chevron*, and some recent opinions (mostly separate opinions, not binding opinions for the Court) that attempt to destabilize it. I will also suggest, however, that these countercurrents are weak compared to the long-term trend of judicial deference to agency legal interpretations, which predates *Chevron* by many decades and which would persist in *de facto* form even if *Chevron* were overruled *de jure*.[24] The trend of deference (to reasonable decisions on either law, fact or policy, or all three) is not derived from any one judicial decision; it is a global feature of law in the administrative state, observable in many legal systems over time.

Viewed in long-term perspective, the strongest, most sustained, and best-known countercurrent to law's abnegation does not involve agency legal interpretations or *Chevron* deference. Rather it is the body of caselaw known as "hard look review," developed in the 1960s and 1970s, which occasionally yields stringent judicial oversight of the rationality of agency decision-making. Lawyers and legal academics, however, chronically overstate the extent and prevalence of "hard look review." In part this is because cases that overturn agency action are more salient and exciting, in part because many legal theorists who lack an appreciation for the practicalities of governance have a congenital horror of administrative discretion. That horror, in turn, is sometimes exacerbated by a political and ideological conjunction: left-wing lawyers fear administrative discretion in the administration of "new property" and welfare benefits,[25] while right-wing lawyers fear administrative discretion over old property and economic regulation.[26] In reality, however, the "hard look" era was never very robust and seems to have passed its peak, as I will discuss in Chapter 5. Textualist judges have even begun to question whether "hard look review," and the closely related notion that informal agency rulemaking should amount to a "paper hearing" subject to judicially developed procedural requirements, can be squared with the text of the Administrative Procedure Act (APA).[27] For the first time in many a year, it has become possible to imagine a judicial retrenchment that would repudiate the doctrinal innovations of the 1960s and 1970s altogether.

Administrative law is a dynamic system, constantly in flux. At any given moment, some development or other will grip the attention of lawyers and judges. As of this writing, for example, the Supreme Court (with eight members) recently decided a challenge to a policy statement by the Obama administration on enforcement, or nonenforcement, of the immigration laws with respect to certain illegal immigrants with children lawfully present.[28] The lower court ruled that the policy statement amounted to a binding regulation and thus should have been promulgated with notice-and-comment, under the APA. The Court split 4–4 on this issue and thus affirmed the lower court, although such split decisions have no binding precedential value, according to the Court's own practice. Headlines and lawyers will make much of the controversy. Within a few years, however, it will recede into the dim recesses of the lawbooks and join the vast collection of administrative-law cases, most of which are forgotten, however heated the controversies when decided. The long-term trends of the law, however, will not be stopped or even redirected by any one opinion. It would take a sustained effort by the Court, over a generation or more, to reverse the arc of law's abnegation; and for internal legal reasons, because of law's internal imperatives, such an effort is impossible, or so I will argue.

The Scholar as Undertaker, and as Midwife

If abnegation is both the shape of administrative law's past and the arc of its future, what is the role of the legal scholar? I will argue that there is a tension at the heart of libertarian and originalist calls for a return to the classical Constitution of separated powers. The tension is that the classical system itself, operating through the institutions of separated powers, produced the administrative state in the first place. It is not as though the administrative state was created by a coup. Its creators were the very institutions that the opponents of the administrative state valorize. If it were abolished, and the classical Constitution reinstated, the same operative processes would ensure that the administrative state would in all probability be created again, in a kind of eternal recurrence. Doubtless the recurrence would not take exactly the same form, but whatever form it did take would serve roughly similar functional purposes.

If there is no possibility of *permanently* reversing or deflecting the arc of the administrative state, what then is the point of theorizing about it? In my view the analyst can still perform useful services as both undertaker and midwife. As undertaker, the analyst can bury law's imperial pretensions, which law itself has decided to abandon, but which still inspire nostalgia in significant sectors of the legal academy. As midwife, legal scholars can help to "shorten and lessen the birth-pangs"[29] as the administrative state is born from the womb of law. Although the arc of law bends toward abnegation in the long run, in the short run counter-eddies and isolated decisions that assert a more intrusive judicial role may cause interim social harms, including the haze of legal uncertainty, deadweight losses arising from unproductive litigation, confusion produced by the minority of decisions that are out of step with the broad trend toward abnegation, and incentives for agencies to engage in the "science charade,"[30] ginning up fake reasons to offer courts that relentlessly demand fully rationalized decision-making even under conditions of severe uncertainty. Judicial decisions that do these things are less frequent than they were, but we will see plenty of them in what follows.

The legal analyst may then play a modest but constructive role in reducing these interim social harms. Analytics may help by refuting bad legalist arguments against judicial deference, by dispelling embedded assumptions that cramp the traditional legal mind, and by explaining theoretical points of direct practical relevance for administrative law, such as the theory of decision-making under uncertainty. I will undertake those tasks here.

Plan of the Book

Chapter 1 begins with some essential preliminary work, both constructive and destructive. The constructive part is that I will explain the baseline from which I measure abnegation, the famous 1932 decision in *Crowell v. Benson*. The attempt to create lines of compromise and demarcation between the law and the state, a compromise central to *Crowell*, largely failed. From the baseline of 1932, law's abnegation is plain. Almost every element of the *Crowell* framework is no longer law, at least not in anything like its original form.

One might reason that since the *Crowell* synthesis that was supposed to legitimate the administrative state is no longer the law, the legality of the administrative state itself comes into question. And indeed a somewhat similar logic seems to underlie the wholesale critiques of the administrative state that I will examine. It is true that the law itself has ceded ever more discretion to the administrative state over time. Entirely false, however, is the suggestion, usually insinuated without being openly defended, that the state has brutally knocked law out of the way, that the state has violated or is constantly violating the rules of law. Not so. Law's abnegation has been essentially voluntary, a working pure of internal legal imperatives, or so I will aim to demonstrate throughout. Law's greatest triumph has been to subordinate itself, to efface itself, in the interests of working out its own logic.

The wholesale legalist critiques of the administrative state come in two broad versions. In one version, originalist constitutional lawyers like Gary Lawson claim that administrative law is inconsistent with the written Constitution of 1789; in a second version, Philip Hamburger portrays American administrative law as inconsistent with deep principles of a putative Anglo-American constitution (small-c), whose centerpiece is the common law. I examine and reject the claims of both; indeed the two views each tends to undermine the other. On the one hand, Lawson's account is unconvincing for the set of judges—and this includes almost all judges, and would emphatically have included all lawyers of the founding generation—who attach any weight at all to common-law norms of "liquidation" of constitutional rules through practice and the development of judicial precedent over time. On the other hand, Hamburger's account fails to understand basic constitutional and statutory principles that underpin American administrative law and that in some cases have done so since the beginning. Although the two critiques of administrative law are in tension with one another, both can be wrong.

Chapter 2 focuses the constitutional analysis on the separation of powers, a centerpiece of classical constitutionalism, and one which many critics claim is flatly inconsistent with the administrative state. I argue on the contrary that American law—constitutional, statutory, and judge-made law—has come to recognize that the separation of powers must not be made into an idol. The separation of powers must be traded off against other considerations and goods; it is to be optimized, not strictly maximized nor treated as an inviolable side-constraint.

Indeed, the separation of powers at the constitutional level itself entails departures from the separation of powers at the level of agency decision-making structure. The separation of powers at the higher level licenses its own violation at the lower level—an abnegation of authority. In this sense, the classical separation of powers is self-undermining. The classical lawmaking process itself has systematically decided to depart from the classical arrangements of separated powers by conferring fused powers and combined functions upon agencies. It follows that there is a pragmatic contradiction in calling for a return to the classical order of separated powers, when that order has in effect overturned itself in a large-scale act of abnegation, generating the very institutions that have partially superseded it. Throughout Chapters 1 and 2, accordingly, I argue that calls for a return to the classical order are self-defeating.

This line of argument would fail if the administrative state had been generated, not by the operation of the classical institutions of the Constitution, but instead by the "abdication" or malfunction of those institutions, somehow defined. I will argue, however, that "abdication" (however defined) is not a plausible account of the genesis of the administrative state. On the congressional side, the process from the beginning of the Republic has been one of considered, cumulative grants of statutory authority to agencies, combined with ongoing adjustment of authority, procedural checks, congressional monitoring, and occasional abolition of agencies. On the judicial side, the whole book is an attempt to show that judges have not somehow abandoned their office in the course of granting agencies ever-broader discretion; rather they have granted that discretion through and by means of ordinary legal argumentation, conducted in good faith, based on ordinary legal sources, and from an internal point of view.

It is not as though the classical institutions were simply overborne by an outside force, like the Japanese Government in 1945, and coerced into creating new legal structures. Nor is it the case that those institutions abdicated their functions in a sudden gust of political passion, like the debased Roman Senate clamoring for an Emperor. Rather the long-run, accumulated institutional operation of separated powers, checks and balances, and judicial decision-making on questions of constitutional and statutory law, together gave birth to the institutions of the administrative state, and nurtured them to maturity. In the fullness of time, those institutions would grow to overshadow their progenitors. But they are the heirs and the offspring of the classical institutions, not alien impositions.

Chapter 3 illustrates law's abnegation in another quasi-constitutional setting, the law of procedural due process. The law of due process is quasi-constitutional because the Court has, in the modern era, consistently tied due process law to nonconstitutional entitlements created by legislatures and agencies. Inconsistently, however, the courts have insisted that the procedural obligations imposed by due process are still a question exclusively for the courts. I take the historical arc of procedural due process law to its logical conclusion, arguing that entitlements and procedure are pragmatically inextricable (although not conceptually fused), and that as a consequence courts should defer to reasonable agency decisions about how much process to afford. Indeed, in this area as in others, the law has already taken just this course, or so I claim. Law has increasingly abnegated its authority over procedural due process to agencies, not because law has been violated or forced aside but because courts have traced out the internal logic of their own commitments and decisions, and worked them pure.

Chapters 4 and 5, a pair, turn to a central component of administrative law proper in the current regime: judicial review of agency decision-making for rationality, under the "arbitrary and capricious" test of Section 706 of the APA. Many agencies shifted from adjudication to rulemaking in the 1960s and 1970s, an especially severe blow to the Hughes synthesis of law and the administrative state, which was largely premised on the implicit assumption that agencies would be constrained by court-like adjudicative procedures in most of their behavior.[31] Accordingly, after the rulemaking revolution, courts turned to rationality review as one of the remaining constraints on agency discretion in rulemaking—especially after *Vermont Yankee*[32] barred judges from adding to the bare-bones rulemaking procedures laid out in the APA. So rationality review of major agency rulemaking has been a battleground for a generation at least.

The fog of war has, apparently, confused many observers. Legal academics often speak of an era of stringent "hard look review" after a decision in 1983, *Motor Vehicle Manufacturers Association v. State Farm.*[33] The case involved review of a controversial deregulatory policy by the Reagan Administration, repealing certain auto safety requirements; the Court clearly felt that the policy was inadequately justified in technocratic terms. In the academic mind, *State Farm* symbolizes stringent arbitrariness review and a strong judicial commitment to oversight of agency rationality. Yet all this is basically a myth. The caselaw simply does not reflect it—certainly not at the level of the Supreme Court, and for the most part not at the level of the lower courts either, as I will detail. What is true is that occasional decisions of lower courts, especially from a subset of judges on the Court of Appeals for the District of Columbia Circuit, employ searching rationality review. But overwhelmingly, the Court itself has been resolute in protecting agency discretion from this sort of episodic interference by aggressive lower courts, as Chapters 4 and 5 both aim to show. The Justices have come to see, quite rightly, that agencies may often have excellent second-order reasons to behave nonrationally or arbitrarily, to fail to compare alternatives, to ignore relevant policy considerations, or to make erroneous decisions. So rationality review is thin, meaning that it is capacious and forgiving, sometimes allowing agencies to provide second-order reasons to explain their inability to give first-order reasons. A corollary is that "hard look review" is more notional than real, certainly at the level of the Supreme Court.

Chapter 4 begins with the role of uncertainty in the administrative state and its relationship to rationality review. Under conditions of uncertainty, where agencies have no choice but to make a leap in the dark one way or another, it may even be perfectly rational, or reasonable, for agencies to make decisions that are arbitrary—using arbitrariness in a decision-theory sense, not a legal sense. Such decisions would be rationally arbitrary, but for that very reason they should not count as "arbitrary and capricious" within the meaning of Section 706 of the APA. Courts should recognize—and, I will claim, do recognize, or at least the Supreme Court recognizes—that a ban on "arbitrariness" in a legal sense permits a wide range of agency behavior that is arbitrary in a larger theoretical sense.

Generalizing this idea, Chapter 5 argues for a chastened form of rationality review—"thin" rationality review. In this form, judges ask agencies for reasons and overturn unreasoned decisions. Yet judges accept a capacious account of what sorts of reasons suffice to validate agency action. They accept, in particular, that agencies often have good second-order reasons to take actions that are erroneous or unreasoned at the first-order level. Courts should overturn agency action as arbitrary, in the legal sense, only when agencies lack this sort of valid second-order reason as well—a situation I label "indefensible decision-making." One collateral implication is that courts have no business requiring agencies to justify their decisions with quantified cost-benefit analysis, not even presumptively. Qualitative reasoning is sufficient, at either the first order or the second, as current law emphatically permits.

Together, Chapters 4 and 5 sketch a picture of rationality review that is very different indeed than the "hard look" stereotype. An appendix to Chapter 5 collects every Supreme Court decision on arbitrariness review since 1983, when *State Farm* was decided, and finds that agencies win such challenges about 92 percent of the time. There are empirical issues here, but at a minimum the facts on the ground are very different than the received wisdom about "hard look review" would suggest. In rationality review, as in separation of powers, due process, statutory interpretation, and other critical areas, the courts have followed out law's logic. Their conclusion has been that, by and large, agencies should be able to make policy as they see fit, unless there are very clear reasons indeed for courts to intervene.

Chapter 6 adds a sociological dimension to the discussion by examining the surprising abnegation of *lawyers* through legal doctrine. As a profession lawyers are not famous for their tendency to abandon power. But the doctrines of administrative law, crafted by lawyers in a ceaseless jostle with other professions and with nonlegal institutions, have the effect in many cases of shifting power away from lawyers and toward nonlegal professionals within administrative agencies, such as scientists, engineers, and economists. This perspective makes sense of some enduring puzzles about the scope and justification of central administrative-law doctrines, such as the *Chevron* doctrine of deference to agency interpretations of law, and the *Chenery* I[34] principle that agency action may be sustained, if at all, only on the ground the agency itself advanced.

The Conclusion returns to the ideas of abnegation, thin rationality review, and indefensible decision-making, and it ties the ideas together in an analysis of the marginal place of law—"marginal" both in the colloquial sense and in the economist's sense. Law is marginal in the sense that it is relegated to the sides of the picture frame, policing only agency action that is indefensible in the sense that agencies have no valid reasons (including second-order reasons) for the action. In the technical sense, the place of law ought to be determined by an analysis of the marginal benefits and costs of additional increments of legal and judicial oversight of the bureaucracy. To a surprising extent, it has already been so determined, by an informal analysis of the marginal benefits and costs of legalism, conducted by judges and lawyers themselves.

Law's informal marginalist analysis of its own value yields a decision in favor of self-abnegation. Given broad, vague, or ambiguous statutory delegations, and a policy-making environment rife with uncertainty and complexity, the gains of additional increments of legalism become at best unclear, and perhaps simply negative, when legal review becomes more robust than review for indefensibility. The abnegation of the law is not solely, not simply, the result of the massive growth of the administrative bureaucracy over the last century-plus. It is the result also of the law's own appreciation of how the logic of law must work in an environment of that sort. The law, working itself pure over time, has come to realize that decision-making works best according to law's own criteria—criteria of rationality, predictability, and conformity to legislative commands—if judges confine themselves to policing the outer boundaries of agency authority and rationality. The requirements of "public reason"[35] turn out to be surprisingly capacious, especially once second-order reasons are seen to be as legitimate as first-order reasons. As the law has recognized this, it has increasingly come to realize that the very principles law generated to check and constrain administrative discretion themselves counsel abnegation. Law has decided that it best serves its own ends by lying more or less quietly under the throne.

1

The Legality of Administrative Law

THIS CHAPTER begins the sketch of law's abnegation in broad strokes, to set the main outlines of the picture. The following chapters fill in critical details. I will begin with the great 1932 decision in *Crowell v. Benson*[1] and its subsequent history. As we will see, *Crowell* attempted to create a synthesis or compromise between the claims of administration and the claims of law. In later decades, however, things fell apart.

Critics of the administrative state, who tend to be either originalist or libertarians or (frequently) both, portray this process as the conquest of law by the state. For concreteness I will examine two wholesale criticisms of the legality of the administrative state offered by Gary Lawson and Philip Hamburger. The significance of these theories, for my purposes here, is that they claim—explicitly or implicitly—that the administrative state and the law are antithetical and that the original Constitution, with its commitments to legality and the separation of powers, was shoved aside by political necessity and the expanding state. I argue to the contrary that from a lawyer's point of view, the main justifications for ever-increasing abnegation were not political but internal and legal. The very institutions of the original Constitution, functioning as they were originally created to function, decided for excellent reasons (from a lawyer's point of view) to create the administrative state and to abnegate authority to it. Together, the two pieces of the chapter try to offer a unified overview of law's abnegation and its internal motivation.

Baselines

We can imagine, if only dimly, a system in which judicial review is even more relaxed than it is today; relative to that baseline, our system is highly legalist and intrusive. But from the internal lawyer's point of view, the right place to begin is not with abstract and rather silly comparisons of hypothetical systems across possible worlds. The right place to begin is doctrinal and historical. The proper benchmark, I believe, is the great hinge between the world of classical legalism and the modern system of administrative law—a great case that attempted to settle a stable equilibrium compromise between the claims of law and the imperatives of bureaucratic government, and that in many ways provided a foundation for the structure of the Administrative Procedure Act (APA). *Crowell v. Benson*, decided in 1932, was a sweeping attempt to mediate the conflict between law and the administrative state in general terms. Although the attempt failed, it was a grand failure, one that casts its author, Chief Justice Charles Evans Hughes, in an admirable light.

The failure both provides the baseline or benchmark for my claim that law has abnegated authority to the administrative state, and structures the elements of that claim—accounting both for what *Crowell* did, and for what it left undone. Every important element of the *Crowell* compromise has become unstable; and in every case, the instability has resulted in a movement in one and the same direction, toward ever-greater judicial deference to administrative discretion. The arc of administrative law bends toward abnegation.

The critical point, or so I will claim, is that the arc results from the law working itself pure. It is not that the law was overcome by external force. Rather, the very arguments that Hughes used to compromise with the administrative state, taken to their logical end, implied that the law should cede authority altogether. The unfolding logic of deference in administrative law represents, not a triumph of state force over reason, but a flowering of reason.

Hughes, between Two Masters

"No man can serve two masters; for either he will hate the one, and love the other; or else he will hold to the one, and despise the other."[2] Charles Evans Hughes, of all people, ought to have understood this; the son of a minister, some of his contemporaries mockingly dubbed him—but only behind his back—"Charles the Baptist." As Dan Ernst has shown, Hughes attempted to domesticate the administrative state, rejecting two alternative visions: the vision of the reactionary lawyers who wanted to subjugate the administrative state to common-law baselines, through constitutional law; and the vision of the radical progressives and New Dealers, who wanted to subjugate law to the administrative state.[3] Hughes attempted to serve both masters, combining and harmonizing both of these impulses in a unifying framework that would adapt the legalist commitments of the common lawyers to new circumstances, while making room for progressive institutional innovation—especially the development of a professional civil service and bureaucracy that would more efficiently process adjudication on the industrial scale needed in the modern state.

Crowell involved the constitutionality of administrative tribunals adjudicating workmen's compensation claims occurring on navigable waters. As Hughes sketched the main outlines of the synthesis:

1. Courts would decide all questions of "law" *de novo,* without deference to administrators.
2. Administrative tribunals could (but need not) be given exclusive power by Congress to decide questions of "fact" in cases involving "public rights"—cases between government officials and citizens.
3. In cases involving "private right," between citizen and citizen— the heartland of the common law—administrative agencies could be given the power to determine the facts, subject to somewhat deferential judicial review for "substantial evidence." Here Hughes split some differences. On the one hand, he rejected legalist proposals that courts should redetermine all facts *de novo,* on a new record generated in the trial court, or should at least review the administrative record without deference,

asking whether the tribunal's determination was supported by the "weight of the evidence." On the other hand, he attempted to preserve a domain in which courts would not wholly defer to administrative determinations of fact.

4. Following on the last point, Hughes also ruled that courts would make *de novo* factual determinations in two subcategories of cases—those involving

    (a) "jurisdictional facts," whose existence or nonexistence supplied the predicate for the statutory "jurisdiction" of the administrative body;[4]
    (b) "constitutional facts," whose existence or nonexistence supplied the predicate for the constitutional power of Congress to confer jurisdiction on the administrative body in the first place. For Hughes, the critical examples involved Congress's power over admiralty cases and its power over interstate commerce.

The Lions of Constitutional Law

An obvious question was how the *Crowell* synthesis, established in 1932, would survive the transition from the old constitutional regime to the new in 1937. In the short run, Hughes's synthesis was enormously influential. Its major outlines were embodied in the administrative state's large-scale treaty with law: the Administrative Procedure Act of 1946, which said that reviewing courts would "decide all relevant questions of law,"[5] specifically including constitutional questions, and that agency factual determinations in formal adjudication would be subject to review only for "substantial evidence."[6] Yet even at the moment of its triumph, there were ominous signs. To understand them, some constitutional background is necessary.

In constitutional law, Hughes had also attempted to steer a middle course. On the one hand, he assembled coalitions in favor of ample congressional lawmaking power under the Commerce Clause and voted to uphold ample grants of statutory authority to administrative agencies. Yet on the other, Hughes also organized judicial resistance to either plenary national lawmaking or to delegations of legislative power so sweeping as to amount to abdication. In perhaps his most famous opinion, *A.L.A. Schechter Poultry Corp. v. United States,*[7] which invalidated the National Industrial Recovery Act on both Commerce Clause and nondelegation grounds, Hughes tried to draw lines, create a narrow but real version of the nondelegation doctrine, and allow judicial intervention in important cases without inviting it in routine cases.

It was not obvious, however, that Hughes's balancing act could survive the sweeping away of the old regime in 1937–1938. In *Jones & Laughlin Steel*[8] in 1938, Hughes himself tacked back, upholding expansive national lawmaking powers. On the nondelegation front, when the reconstructed Court decided in 1944 in *Yakus v. United States*[9] that Congress could grant agencies the power to set prices in the "public interest," it was hardly clear what if anything was left of Hughes's version of the nondelegation doctrine or of his moderating approach to constitutional law proper. A book by Charles Curtis, writing in 1947, described the Justices as "Lions Under the Throne" and said that Bacon's metaphor "hit . . . precisely on the relation of the Court with the New Deal."[10] In a world that could be so described—and with a great deal of justice—the Hughesian synthesis of administrative law seemed vulnerable in the extreme. Despite its triumph in 1946, the Hughesian synthesis was unstable and eventually came undone.

To be sure, one might see the Hughesian synthesis and the APA as a set of "substitute safeguards" that implement constitutional values of legality and rationality under changed circumstances, under a new constitutional order. On this view, the Hughesian synthesis became all the more necessary and desirable precisely because of the collapse of the classical constitutional safeguards of the old regime, such as the separation of powers. But that turns out not to be a view that the law has subscribed to over time. As I will discuss in this chapter (with reference to the general notion of "substitute safeguards"), in Chapter 2 (with reference to the separation of powers), and indeed throughout, the law has progressively relaxed the safeguards that Hughes wanted to put into place at the level of administrative law. Those safeguards, especially *de novo* and nondeferential judicial decision of legal questions, have seemed to modern judges and lawyers to be indefensible on legal grounds themselves.

Internal Tension and Instability

The reason for this basic instability in the framework is that the elements of Hughes's synthesis sat uneasily together. Indeed there was a warning sign written right across the face of Hughes's opinion. To many readers, *Crowell* did not convey the impression of an integrated synthesis, but instead seemed internally conflicted. The great public law scholar David Currie later characterized *Crowell* as schizophrenic.[11] In its first part, allowing agencies principal control over factual determinations even in cases of private right, *Crowell* extolled the benefits, in accuracy and efficiency, of entrusting workmen's compensation claims to administrative tribunals. Indeed Hughes implicitly praised the new system for furthering the cause of justice for all, relative to the expensive baseline of common-law litigation. In its second part, carving out jurisdictional and constitutional facts for *de novo* review, *Crowell* warned darkly that the administrative state represented a "government of a bureaucratic character, alien to our system."[12] Logically, there was no necessary contradiction between the specific holdings of the two parts, but the deep premises and attitude of each were inconsistent with the deep premises and attitude of the other. The overall impression was that of a house divided against itself, one that could not stand. The first half, extolling the efficiencies of administrative justice, and the second half, fearing the advent of an alien bureaucracy, seemed as though written by different pens. Hughes was attempting to serve two masters simultaneously, and ended up serving neither wholeheartedly.

Hughes had tried to go so far and no further. However, it was hardly obvious that the logic of his arguments could be confined in such a way. After all, no one has ever drawn clear and crisp distinctions among fact-finding, law-interpretation, and policy-making; the three activities bleed into one another in an integrated course of activity by which agencies set legally enforceable government policies within a certain domain. What would happen if the arguments that persuaded Hughes to commit fact-finding to administrative tribunals—arguments from justice, the inadequacy of the common law, expertise, and efficiency—also applied to law-interpretation, for example? In that case the rationales for one half of the synthesis would sweep too broadly, undermining the other half of the synthesis.

And in fact the *Crowell* synthesis has proved unstable over time and has come largely undone; the balance Hughes attempted to strike has tilted ever farther in the direction of administrative power. The judges, working through the implications of the doctrines and principles by which law constrains the administrative state, have decided that the logic of the Hughesian synthesis, fairly understood, implied greater deference to administrative agencies than even Hughes himself understood. The judges have thus discarded a number of *Crowell*'s central tenets.

The Collapse of *Crowell*

Consider the elements of Hughes's synthesis and how they have fared.

(1) *Legal Interpretation.* For many of the same reasons that *Crowell* offered to justify deference to agency fact-finding, federal courts now also defer heavily to administrative agencies on questions of law, in virtue of the 1984 decision in *Chevron U.S.A., Inc. v. Natural Resources Defense Council, Inc.*[13] Deference to agency fact-finding in *Crowell* was justified by expertise and efficiency, and by the tribunal's status as an agent of Congress and an adjunct of the court.[14] Appropriately modified versions or relatives of all these rationales have been offered for *Chevron,* including expertise, political accountability, and centralization, which produce greater efficiency in rulemaking and greater consistency across adjudicated cases.[15]

Although the original *Chevron* decision primarily emphasized factors of this sort, later cases have offered a traditionalist rationale.[16] The demise of *de novo* judicial review of legal questions, which to Hughes was an unquestionable element of the judicial power, is papered over by the legal fiction that Congress itself generally intends to delegate law-interpreting power to agencies. The fiction attempts to reconcile the traditional lawyer's conscience to a regime in which agencies, not courts, have the power to say what the law is.[17] But the only real reason to posit *that* fiction, as opposed to the opposite fiction that Congress intends courts rather than agencies to decide legal questions, is that the reigning fiction promotes expertise and accountability, which just returns us to the practical observations built into both *Crowell* and the original *Chevron* decision. The delegation fiction is modern administrative law's equivalent of the fiction that the Queen-in-Parliament still rules England—although she is bound always to act on the advice of her ministers.

Commentators sometimes point out, thinking to say something important, that judges and Justices do not always defer to agencies even under *Chevron*, in the sense that sometimes judges and Justices read the statute as clear, overriding the agency interpretation (the so-called "*Chevron* Step One"). Deference does not mean total abdication, and courts retain a residual power to set outer boundaries. But deference never meant that agencies would always win; it was always deference where law is silent or ambiguous. That is still a world away from the traditional lawyer's approach, which assumed that *unclear or ambiguous statutes were for courts and lawyers to interpret de novo* through ordinary legal tools. Relative to the classical baseline of 1932, the shift judicial deference where statutes are ambiguous is strictly an abnegating move, however important the residual power to enforce clear statutes.

More recently, a countercurrent to *Chevron* deference involves the so-called "major questions" canon, under which courts sometimes say that they will not defer to agency decisions on questions of major economic and political significance.[18] But the canon is invoked episodically and unpredictably, and so far in a mere handful of cases. To the extent it is an unpredictable and low-probability occurrence, it will have little *ex ante* effect on the anticipated reactions of other bodies, who will rationally ignore it.

Above all, it will not do to focus to excess on the most recent and most salient decision.[19] The "major questions" canon is not a strong, predictable doctrine but a sort of wild card that the Court occasionally pulls from its back pocket, invariably in cases of great "political" significance in the conventional sense. In everyday administrative law, both at the Supreme Court level and especially at the level of lower courts, deference to administrative interpretations of law is routine. Thus we ought not overreact to *King v. Burwell*,[20] which applied the "major questions" canon to interpret the Affordable Care Act without the use of *Chevron* deference. *King v. Burwell* was of course merely the latest by-product of a titanic partisan struggle over the Affordable Care Act, one that has resonated through the agencies and courts for years now. Great cases—in the sense of cases with maximum political salience—make bad law.

Apart from *King v. Burwell*, there are also a handful of concurrences and dissents from the late Justice Scalia, and from Justices Thomas and Alito, which question *Chevron* deference or reject it outright.[21] So far, however, there is no indication whatsoever that the Court as a body has any interest in overruling *Chevron*. The center holds.[22]

Most importantly, supposing *Chevron* to be overruled tomorrow, in all likelihood nothing of substance would change. Judicial deference to administrative interpretations of law, in various forms and with varying weights, preceded *Chevron* by decades,[23] in a kind of twilight between *de jure* and *de facto*; the caselaw was inconsistent, but deference was always one major strand. And deference (not necessarily on questions of law, but in some form or other to reasonable agency decisions) is, as I have mentioned, a staple of legal systems around the Anglo-American world.[24] Its roots run far deeper than this or that recent opinion. Rather deference arises from the long-term working out of legal principles by judges who, over time, become aware of the limits of their own knowledge and who build deference into law itself—the essence of abnegation.

(2)–(3) *Adjudication of Public and Private Rights.* In a series of cases since *Crowell*, the Court has steadily expanded the constitutionally permissible scope of adjudication by administrative agencies. As the law currently stands, very roughly speaking, the only civil cases that must be committed exclusively to Article III courts exercising the "judicial power of the United States" are pure common-law claims between private parties A and B, claims that are not ancillary to an administrative cause of action in the case.[25] The protected heartland of Article III jurisdiction has shrunk to almost nothing.

(4) *Jurisdictional Fact.* The categories of "jurisdictional fact" and "constitutional fact" have become vestigial. Indeed the former has more or

less vanished altogether; the caselaw essentially confines it to the facts of *Crowell* itself. The "constitutional fact" category is slightly more robust; judges do sometimes still assert that the Constitution requires *de novo* judicial determination of factual matters. But the category is not robust in the areas Hughes thought critical, the scope of national lawmaking power, which is far larger than any lawyer could have imagined when *Crowell* was decided. Rather it tends to appear, if at all, in free speech cases and scattered areas of criminal procedure and individual rights.

The larger problem here is that Hughes's category of "jurisdictional fact," although absolutely indispensable to the common-law mind, was always unclear even at a purely conceptual level, let alone at the level of application. If Congress creates N statutory prerequisites to the alteration of legal rights and duties by an administrative agency, then there is no subset of the N that can be carved out and labeled "jurisdictional." The agency's power is present if, but only if, all N of those statutory prerequisites are present; all are on exactly the same footing.

For exactly this reason the Court, in *City of Arlington v. FCC*,[26] recently rejected and indeed exploded the longstanding idea, which had been floating around the lower courts, that agencies would get no deference on the legal question of the scope of the agency's statutory "jurisdiction." As I will explain shortly, the Court denied the coherence of the idea itself, and the same logic applies to jurisdictional facts. Happily, lower courts have long since stopped trying to police the category of jurisdictional fact anyway.

(5) *Rulemaking.* Finally, Hughes's framework made a major error of omission as well as commission: it essentially neglected the central role of legislative rulemaking in the modern administrative state. *Crowell* implicitly presupposes that adjudication, meaning formal adjudication on the record, would be a principal method, or even the principal method, of administrative decision-making. In the 1960s and 1970s, however, the Court began, in effect, to increase the relative benefits to agencies of engaging in rulemaking and to loosen the constraints on agencies by encouraging informal as opposed to formal rulemaking. One of the critical developments occurred when the Court, beginning after World War II, allowed agencies to make rules

whose terms would predetermine the issues in subsequent adjudication,[27] thereby effectually denying regulated parties a case-specific hearing on those issues at the point of application.

Since the rulemaking revolution, it is indisputable that rulemaking has displaced formal adjudication as the central mode of administrative decision-making. In turn, legalist judges have attempted to develop two types of constraints on rulemaking. One involved "hybrid rulemaking," in which judges would require agencies to afford more elaborate procedures for rulemaking than the APA itself requires. The Supreme Court, however, stepped in to squash that development in *Vermont Yankee* in 1978,[28] warning that procedural obligations must be grounded in the text of the APA.

A second type of constraint involved judicial requirements of reason-giving, developed through aggressive interpretations of the bare-bones rulemaking provisions of Section 553 of the APA, and of Section 706's instruction that courts shall set aside agency action that is "arbitrary [and] capricious." (Because these two grounds are both nominally rooted in statutory text, they evade the narrow holding of *Vermont Yankee*[29]—although I will argue that they stand in patent tension with the larger institutional premises of the decision.) Under the latter provision, courts developed an intrusive form of oversight known as "hard look review," whose signature decision is *Motor Vehicle Manufacturers Association v. State Farm*, from 1983.[30]

We are by now far from Hughes's own vision, which did not envision deep judicial involvement in checking the reasoning process of administrators, as opposed to their "jurisdiction" and statutory authority. In any event, however, the development of "hard look review" is overblown, or so I will argue in Chapters 4 and 5. Law professors who are generally suspicious of administrative discretion have exaggerated the import of *State Farm*, at least at the level of the Supreme Court. As we will see, the Court has vindicated agencies against arbitrariness challenges about 92 percent of the time, contrary to the impression conveyed by most of the administrative-law textbooks.

If, to some lawyers, *State Farm* is the canonical case on rationality review, there is by now a large *counter-canon of deference to administrative rationality*. In this counter-canon is a phalanx of highly deferential cases. *Baltimore Gas and Electric v. Natural Resources Defense*

Council,[31] decided the same term as *State Farm,* allows agencies to make optimistic assumptions under uncertainty; *Pension Benefit Guaranty Corp. v. LTV Corp.*[32] allows agencies to limit their consideration to a subset of relevant legal and policy factors; *Mobil Oil Exploration and Producing Southeast, Inc. v. United Distribution Co.*[33] allows agencies to proceed "one step at a time"; *FCC v. Fox*[34] allows agencies to change policies without comparing the new policy to the old, and without showing that the new is better than the old; and so on and on. It is ultimately a cultural question why so many lawyers and legal academics fixate on *State Farm,* in many respects an outlier decision that is unrepresentative of the law.

These details are not yet important; Chapters 4 and 5 will amplify. The larger point is that, by and large, and with necessary qualifications, the Hughesian synthesis of administrative law has collapsed. Hughes fought a rear-guard action, most of all, to contain the spread of deference—to reserve some heartland of legalism in which judges would exercise *de novo,* entirely independent judgment. But deference escaped the enforced quarantine. And I will argue throughout the book that it escaped because the internal logic of legal principles and doctrines, properly understood and worked through to their logical conclusions, indicated that the quarantine should be lifted. In the end, judges and lawyers decided that the best legal arguments indicated a far more permissive scope for legal recognition of administrative discretion than Hughes realized. Of course this does not mean that law has no role left to play, but it has the sort of circumscribed role that highly constrained reviewers play in many domains of institutional design. In administrative law, judges check for clear and indefensible legal error or irrationality; where they exceed that role, as some of them occasionally do, they are acting contrary to the law's own instructions, and are often chastised accordingly by the Supreme Court.

City of Arlington and the Final Abnegation of Law

Indeed, the law, working itself pure, has even made central elements of traditional legalism, and central elements of the Hughesian synthesis, unintelligible at a conceptual level. In *City of Arlington v. FCC,* decided in 2013, the main legal issue was one that the Court had danced around for a generation, without ever resolving: whether the *Chevron* frame-work would apply to "jurisdictional" interpretations by agencies.[35] That issue was not a minor problem at the periphery of *Chevron*. Rather an exception for "jurisdictional" determinations reflected the deep prem-ises and assumptions of traditional legalism, of the Hughes variety.

Quite obviously, the traditional lawyer thinks, agencies cannot set the legal limits on their own authority; a regime of that sort would pro-duce a "government of a bureaucratic character alien to our system."[36] On this view, "jurisdiction" to make decisions is necessarily a legal issue, belonging to courts, no less when the jurisdiction is that of agen-cies than when it is the jurisdiction of the courts themselves. Any other approach would license a form of agency self-dealing and power-grabbing, as agencies relentlessly expand their domains through ex-pansive interpretation of jurisdictional provisions. Agencies' power to determine their own jurisdiction would make agencies "judges in their own cause"—so the thinking ran.

The assumptions and indeed confusions underlying this thinking are legion, and I will discuss them in full later. What matters here is that the law itself has now repudiated the view beloved of tradi-tional legalists, in a spectacular moment of self-abnegation. In *City of Arlington* the Court, through Justice Scalia, decisively rejected the "jurisdiction" exception to *Chevron*, and indeed denied that the very concept of such an exception could ever be coherent. Under an agen-cy's organic statute, there are a set of legal conditions or prerequisites that must be fulfilled before an agency has the delegated authority to make rules or orders, including those with binding legal effect on pri-vate parties. All of those prerequisites are on the same footing; absent any one of them, the agency cannot proceed. There is thus no basis for singling out some subset of them and labeling that subset "jurisdic-tional." If agencies are to have deference on the interpretation of any, they must have deference on the interpretation of all.

City of Arlington was not unanimous, and the dissenters worried openly about the swelling power of the administrative state.[37] For my purposes, however, the key point is that *even the dissenters* refused to defend the line between "jurisdictional" determinations and other de-terminations in judicial review of agency authority. They defended in-stead an entirely different line, between general and specific statutory delegation. Not a single Justice renewed Hughes's insistence that absent *de novo* judicial control over the determinants of agency "jurisdiction," the result would be a bureaucratic government of an alien character. Even to the dissenters, the traditional categories seem to have become unintelligible at a deep level. The deep conceptual structure of administrative law has changed, irrevocably.

On the majority's view, and seemingly to the dissenters as well, the inner logic of deference to agency interpretations of law, worked pure, makes it not merely wrong, but actually incomprehensible, that there should be an exception for "jurisdictional" issues. To the traditional legal mind, by contrast, it is incomprehensible to say that there *shouldn't* be such an exception. *City of Arlington* is the anti-*Crowell*. We are in a different world, one in which a lynchpin of the Hughes synthesis, and a deep premise of the traditional lawyer's thinking about law, appear incoherent. *City of Arlington* is a very late stage of legal abnegation.

The Constitutionality of the Administrative State

What sort of tale does the collapse of the *Crowell* synthesis represent? For some, it is a tale of the conquest of law's empire from without. On this account, the original understanding of the Constitution and the settled axioms of our law were crushed by the swelling power of the state. I believe this sort of vision is wrong both in the large and in the details.

I begin at the macro-level, by addressing a suite of constitutional critiques of the administrative state. Among these, I will focus on two, offered respectively by Gary Lawson of Boston University and Philip Hamburger of Columbia University. I disagree with both; but the important issue is why the disagreement arises. The ground of disagreement is emphatically *not* that Lawson and Hamburger are offering legal critiques that fail in light of the institutional practicalities of the modern administrative state. Rather the objection to Lawson and Hamburger is that they get the law itself wrong. They fail to recognize the arguments *internal* to law that have induced judges and lawyers to step out of the way, to abnegate their claim to authority.

The stakes could not be higher. Lawson has given us the best possible version of the argument that the administrative state violates the

Constitution of 1789, and if that argument fails on legal grounds, as it does, then it means that no such argument is tenable. Hamburger expresses a deep anxiety over the death of the common law as an ordering framework for Anglo-American constitutionalism; if his argument fails, as it does, then that anxiety is merely a lingering neurosis that should be firmly quelled, not indulged. (I bracket the point, recently made by Paul Craig, that Hamburger's vision is simply wrong about English legal history in any event.)[38]

A Matrix of Views

Let me distinguish two different questions: (1) whether the administrative state was unconstitutional at its inception, against the baseline of the original Constitution of 1787; (2) whether the administrative state is unconstitutional against a nonoriginalist baseline of the Constitution as rightly understood today. The answers to the two questions are independent of one another. The resulting matrix of logical possibilities yields four distinct views. One might hold that (A) the administrative state was unconstitutional as an original matter and still is; (B) the administrative state was unconstitutional as an original matter, yet no longer is; (C) the administrative state was constitutional as an original matter and continues to be so; (D) the administrative state was constitutional as an original matter, yet has become unconstitutional.

As far as I am aware (D) has no proponents. The closest is Richard Epstein, who objects to the administrative state as inconsistent with a view that he calls "classical liberalism," but who denies the label of originalist; he characteristically argues that a classical-liberal approach would make for the best possible constitutional order. In that sense his view resembles that of Ronald Dworkin more than the originalist critics of the administrative state.[39]

Lawson and the Constitution

The first view, the one I have labeled (A), is Lawson's own view, expressed in clear and arresting terms. Lawson holds that the administrative state was unconstitutional as an original matter and remains so. It is impossible to square its main features with the original

Constitution, and because originalism is the correct theory of constitutional interpretation, the administrative state continues to be unconstitutional. The Progressive Era and the New Deal worked an irrevocable departure from the constitutional structure—although there is a separate question whether anything can be done about this.[40] One might or might not combine the originalist baseline of this argument with an account of precedent holding that some mistakes are too costly to reverse. That fillip, however, merely accentuates the constitutional illegitimacy of the administrative state.

On this view, the administrative state has at least five features that cannot be squared with the original Constitution: (1) the vastly increased scope of federal governmental powers under Article I, particularly the Commerce Clause; (2) massive delegation from Congress to the President and bureaucracy, amounting to a *de facto* transfer of legislative power to nonlegislative officials; (3) the creation of independent agencies, which is said to be inconsistent with the "unitary executive" created by Article II; (4) the vesting of adjudicative power in executive agencies, subject only to deferential review by Article III judges; (5) and the combination of legislative (rulemaking), executive, and adjudicative functions in administrative agencies. Jointly and severally, the consequence of these violations is that the original scheme of separated legislative, executive, and judicial powers has fallen by the wayside.

Surrogate Safeguards

Before laying out my own response to Lawson, let me examine a different line of response, one that is theoretically important but ultimately unsuccessful. This response—corresponding to position (B) in my matrix—is typically discussed under the heading of "surrogate safeguards." The main theme of this response is that violations of the original Constitution are cured by later developments; but several different versions are possible.

In one version, the administrative state has been blessed by a *de facto* constitutional amendment implicitly embodied in the electoral victories of the New Deal coalition.[41] That view has been widely criticized, and in withering terms. The principal criticism is theoretical arbitrariness; it is deeply unclear when, and why, electoral victories should count as constitutional moments that effectively amend the constitution, rather than as ordinary politics.

In a far more plausible version, although the administrative state violates the structural features of the original Constitution, "the principal concern of administrative law since the New Deal . . . has been to develop surrogate safeguards for the original protection afforded by separation of powers and electoral accountability."[42] These safeguards may be understood as second-best arrangements that produce compensating adjustments for unavoidable violations of the original Constitution, thereby preserving the substance, if not the form, of separation of powers and electoral accountability.

The pioneer of this sort of response was James M. Landis, who defended the existence of independent agencies and "administrative tribunals" in second-best terms. In Landis's argument, the unavoidable violation of the original Constitution was the swelling power of the Presidency and the executive bureaucracy. Given the inability of direct legislative and judicial checks to constrain the executive, the creation of administrative tribunals with some autonomy from the Presidency created a new balance of powers, in accord with the spirit if not the form of the original. "Though [the partially autonomous administrative tribunal] may seem in theoretic violation of the doctrine of the separation of power . . . [it] may in matter of fact be the means for the preservation of the content of that doctrine."[43] Landis's second-best idea here is theoretically crucial, as becomes clear once we notice that the independent tribunals and agencies to which he refers were themselves created by the separated-powers institutions established by the Constitution of 1789. The institutional scheme of 1789, in other words, *created the means of its own supersession.* I return to this crucial point shortly, and indeed throughout the book.

Later scholars have expanded the scope of the response by classifying the APA, the fundamental charter of the U.S. administrative state, as a surrogate safeguard. On this view, the APA's central notice-and-comment provisions create a kind of surrogate legislative process that allows for representation of all affected interests; APA provisions that ensure the independence of agency adjudicators, and that separate functions at lower levels of the agency, constrain politicized adjudication; and the APA's expansive judicial review provisions enlist courts to monitor the executive on behalf of Congress and the citizenry. Although the *de facto* delegation of legislative powers to agencies and the combination of functions threaten the purposes that animate the original scheme of separation of powers, Congress itself has created a second-order structure that reproduces at least some of the original constitutional goods.

The Failure of Surrogate Safeguards

The fatal problem that afflicts the surrogate-safeguards view is the collapse of the Hughes synthesis. Recall that in many of its broad outlines, the APA, chief source and font of surrogate safeguards, reflects the Hughes synthesis laid down in *Crowell*. Courts are to review questions of law *de novo*, afford deference to agencies on factual determinations, but not on matters constitutional or "jurisdictional," and so on. And we have seen that the Hughes synthesis has come undone in almost every crucial element—most notably the development of judicial deference to agencies on matters of law, under the *Chevron* doctrine.

But the surrogate safeguards of the APA have become increasingly loose as well, in area after area. Beyond the *Chevron* doctrine, Chapters 4 and 5 will argue at length that the APA's provisions for judicial review of agency rationality, principally the "arbitrary and capricious" test of Section 706, have been applied in a heavily deferential way over time by the Supreme Court. There are imponderable questions, of course, about the anticipated reactions of agencies and the selection of cases for litigation. But at a minimum, there is no evidence-based reason to think that arbitrariness review creates a strong check on agencies. The recent wave of studies finding no "ossification" of agency decision-making by arbitrariness review supports the point. Similar points might be made about other putative safeguards. The notice-and-comment process, for example, has been frequently criticized on the ground that it favors well-organized groups with time and money to invest in providing information and arguments to the regulators, perhaps even resulting in a kind of "epistemic capture." Those debates are outside my remit, because they do not directly involve judicial review of administrative action, my subject here. Yet the point remains that the effect of the safeguards is not at all what their formulators hoped for and intended.

The surrogate safeguards are neither nonexistent nor unimportant. They are just marginal. Judges and lawyers, working them out over time, have settled on highly deferential modes of review that amount to an abnegation of law's authority.

An Uncompromising Response

The surrogate-safeguards response to Lawson grants the premise that the administrative state is inconsistent with the original Constitution, but then denies that this makes the administrative state unconstitutional. A distinct, third view—view (C) in my matrix—denies the premise altogether. The administrative state is not unconstitutional in any sense, and never was. Those who charge that it is have over-read the Constitutional text and ignored the rich history of administrative institutions in the United States,[44] a history that extends far back beyond the Progressive Era, indeed to the founding era. What has changed is that the observed scope of federal government action, and the federal government's regulatory jurisdiction, have expanded radically. That enlargement stems from a long series of statutes that have wielded Congress's Article I powers, particularly its powers over "commerce," in expansive ways. So it is not that the administrative state has grown, exactly; it is that the federal government has grown, and due to institutional constraints on congressional and presidential capacities, the growth of the bureaucracy has inevitably followed. There is a separate question whether the expansive use of Congress's Article I powers is valid, but that is in effect a question about the constitutional scope of the federal government *as a whole*, not about the administrative state as distinct from the original branches.

The Abnegation of the Constitution

The last point goes a long way as a response to Lawson, but not all the way, for he also thinks that the scope of the national government's regulatory jurisdiction is unconstitutionally broad. True enough, though that is not exactly a tailored objection to the administrative state, as opposed to the overall power of government, however that power might be distributed across branches. Even if Congress did everything itself, without creating any bureaucracy at all, the scope-of-government issue would be the same. But it is also true that absent the expansion of national power, the vast administrative bureaucracy would not exist; in that sense it is still true that the administrative state is a direct consequence of unconstitutional innovations (as Lawson sees them).

Yet Lawson's view is unpersuasive in any event, and it is unpersuasive for internal legal reasons (whether or not there are other objections to it). The inescapable fact is that *the institutional innovations that appall Lawson were themselves generated by the very system of lawmaking-by-separation-of-powers that he wants to defend.* Lawson never comes to grip with the problem of abnegation, the brute fact that everything Lawson deems inconsistent with the Constitution of 1789 emerged *through and by means of* the operation of that very Constitution, not despite it.

Here is another way of putting the issue. Suppose magically that the American constitutional order of 1789 were somehow restored to the baseline of 1789. (Ignore all the questions about how exactly this would work.) Would we have any reason to expect a different outcome? The same classical lawmaking, through the same classical separation-of-powers system, might well generate the same administrative state that it generated before, or some functionally equivalent substitute, quite possibly with different concrete arrangements. (Just as, in the epigraph at the beginning of the book, Valéry Giscard d'Estaing observed that a return to the state of affairs in France before the shattering events of 1968 was impossible, because it would include the conditions that had produced 1968 in the first place.) Legislators legislating by virtue of Article I, Presidents exercising their functions under Article II, judges judging under Article III—these, not some sinister cabal of New Deal lawyers, were the source of all the institutional innovations, like agencies exercising combined functions, that Lawson abhors. These institutions, acting in their classically separated ways, together decided to create institutions that did not follow the pattern of the creating institutions themselves. They made creatures *not* in their own image. Thus the Constitution superseded itself from within, in a gigantic act of self-abnegation. In that sense Lawson's posture is self-defeating; there is an inconsistency in its deep structure.

Abdication?

This point is critical; let me come at it from another direction. From a lawyer's perspective, an odd feature of many critiques of the administrative state is that the critics are hazy at best about its constitutional origins. It is somehow just there, looming ominously over the constitutional order. From the more feverish of the critics one gets the impression that the federal bureaucracy was imposed by a Stuart monarch, or at best by Franklin Roosevelt, acting extra-constitutionally. The haze contributes to the suggestion of illegitimacy, as though the administrative state were an alien construct.

In fact the administrative state is entirely the product of the constitutional institutions of 1789. It is a creature of Congress, acting through the constitutionally prescribed processes of lawmaking; of the President, both as participant in the lawmaking process and as head of the executive branch; and of the courts, who review and (almost always) approve grants of statutory authority to the President and agencies. This lawmaking process is conventionally called "delegation" to agencies, but it is delegation of statutory authority, not delegation of Congress's own legislative powers. Federal agencies, with a few exceptions related to the President's core constitutional powers, are entirely creatures of statute; they are brought into being by legislation, given their powers by legislation, and constrained by legislation—including constraints that appear not only in the agency's organic statute, but in the APA. (Not to mention constraints stemming from relevant constitutional provisions, such as the Due Process Clauses of the 5th and 14th Amendments, which I discuss in Chapter 3.)

The main rejoinder is that Congress has unconstitutionally "abdicated" to the administrative state through delegation. (Alternatively, the rejoinder may be that the courts have done so by upholding delegations.) It is interesting that the moment of abdication varies, however. Sometimes it is the creation of the Interstate Commerce Commission in

1889; sometimes it is World War I, sometimes World War II; if the author is especially overheated, references to the Reichstag's Enabling Act of 1933 will start flying about.

In any of these versions, however, abdication is not actually a plausible description of what has occurred. As Jerry Mashaw has shown, the creation of the administrative state has in fact been a long-term, consistent, bipartisan project of the Congress as an institution, initiated more or less co-terminously with the birth of our Republic (the First Congress delegated wide powers to the President).[45] That project has included an enormous amount of shaping and constraining of agencies, abolition of agencies that have outlived their usefulness, and oversight of agencies to check their excesses. This is no abdication of Congress's functions, but a deliberate, sustained, and nuanced exercise of those functions. If the administrative state were somehow abolished tomorrow, Congress would in all probability start laboring to re-create it, in a cycle of eternal recurrence.

On the judicial side, with the arguable exception of Justice Thomas, no modern Justice has fundamentally contested the legitimacy of delegation, whatever their complaints as to particulars. Its basic validity commands assent from Ginsburg to Alito. And the Court has invalidated delegations only twice in its history, both in 1935. Just as the critics are interestingly taciturn about the legislative origins of the administrative state, they are interestingly silent about the elaborate and conventionally *legal* arguments for sustaining delegation that the Court—as a corporate institution—has consistently given over time.

An example is *Yakus v. United States*, the 1944 opinion that sustained delegation to executive officials of power to set maximum prices in wartime.[46] *Yakus* has recently and correctly been described as foundational to the triumph of the administrative state.[47] Right or wrong, however, "abdication" does not capture anything interesting about *Yakus*. Rather, the Court, in a long and thoughtful opinion, upheld the delegation on the basis of a particular legal *theory* about the distinction between legislative and executive power:

> The essentials of the legislative function are the determination of the legislative policy and its formulation and promulgation as a defined and binding rule of conduct—here the rule, with penal sanctions, that

prices shall not be greater than those fixed by maximum price regulations which conform to standards and will tend to further the policy which Congress has established. . . . Congress is not confined to that method of executing its policy which involves the least possible delegation of discretion to administrative officers.[48]

Later in the chapter I will expand upon the theory of legislative and executive power that underpins *Yakus* and many other delegation precedents, and explain why I believe that theory is truer to the Constitution, and to the Court's consistent jurisprudence, than alternatives. The point here, however, is just that it is indeed a good-faith legal theory, derived in a conventional way from conventional legal sources. There is no illuminating or interesting sense in which it might be dismissed as "abdication." It is just decision-making.

Abdication and Legitimate Mistakes

The constitutional theory underlying delegation might of course be wrong. But a charge of "abdication" must mean something more than, and different than, "I disagree with it." The critics of the administrative state must have some room in their theory for reasonable disagreement and legitimate mistakes—for legislative and judicial decisions that, although constitutionally mistaken in the critics' eyes, are nonetheless *legitimately* mistaken, rather than a dereliction of duty. Absent a theory of legitimate mistakes, the critics must divide all official acts into two categories: constitutionally correct, or treachery to the Constitution. Such a perspective is a sure sign of fanaticism, and is surely unfaithful as well to the original public understanding of the Constitution. It has been shown that the founding generation allowed for "liquidation" of ambiguous written legal rules by practice and precedent[49]—no surprise for anyone who has read Blackstone. Nor is it possible to dismiss delegation as demonstrably wrong, as I will discuss shortly; given the consistent practice of it and approval of it by all principal branches of government in the constitutional system, such a claim merely indicates hubris on the part of the claimant. Any originalist theory, then, will have to acknowledge the liquidating force of the consistent recognition by Congress, President, and Court that capacious delegation of statutory authority is fundamentally legitimate, as in *Yakus*; and if delegation is granted, the administrative state follows. Lawson, however, despite calling himself an originalist, is famously or notoriously proud of having no such theory of legitimate mistake; he thinks that all or at least most precedent is unconstitutional.[50]

The Administrative State as the Offspring of the Constitution

To sum up: We have an administrative state that has been created and limited by the sustained and bipartisan action of Congress and the President over time; that is supervised and checked by the President as it operates; and that has been blessed by an enduring bipartisan consensus on the Supreme Court. The classical Constitution of separated powers, cooperating in joint lawmaking across all three branches, *itself* gave rise to the administrative state. When critics of the administrative state call for a return to the classical Constitution, they do not seem to realize they are asking for the butterfly to return to its own chrysalis. If political legitimacy is not to be found in this long-sustained and judicially-approved joint action of Congress and the President, the premier democratically elected and democratically legitimate bodies in our constitutional system, then legitimacy resides nowhere in that system, and the real complaint of the critics is not that the administrative state is illegitimate, but that our whole constitutional order is intrinsically misguided.

It is no good simply saying that the classical institutions "abdicated" their position by creating the administrative state. It is not as though the classical institutions simply gave way, in a moment of weakness or irresponsibility. Rather they affirmatively labored over decades, even centuries (on Mashaw's account), and labored with sustained purpose and great care, to bring the administrative state into being. Exercising their institutional capacities, they concluded that delegation of sweeping powers to the administrative state would help them to carry out their constitutionally assigned functions. Their internal reasons—the good stories—were familiar: specialization and expertise, the compacted agenda of Congress and other principal institutions, the rule-of-law virtues of bureaucracy and its representative character, and the increasing rate of change in the policy environment, which favors delegation to agencies that combine functions. Those reasons are both plausible and contestable; they may be right or wrong, in general or in particular cases. But the merits are irrelevant for my purposes here. What does matter is that the classical institutions deliberately adopted those reasons. "Abdication" by the classical institutions is not conceivably a proper description of the process—law's self-abnegation—by which the administrative state came into being.

Hamburger and the Common Law

The theme of law's abnegation also applies to a distinct variant of the wholesale critiques of the administrative state: the critiques founded on a putative common-law order of Anglo-American constitutionalism. In the United States, the most prominent exponent of this view is Philip Hamburger of Columbia University, whose most prominent work is a book titled *Is Administrative Law Unlawful?*[51]

Hamburger urges that American administrative law is "unlawful" root-and-branch, indeed that it is tyrannous—that we have recreated, in another guise, the world of executive "prerogative" that would have obtained if James II had prevailed and the Glorious Revolution never occurred. Administrative agencies, crouched around the President's throne, enjoy extralegal or supralegal power; the Environmental Protection Agency, with its administrative rulemaking and combined legislative, executive, and judicial functions, is a modern Star Chamber; and the *Chevron* doctrine is a craven form of judicially licensed executive tyranny, a descendant of the Bloody Assizes.

For Hamburger, the hallmarks of extralegal absolutism are everywhere to be seen in the system of administrative law created since the Progressive Era. Agencies engage in "extralegal legislation," meaning the issuance of binding general rules, and "extralegal adjudication," meaning the issuance of binding orders. Procedurally, agencies wield combined powers and functions. In contrast to a system of separated powers and specialized functions, their decisions are "unspecialized," "undivided," and "unrepresentative," among other failings. The judges, cravenly, have created an "entire jurisprudence of deference" that provides a sinister twist on the ideal of rule "through the law and its courts." The jurisprudence of deference amounts to "an abandonment of judicial office."[52]

What then is to be done? In a few cursory final sections, Hamburger offers some brief suggestions, vague and ill-defined. The main one is that judges should engage in an "incremental approach to administrative law," meaning "step-by-step corrections" that will "bring judicial opinions back into line with the law."[53] (In a moment, I will suggest that by "law" here, Hamburger seems to mean law in a substantive and unwritten sense—"law" as the deep principles of a common-law Anglo-American constitutional order.[54]) The resulting pragmatic problems are dismissed in the most cursory fashion imaginable; Hamburger merely says that "[u]ndoubtedly, in some areas of law, concerns about reliance, the living constitution, precedent, and judicial practicalities can be very serious. It is far from clear, however, that they are substantial enough to justify absolute power. . . ."[55] Hamburger's interest obviously flags in this section; his passion lies in articulating his dark vision, in the diagnosis of our ills, rather than in prescribing remedies.

"Unlawful"?

What exactly does Hamburger's title mean? Patently, he must be using the word law in two different senses to say that a body of "law" is "unlawful." Given his historical interests, the most obvious possibility is that Hamburger means to advance an originalist claim: that administrative law is inconsistent with the original understanding of the Constitution of 1789. But if Hamburger were an originalist in the conventional American sense, he would spend far more time on the ordinary meaning of the text as of 1789, and on the ratification debates, and far less time on subterranean connections between the Stuart monarchs and German legal theory. His main interest, his intellectual center of gravity, is elsewhere.

One perceives, through a glass darkly, what Hamburger means by "unlawful." Although the ambiguities and obscurities of the tome make it irreducibly unclear,[56] the key to understanding Hamburger is that he is not an ordinary constitutional positivist. The main point, for him, is not that administrative law is inconsistent with this or that constitutional clause, or even with the best overall interpretation of the Constitution. Hamburger is emphatic that "popular and scholarly debates" get off on the wrong foot by addressing the problem of administrative law "as if it were merely a flat legal question about compliance with the Constitution."[57] Passages like this one abound: "[T]he legal critique of administrative law focuses on the flat question of unconstitutionality, and . . . this is not enough. Such an approach reduces administrative law to a question of law divorced from the underlying historical experience and thus separated from empirical evidence about the dangers [sic]."[58]

Hamburger has, in other words, a historically grounded but entirely *substantive* and ironically extra-Constitutional vision of the true Anglo-American constitutional order, emphatically with a small *c*. Whatever he says when on the defensive, Hamburger's deepest commitment is to this common-law version of Anglo-American constitutionalism. It is of secondary interest to him whether the written constitutional rules of the United States, as of 1789, correspond to that substantive vision.

In the reconstruction I suggest, Hamburger offers a highly stylized constitutional vision derived from the English experience, interestingly crossbred with American high school civics—and also premised on a desperately shaky understanding of administrative law, or so I will argue. In this vision, legislatures hold the exclusive power to "legislate," while judges exercise all "judicial" power and exercise independent judgment in the sense that they decide all legal questions for themselves, without "deference." As for the executive, its only power is to "execute" the laws, understood very narrowly—basically the power to bring prosecutions and other court proceedings to ask judges to enforce statutes. The thing to avoid at all costs is that the executive should issue "binding" orders or rules; where that occurs, the executive is necessarily exercising "legislative" power and has arrogated to itself "extralegal" or "supralegal" prerogative, of the sort claimed by the Stuart monarchs in their most extravagant moments.

When Hamburger says administrative law is "unlawful," this, I think, is the way to understand him. He means, in other words, that American administrative law is out of step with the deep substantive principles of the small-*c* constitutional order of the Anglo-American legal culture. Administrative law allows the executive to exercise "legislative" power by allowing agencies, and the President, to issue "binding" orders and rules, and in that sense allows the agencies a prerogative to act extralegally or supralegally, like the Court of Star Chamber.

Administrative Law Is Lawful

Even given Hamburger's reconstructed premises, administrative law is lawful. Above all, Hamburger fails to realize that law's abnegation—especially in its most critical manifestations, evincing a relaxed approach to legislative grants of authority to agencies and judicial deference to agency interpretations of law—flows from law's own internal logic. The central issue is delegation.

The delegation issue hangs over the whole book. Hamburger's basic charge, recall, is that administrative law rests on "prerogative" and is thus "extralegal." Whatever that means exactly, it would become a far more difficult claim to defend to the extent that administrative law enjoys valid statutory authorization. If administrative agencies exercise whatever powers they possess under the authority of valid statutory grants, then they act lawfully in the ordinary sense. Now of course agencies may go wrong in other ways—for example, they may happen to exercise their delegated powers in an arbitrary and capricious manner—but that is not a wholesale problem with the administrative state, and it is not the sort of wholesale critique of the administrative state's lawfulness that Hamburger wants to offer.

So Hamburger will have to deny that the statutory authorizations are indeed otherwise "lawful," in his special sense. He will have to say that even if the authorizing statutes are valid, in the ordinary legal sense, they violate the deep principles of Anglo-American constitutionalism. As we will see, he does say that—on the basis of an argument that is predicated on a straightforward mistake about American administrative law.

What then does Hamburger say about delegation? How does he attempt to show that the authorizing statutes are themselves "unlawful"? With an argument, it turns out, that rests on a simple misunderstanding of American administrative law. Hamburger's major charge is that administrative law permits "subdelegation" or "re-delegation" of legislative power from Congress to agencies. With the exception of a few asides, to which I will return, Hamburger relentlessly, repetitively, urges that when the people have delegated legislative power to a certain body (Congress) in the Constitution, subdelegation or re-delegation of legislative power by that body to another is forbidden, under the old maxim *delegata potestas non potest delegari.* The whole of chapter 20 is devoted to elaborating this argument.

Unfortunately there is no one, or almost no one, on the other side of the argument. Administrative law is in near-complete agreement with Hamburger on this point. The official theory in administrative law is *precisely* the one Hamburger thinks he is offering as a *critique* of administrative law: namely that Congress is constitutionally barred from subdelegating or re-delegating legislative power to agencies. Very oddly, Hamburger never cites the main line of delegation cases that say exactly this, including most centrally *Loving v. United States,* which doesn't appear in Hamburger's index. *Loving* is explicit about all this: the official theory is that "the lawmaking function belongs to Congress and may not be conveyed to another branch or entity."[59] More recently, in *City of Arlington v. FCC,* the Court emphatically reaffirmed that legislative power is "vested exclusively in Congress."[60] Hamburger's elaborate proof that subdelegation of legislative power is forbidden amounts to pounding on an open door.

I said that administrative law is in near-complete agreement about the official theory of delegation. The qualifier is necessary only because of a few judges here and there, most notably Justice Stevens, who have advanced a different, nonstandard theory: that some delegations of "legislative" power are valid, while some are not (with the "intelligible principle" test sorting between the two). But this has never been the mainstream of American legal theory, as Stevens himself very candidly showed, with a long string citation.[61]

The difference between Hamburger and the official theory is that administrative law denies that there *is* any delegation of legislative power at all, so long as the legislature has supplied an "intelligible principle" to guide the exercise of delegated discretion. Where there is such a principle, the delegatee is exercising executive power, not legislative power. As the Court put it in *City of Arlington,* "[a]gencies make rules ('Private cattle may be grazed on public lands X, Y, and Z subject to certain conditions') and conduct adjudications ('This rancher's grazing permit is revoked for violation of the conditions') and have done so since the beginning of the Republic. These activities take 'legislative' and 'judicial' forms, but they are exercises of—indeed, under our constitutional structure they *must be* exercises of—the 'executive Power.' "[62] One might think this distinction merely semantic. Nothing could be further from the truth. The distinction results from a serious, substantive view of the nature of executive power, a view worked out in a line of cases beginning, at the latest, with *Field v. Clark*[63] in 1892, and continuing with *United States v. Grimaud*[64] in 1911 and *J. W. Hampton v. United States*[65] in 1928.

On that view, the whole problem of delegation is to navigate between Scylla and Charybdis. On the one hand, if the only requirement were that the delegatee must act within the bounds of the statutory authorization—the *Youngstown* constraint[66]—the legislature could in effect delegate legislative power to the executive by means of an excessively broad or open-ended authorization. On this view, requiring the agency to act within the bounds of the statutory authorization is not enough. *Youngstown* must be supplemented by an additional standard—in the rules-and-standards sense—that courts use as a backstop to police overly broad or vague statutory authorizations. Excessive breadth or vagueness means that the authorization *in effect* amounts to a delegation of legislative power *de facto*, even if not *de jure*.

On the other hand, the dilemma continues, it would itself be a misunderstanding of the constitutional scheme to require the legislature to fill in every detail necessary to carry its chosen policies into execution, and to adjust those details as circumstances change over time. To require that would equally confound legislative power with executive power, just in the opposite direction. In order to prevent legislative abdication to the executive, such a requirement would in effect force the legislature to act as the executive itself. The "intelligible principle" doctrine steers between these perils, attempting to sort executive power to "fill in the details" from legislative power to set the overall direction for policy.

And here is the essential point: critics of the administrative state, Hamburger very much included, tend to go wrong by assuming that the argument in favor of allowing the executive to fill in the details, and against requiring legislatures to handle all the details themselves, is all just an argument from practicality, or expediency, or necessity. It is not; it is emphatically an *internal* legal and constitutional argument, just as much as any of the arguments against delegation. The internal legal argument is that the power to fill in the details is an indispensable element of what "executive" power means; that to execute a law inevitably entails giving it additional specification, in the course of applying it to real problems and cases. General legislative lawmaking can never go all the way down, as it were, to the actual facts of particular cases. (Of course *legislators* may act as executive officials, or try to; but that is a different issue, raising different constitutional questions.)

To be clear, the official theory of delegation in American administrative law is not a view that I agree with. The better theory, and indeed the one with better founding-era credentials, is that so long as an agency acts within the boundaries of the statutory authorization, obeying the *Youngstown* constraint, the agency is necessarily exercising executive rather than legislative power, intelligible principle or no. But right or wrong, the merits of that nonstandard view are not relevant here, and the official theory of American administrative law is by no means trivially or obviously flawed. Before one discards it, one must first understand and respond to it. Hamburger's main, exhaustive argument about delegation simply fails to come to grips with the official theory.

So Hamburger seems largely unaware of the true grounds of his central disagreement with American administrative law. The true issue in controversy is not whether legislative power can be delegated (all concerned agree that it cannot); the issue is whether administrative issuance of "binding" commands, under statutory authority, always and necessarily *counts as* an exercise of "legislative" power. Hamburger would have to say that it does; the main line of American administrative law says that it does not, at least not necessarily. So long as agencies are guided by an "intelligible principle," they are exercising executive power, not legislative power, even when they issue binding commands.

Self-Defeating Solutions

A final point about solutions, bracketing everything I have said so far. Assume Hamburger's critique is correct. His main proposal for rolling back the administrative state, step-by-step judicial correction, verges on self-refutation. Were not the American judges who decided cases like *Chevron* the ones who helped get us into this mess in the first place, on Hamburger's view? If they are a large part of the problem, why does he think they are also the source of the solution? Hamburger has not thought through the relationship between his diagnosis and his prescription, which are patently in tension with one another.

This is a version of the abnegation problem that afflicts Lawson, *mutatis mutandis*. The very innovations Hamburger describes were developed by judges exercising the intrinsically and quintessentially judicial power to set rules for statutory interpretation and judicial review—rules such as the default rule that Congress intends agencies, rather than courts, to have law-interpreting power. And those judges, exercising the very same plenary judicial power Hamburger wants them to exercise, decided—on the basis of *internal* legal arguments about delegation, congressional meta-instructions or meta-intentions, and judicial respect for the authority and expertise of other institutions and officials—that abnegation was the best course for law to take.

The Abnegation of the Law—Redux

At a general level, the point about Lawson and Hamburger is the same. Both overlook that the institutional innovations they condemn as unconstitutional (in their two very different senses of "unconstitutional") are themselves internal products of law's own reasoning, as conducted by the very pre-innovation institutions they admire. Both want to take the sweet without the bitter; they want to return to a baseline set of legal arrangements that proved unstable, because the lawyers and judges *within* those arrangements decided that abnegation had the better of the internal legal arguments. Again, it is like admiring the chrysalis, while abhorring the butterfly that will in the course of time be born out of it.

The abnegation of the law accompanied, and was certainly influenced by, the external and pragmatic institutional pressures of the burgeoning welfare state and regulatory state. But law's abnegation is not reducible to a kind of coup, or forced abdication. The lawyers and judges who arranged for law's abnegation debated, seriously and in good faith, a complex array of internal legal arguments, prominently featured in the delegation caselaw at least since *Grimaud*, and in the deference caselaw and its accompanying scholarly commentary. The balance of these arguments, according to the now-settled consensus of the legal profession, weighed in favor of a conditional surrender of law's grandest pretensions. That chastened and self-effacing version of law is itself a product of law's processes, working themselves pure.

2

Separation of Powers without Idolatry

THEORISTS like Lawson, Hamburger, and other originalists and legalist-libertarians believe that the administrative state systematically violates the separation of powers, by consolidating vast powers in the hands of the executive, somehow defined. The administrative state tolerates sweeping grants of authority to agencies, which some describe as a forbidden "delegation" of "legislative power" (as we saw in Chapter 1); and it combines functions of rulemaking, enforcement, and interpretation in the hands of agency officials. For the legal-libertarian critics, all this is a betrayal of the central tenets of the classical constitutional order. The result is abuse of power by administrators, the inevitable result of collapsing powers into a single set of hands.

My thesis in this chapter is that the classical arguments do not survive the abnegation of the law. A critical part of law's self-effacement has been to jettison the classical constitutional ideal in this regard, as in others. The law has decided, for good internal legal reasons, that the classical separation of powers was *idolatrous*—that it treated the separation of powers as an inviolable command, whatever the sacrifices required to respect it, even if those sacrifices worked to the overall detriment of law itself. Lawyers and judges, working out the internal logic of law in the administrative state, have decided that the separation of powers is not to be seen as a sacred constraint that must be strictly obeyed, but instead that the separation of powers should be optimized. The benefits of separated powers must be traded off against other goods and considerations.

The resulting regime, toward which the law has groped, is something like separation of powers without idolatry. The point is certainly not to claim, quite implausibly, that the law has at any given time reached a single identifiable optimum. Rather it is that the law is best understood, from the internal point of view, as having been engaged in an ongoing process of balancing competing concerns, a process that trades off and equilibrates various considerations that all have perfectly legitimate standing, as it were, from the internal legal point of view, yet that cannot be simultaneously fulfilled. Competing with the goal of preventing governmental abuses are many other goals, including preventing "private" abuses by actors wielding delegated common-law powers; encouraging a desirable activity level on the part of officials; and ensuring that officials are well-informed. On the last point, there is a well-known trade-off between bias on the one hand, and expertise or information on the other.

In reality, of course, not all the relevant actors are or were deliberately attempting to balance, reconcile, and optimize the competing considerations. Some of the actors undoubtedly *were* doing that; architects of the modern administrative state, such as James Landis and the Justices in the majority in *SEC v. Chenery (II)* in 1947,[1] were sensitive to relevant trade-offs, as we will see. In part, however, the appearance of a process of optimization and equilibration arises from conflicts between different views, officials, and groups. The equilibrium of American administrative law, at any given time and over time, is an equilibrium of "opposing forces" that have "come to rest" on a legal "formula," as Justice Jackson put it in *Wong Yang Sung v. McGrath* in 1950.[2] But that does not mean that the external standpoint of political science or economics is the only way to understand the resulting arrangements. The synthesis of the competing views that we call "administrative law" has developed a weighing of competing institutional considerations—an approach to the separation of powers that refuses to engage in idolatry.

Separation of Powers and the Abuse of Power

But I have gotten ahead of the story. Let me begin with the general outlines of the classical view, and with a sketch of the main problems.

On the classical view, the master aim of the separation of powers is to prevent the abuse of power. Indeed much of classical constitutional theory is haunted by the prospect that some official, somewhere, might commit abuses.

Now different strands of classical constitutionalism define "abuse" differently. Abuse may be defined in legal terms, as action that flagrantly transgresses the bounds of constitutional or statutory authorization, or—implicitly of course—in welfare-economic terms, as action that produces welfare losses, either because officials have ill-formed beliefs or because they act with self-interested motivations. My objections apply equally to all these versions, and so I need not specify any one of them in particular.

In the modern administrative state, there are three major problems that undermine the abuse-prevention justification for the separation of powers. The first and most obvious problem is that it is excessively costly to strictly minimize the abuse of power by government officials. Strict minimization is excessively costly both because it is costly to set up the enforcement machinery to prevent abuse, and because the enforcement machinery will itself be staffed by officials who may abuse their power in turn. Given these costs, the optimal level of abuse of power will be greater than zero.

The second problem is that the goal of preventing official abuse trades off against the goal of producing the myriad of welfare goods that the administrative state supplies, such as poverty relief, health, safety, environmentalism, and consumer protection. There are substitute risks, as well as trade-offs across and among risks, on all sides of the relevant institutional questions. The largest trade-off is that abuses of power can occur on both sides of the divide between "public" and "private" actions. The architects of the modern administrative state were not only worried about abuse of power by governmental officials. They were equally worried about "private" abuses—abuses effected through the self-interested behavior of economic actors wielding delegated state power under the rules of the common law of property, tort, and contract, and under corporate law. The administrative state thus trades off governmental and "private" abuse; it accepts increased risks of official abuse and distorted decision-making in order to give governmental officials more power to suppress "private" abuses, in order to increase the activity level of the government as a whole, and in order to give administrators sufficient information to combat the evils that arise in complex sectors of the economy.

The third and final problem is that the great flowering of constitutional theory in the late eighteenth century addressed institutions—principally elected legislatures, constituent assemblies, and juries—that together represent a different world from our own. Our governments are, to a first approximation, essentially bureaucracies. The elaborate body of eighteenth-century classical constitutional theory on the separation of powers simply has little to say about bureaucracy in any form recognizable to us today; for the most part, it fails to speak to us where we are now, given how bureaucratized our government has become.

The main reason for the transformation of our government into an administrative state is that the rate of change in the policy environment, especially in the economy, is much greater than in the late eighteenth century—so much greater that the state has been forced, willy-nilly, to speed up the rate of policy adjustment. And the main speeding-up mechanism has been ever-greater delegation to the executive branch, accepting the resulting risks of error and abuse. We inhabit a different world of policy-making than did the theorists of the eighteenth century. One of the main differences is that, for us, time is always of the essence, so institutions are forced to trade off the quality of policy against its timeliness.

The Abnegation of the Separation of Powers

Recognizing these three points, modern administrative law has sharply qualified the very goal of minimizing abuses of power. In the administrative state, the abuse of power is not something to be minimized, but rather optimized. Law has come to recognize that a well-functioning administrative regime will tolerate a predictable level of abuse of power, as part of an optimal package solution—as the inevitable by-product of attaining other ends that are desirable overall. So one way of describing the basic movement of modern administrative law is the abnegation of the separation of powers.

Critically, this process of abnegation arises from *within* the classical system of separated powers. It was not imposed by force, from the outside; although institutional pressures undoubtedly influence legal decision-making, they influence decision-making by all other institutions as well. Rather it is that the classical lawmaking institutions themselves generated an emergent solution that partially compromises the separation of powers in pursuit of other goods, with those goods arising from the aggregate of statutory grants of authority to administrative agencies and from statutory provisions combining functions in administrative agencies.

Benefits, Costs, and Trade-offs

What exactly are those other goods? What is to be gained through an optimizing, compromising approach to the separation of powers? The architects of modern administrative law believed that a government that always forms undistorted judgments and always acts from welfare-maximizing motives, and that therefore never abuses its power, will do too little, do it too amateurishly, and do it too slowly. Institutional design in the administrative state must therefore consider the pervasive trade-off between impartiality and expertise, such that more informed bureaucrats systematically tend to have agendas or stakes that threaten their impartiality; must consider the activity level or output level of governmental institutions; and must consider the rate of policy adjustment. Hence administrative law constantly trades off the ideal of undistorted decision-making against the activity level, expertise, and speed of the bureaucracy. Moreover, the sheer costs of constitutional enforcement ensure that some positive rate of abuse is inevitable, at least in the practical sense that it would be unthinkable to spend the resources or to create the institutional structure needed to reduce official abuses to zero. Given all these reasons, administrative law constantly gropes toward arrangements that embody an optimal abuse of power.

I will articulate the positive thesis by addressing enforcement costs, the threat of "private" abuse of power, and the rate of policy adjustment. I then turn to a more critical register, examining important recent attempts by a philosopher and a judge to rehabilitate—in different ways, as appropriate to their different roles—classical versions of the separation of powers. The philosopher is Jeremy Waldron, who offers a conceptual analysis of the separation of powers; the judge is Justice Antonin Scalia, who has invoked classical principles to criticize the judicial practice of deference to rule-interpretation by administrative agencies. Both arguments fail, I believe, and in ways that illuminate the optimal scope and limits of the separation of powers in the administrative state.

Enforcement Costs

Whatever the constitutional and institutional rules, the costs of enforcement—of preventing official abuses—will inevitably be positive. The problem is two-fold. Obviously enough, the costs necessary to produce full enforcement of constitutional rules might simply not be worth paying, in light of other possible uses for those resources. It might take a large percentage of GDP to eliminate all official abuses whatsoever, leaving too little for the actual functioning of government and for the welfare goods that government supplies.

Somewhat less obviously, eliminating abuses requires setting up an enforcement machinery that is itself a source of possible abuses. In order to police officials who may abuse their powers, one must set up a new cadre of monitors—such as Inspectors General, prosecutors, or judges, or all of these—who may proceed to commit abuses in their turn. The resulting question, "Who guards the guardians?" has a neat answer in principle: The guardians must be arranged in a circle of mutual monitoring.[3] But the necessary institutional arrangements produce costs of their own, as the circle of mutual monitoring inevitably operates with a certain degree of friction, disagreement, conflict, and delay.

The upshot is that given positive costs of enforcing constitutional rules, some level of official abuse of power will be inevitable. In a thin second-best sense, it will even be desirable: insofar as there is no feasible improvement, no alternative regime that would do better. A certain level of abuse of power will necessarily be part of the best overall package solution to the problems of constitutional design.

"Private" Abuse of Power

Let me turn now to a more complex issue: the abuse of power by nongovernmental actors, wielding delegated legal powers under general common law rules or under corporate law. James Landis argued, in his 1938 Storrs Lectures—along the lines of Berle and Means's 1932 manifesto—that increased economic interdependence, the sheer density of economic interactions, had generated "pressure for efficiency" that in turn generated massive corporations. These corporations represent "concentrations of power on a scale that beggars the ambitions of the Stuarts."[4] In spheres dominated by the lords of capital, there is an absence of "equal economic power" between corporation and individual. The consequence is that the "umpire theory of administering law is almost certain to fail. . . . [G]overnment tends to offer its aid to a claimant . . . because the atmosphere and conditions created by an accumulation of such unredressed claims is of itself a serious social threat."[5] The administrative state, whose defining feature is tribunals exercising active and ongoing supervision rather than reactive common-law adjudication, is necessary to redress this imbalance of economic power.

Conditional on creating a tribunal with active, supervisory regulatory jurisdiction, which form should the tribunal take? Here emerges Landis's famous argument for the combination of powers or functions in agencies—the fusion of legislative, executive, and judicial powers. The late eighteenth century was anxious to keep these powers apart, as a fundamental precaution against abuse. Landis argues by contrast that "[i]f in private life we were to organize a unit for the operation of an industry, it would scarcely follow Montesquieu's lines."[6] The form of the agency must follow the form of the concentrated entities it regulates.

This is not simply magical thinking, although there may be a dash of that. Rather, the point is that the supervisory character of the agency's role implies that it will be performing the same sort of tasks as the entities it regulates; it is thus "intelligent realism" for government to adopt a functionally similar form. The imperative is to counterbalance concentrated corporate power by means of expert supervisory agencies; this imperative dictates not only the scope of regulatory jurisdiction, but also the organizational form for exercising that jurisdiction. That form sharply qualifies a central, classical precaution against abuse—the separation of powers—in order to ensure an adequate level of information and an adequate activity level on the part of official bodies charged with countervailing private power. Although Landis is too much the politician to say this explicitly, the structure of the argument necessarily implies some degree of official blundering, even abuse of power, as the anticipated, necessary, and unavoidable by-product of a level of governmental information and vigor that is desirable overall.

Let me offer two illustrations within contemporary administrative law: first, the combination of prosecutorial and adjudicative functions, and second, the combination of the power to make law with the power to interpret law.

Separation of Functions

A central topic of administrative law is the combination of functions in bureaucracies and agencies—the brute fact, which horrifies separation-of-powers traditionalists, that agencies quite often combine the powers to legislate binding rules, to enforce the rules through the prosecution of complaints, and to adjudicate whether the rules have been violated. Shockingly, the Federal Trade Commission, or FTC, (to choose only one example) may legislate rules about unfair competition, within the bounds of its statutory delegation from Congress; authorize its legal staff to file a complaint that alleges a violation of the rules; and then, rapidly switching its hat, assume the mantle of judge and hear and decide the complaint that it has caused its own creatures to prosecute.[7] What could possibly make this constitutional? What happened to venerable maxims like "no man shall be judge in his own cause"? And what of all the decisional distortions that such a scheme risks—most obviously, self-serving bias, as well as the reputational cost that a decision-maker would pay by finding invalid a complaint that the decision-maker itself had put forward?

In a case called *Withrow v. Larkin*,[8] the Supreme Court recognized all these institutional risks, yet upheld the combination of agency functions, essentially on the ground that the administrative state could not go on otherwise. The legal challenge in the case was brought under the constitutional provision that prohibits deprivation of "life, liberty or property without due process of law";[9] the claim was that due process forbids a biased tribunal, and that a tribunal that combines prosecutorial with adjudicative functions must be a biased tribunal. Surely, the complaining party said, there is an intolerable risk of biased decision-making when the same decision-maker who lodges the charges is also the one who decides (at least in the first instance) whether those charges are correct. The pattern is typical for the cases; the central harm that flows from violation of the classical separation of functions is thought to be a distortion of decision-making.

The Court, however, said that the principle of separation of functions, such as the functions of law-execution and judging, was too much of a straitjacket to be tolerable in the administrative state. "[T]he growth, variety, and complexity of the administrative processes have made any one solution highly unlikely. . . . The incredible variety of administrative mechanisms in this country will not yield to any single organizing principle."[10] In other words, were the principle of separation of powers to be enforced, too much of the vast and heterogeneous administrative state would have to be jettisoned—an intolerable result, given everything the administrative state does.

Withrow v. Larkin built on an earlier case, *FTC v. Cement Institute*,[11] that had upheld a similar combination of functions in the FTC itself. The case involved monopoly price-fixing in a regulated industry— exactly the sort of "private" abuse of market power that is a central concern of the regulatory state. The regulated firms complained that the structure of the FTC, which combined investigative functions with adjudicative ones, was an affront to the separation of powers and to due process, because of the risk of a biased tribunal.

With either stunning naïveté or a sophisticated faux-naïveté, the Court rejected the constitutional challenge on the ground that the complaining party's "position, if sustained, would to a large extent defeat the congressional purposes which prompted passage of the Trade Commission Act."[12] Both expertise and activity levels were at issue. As to expertise, investigation of the industry by the same Commissioners who would judge violations was a feature, not a bug; the experience gained through those investigations would be the necessary precondition for the Commissioners to form genuine expertise in the trade practices they are charged with regulating. As to activity levels, requiring a separation of prosecution from judging would disqualify the entire membership of the Commission, with the result that "this complaint could not have been acted upon by the Commission or by any other government agency."[13] To the Court, in other words, it seemed intolerable that government should be forbidden to act against monopolistic distortions of the market—against the "private" abuse of power—even if the price of avoiding that intolerable passivity of government would be predictable distortions of governmental decision-making.

The Constitution, then, does not generally require a separation of prosecution from judging. But statutes may; I have simplified the legal situation a bit by leaving that out. In fact, the Administrative Procedure Act creates another layer of complication that illustrates how the administrative state gropes toward optimal trade-offs between and among institutional risks. When the Federal Trade Commission's lawyers file a formal complaint against a firm, the first adjudicator to decide the case will not be the Commission itself. Rather there will be an initial, formal adjudication on the record, conducted by an official called an "administrative law judge" (ALJ), with an appeal lying from that decision to the Commission itself. The ALJ emphatically does not combine prosecutorial functions with adjudicative functions, and the ALJ has no legislative rulemaking functions either. Rather, the Administrative Procedure Act puts into place a set of protections for the independence and disinterestedness of the ALJs, who may neither prosecute themselves nor be subject to the supervision of the prosecuting staff. But the Act exempts from those strictures the agency itself, meaning (in the case of the FTC) the top-level Commissioners, who review and may reverse the decisions of the ALJs.

Consider the odd patchwork of rules that results: functions are separated at the lowest level of the agency, but only for formal adjudication on the record, not for either informal adjudication or the agency's legislative rulemaking functions. And in any event, when the case is appealed to the top level of the agency—the level of the Commissioners themselves—there is no separation of functions at all. This patchwork is clearly an equilibrium compromise—the Supreme

Court has described it as such[14]—that trades off competing considerations, involving the risks of biased decision-making on the one hand and on the other the risks of insufficient activity levels and insufficient expertise. It seems unlikely that the compromise is optimal in any strong sense, but historically it was designed to protect multiple values, each to some degree but none fully, and in that weaker sense has an optimizing character.

Separation of Lawmaking and Law-Interpretation

So far I have discussed the combination of prosecutorial with adjudicative functions, but there is also the recurring issue of the combination of lawmaking with law-interpretation. Agencies often do both things, to the horror of separation-of-powers devotees. Here, the classical worry about abuse of power is not so much a worry about cognitive distortion as it is about motivational distortion: A decision-maker who knows that it will have license to interpret the very same laws it creates will have incentives to write vague laws in order to maximize its own interpretive discretion farther downstream.

The modern Supreme Court, however, largely ignores this concern (with the exception of Justice Thomas, the late Justice Scalia, and the possible exception of a few others, as I will explain later). In fact, it not only allows agencies to interpret the legislative rules agencies themselves create, but also holds that judges have to defer to the agencies about what those rules mean.[15] The Court does that because it believes that agencies have special expertise about the meaning of the rules they themselves have created, and—even more importantly— because interpretation is not cleanly separable from policy-making, so that the power to interpret the rules is a necessary component of the agency's policy-making expertise with respect to the given problem or industry.

This is essentially to accept a trade-off. The Court has never said that the motivational distortion posited by the classical separation of powers is not a real one; what it seems to think is that the costs in distorted incentives are worth paying in light of the benefits to policy-making by expert agencies. In other words, a certain risk of abuse is tolerable in the service of overall institutional gains.

Here I merely introduce this point. Shortly, I will offer a more extended analysis of the modern jurisprudence on judicial deference to agencies' interpretation of their own rules. The topic, although seemingly technical, represents an important component of law's abnegation.

Rate of Adjustment

I turn now to the third principal point. Holding constant the institutional variables we have already discussed, there is a separate question about the rate at which governmental policy adjusts over time, as the rate of change in the economic and policy environment itself changes. Here I follow William Scheuerman's insight that the engine of the administrative state is the increasing rate of change in the policy environment, relative to any baseline we choose. That is, the rate of change in the economy, technology, and so on, was plausibly greater in 2000 than in 1900, and greater in 1900 than in 1800.[16]

Legislative institutions are structurally incapable of supplying policy change at the necessary rates, a point made by students of constitutional law as radically dissimilar as Chief Justice Harlan Fiske Stone and Carl Schmitt.[17] The veto-gates; second, third, and nth opinions; and interbranch checks and balances that—in a Madisonian system—are intended to promote reasoned deliberation and launder out passion and interest, together ensure that legislatures will "come too late"[18] to the resolution of an increasing fraction of policy problems. To some extent, legislatures may solve the problem by internal specialization, through an ever-more-elaborate committee system and an ever-larger staff. But there is an upper bound to the capacity of legislative institutions to do this; the constraint arises from the increasing complexity of legislative institutions as they are scaled up, and the increasing transaction costs of conducting legislative business. The U.S. Congress has gone about as far as it is possible to go in this regard, with its 20,000-odd employees and staff, dozens of principal committees, and more than a gross of subcommittees. Even so, Congress's agenda is so radically compacted and constrained that it is routine for critical policy problems to languish indefinitely on the congressional docket, even as extant law becomes risibly maladapted to the relevant problems as the policy environment changes over time.

Under the pressure of necessity, three institutional developments occur in tandem. First, Congress's main response to the increasing rate of change in the policy environment is ever-increasing delegation to the executive and to independent agencies. Second, courts defer ever more strongly to agencies, who are better positioned than courts to update policy under obsolete statutes, in a world in which Congress had increasingly abdicated its policy responsibilities. And, third, the executive itself expands its own power of unilateral action, exploiting broad and vague delegations, vague constitutional powers, and traditional pockets of discretion, such as power over prosecution and enforcement, in order to change policies without going to Congress for statutory authorization.

Constitutional law's main response to these developments, after an initial period of resistance, has been to get out of the way. In the United States, judicial resistance to delegation began in earnest in 1935 and ended, at the latest, in 1944.[19] Judicial deference to agency interpretations of law is not constitutionally problematic; the reigning justification, however fictional it may be, is that Congress itself intends for such deference to occur.[20] Unilateral presidential action has occasionally been invalidated if it goes very far, but for the most part it has become the routine stuff of government in the United States. Consider that President Obama, having failed to obtain a liberalization of the immigration laws from Congress (the "DREAM Act"), instituted roughly the same policy merely by announcing a very broad policy of deliberate nonenforcement of the extant immigration statutes. (That policy languishes in legal uncertainty, due to ongoing litigation, but the very attempt to institute it is nonetheless revealing.)

The cause or consequence of all this is a trade-off. In a simple model, broader and looser delegation, with fewer veto-gates or checks and balances, allows the executive to put new beneficial policies in place more easily, while also allowing more expropriation—more abuse of delegated power.[21] As the rate of change in the policy environment increases, the benefits of loosening the constraints on new executive action increase, despite the greater risk of abuse. The basic approach is to justify abuses of power as the unavoidable by-product of a package solution that is increasingly desirable overall, as the rate of policy change increases.

Waldron on the Separation of Powers and the Separation of Functions

Having laid out the main line of the argument, let me examine two important challenges to it. The first is by Jeremy Waldron, who offers a sophisticated and deeply felt elegy for the classical separation of powers; the second is by the late Justice Antonin Scalia, by Justice Clarence Thomas, and by some associated legal scholars, who invoke the separation of powers to criticize the principle that courts should defer to agencies on the interpretation of their own rules. In both cases, the argument fails, and fails in ways that illuminate modern administrative law's optimizing and desacralized approach to the separation of powers.

I have suggested that the separation of powers has been deeply compromised by the administrative state, and for good reasons. However, not everyone agrees that the compromise is desirable. Jeremy Waldron offers us a late flower of classical constitutional thought—a deeply considered parsing of the notion of separation of powers, one that aims to distinguish it from neighboring notions like checks and balances, and to isolate and identify its inherent value.[22] Waldron's argument is not (mainly) consequentialist. His main point is not that the separation of powers is a useful prophylactic against the abuse of power. Nonetheless I have to address it, because if his argument is correct, then the separation of powers has a special inherent value that ought not to be tossed into the soup of institutional trade-offs. But I think that his argument is incorrect, and indeed that it makes the classical separation of powers into an implacable idol, deaf to all other considerations and to all other goods that law properly cares about. For precisely that reason, modern administrative law has itself decided that an idolatrous respect for the separation of powers is *legally* objectionable.

The Idol of Separation

Waldron acknowledges that the separation of powers may not, in the United States anyway, have the status of an enforceable legal norm. The Constitution's text does not mention it as such, and it is hardly obvious that a freestanding principle of the separation of powers may validly be inferred from the larger constitutional structure.[23] But Waldron observes rightly that even if the separation of powers lacks legal force in the narrow sense, it may still have force as a principle of constitutional politics, a principle of our legal and constitutional culture in a broader sense.

The principle of separation of powers, Waldron argues, has value that is conceptually distinct from the values underpinning checks and balances, the division of powers, or even the rule of law. The value underpinning separation of powers is respect for "the character and distinctiveness of each of the three main functions of government."[24] Rather than collapse all official decision-making into an undifferentiated mass, as in the dictates of a kadi or monarch, it is desirable that there should be *articulated government through successive phases of governance each of which maintains its own integrity.*[25] Power must flow through differentiated institutions; "[t]he legislature, the judiciary, and the executive—each must have its separate say before power impacts on the individual."[26]

Why is this not tautological? If powers should be separated because there is a value to institutions with differentiated and distinctive powers having a "separate say," are we just saying that powers should be separated because there is a value to the separation? Waldron does *not* appeal to the functional consequences of such differentiation; his argument is not that (or is only incidentally that) separating powers produces institutional benefits, such as slower decisions or better decisions. That sort of justification would implicate the countervailing considerations and trade-offs I have detailed. Rather, Waldron is looking for something more conceptual, more enduring. He speaks in the language of the sacred, the language of "integrity" and "contamination": "The Separation of Powers Principle holds that these respective tasks have, each of them, an integrity of their own, which is contaminated when executive or judicial considerations affect the way in which legislation is carried out, which is contaminated when legislative and executive considerations affect the way the judicial function is performed, and which is contaminated when the tasks specific to the executive are tangled up with the tasks of law-making and adjudication."[27] The idea seems to be that functionally separated decision-making has an intrinsic or inherent value from the standpoint of political morality. But it is not clear that Waldron has identified any such value in terms that are distinct from merely describing the separation itself, albeit with a normative glow drawn around it in Waldron's palette of brilliant colors.

Furthermore, it is not obvious that what are, after all, merely *institutional* arrangements could ever be the sorts of things that could be "contaminated," even in principle. The language of the sacred is simply misplaced as to such highly contingent matters of institutional design. Classical Westminster forms of government have no separation of powers, at least in any U.S.-style sense; even today, many constitutional-democratic polities separate legislative from judicial power, but do not separate legislative and executive powers in the way Waldron thinks essential. Waldron has made a particular, highly contingent institutional pattern, the classical separation of powers, into a kind of idol.

Separation of Functions—and the Self-Defeating Separation of Powers

Let us put all this aside, however. Suppose that Waldron's justification manages to avoid tautology; suppose that the justification stands independently of the thing to be justified. An entirely separate question is the *level* at which the justification is supposed to operate. For clarity, let us refer to the separation of *powers* at the constitutional level and the separation of *functions* at the administrative level.

In the administrative state, the great bulk of rulemaking is accomplished by legislative delegation of power to agencies, which then make rules while exercising combined functions, in whole or in part. Waldron clearly wants to condemn this in principle, but it is not obvious that it should pose any problem for him. If the delegating statute itself has been deliberated by the legislature, approved by the executive, and reviewed for constitutionality by the judiciary, why has the force of the separation-of-powers principle at the constitutional level not been entirely exhausted? When the agency then exercises its (combined) functions as authorized by that statute, it *is* true that "[t]he legislature, the executive, the judiciary—each [has had] its separate say before power impacts on the individual."[28] It is unclear, then, why Waldron should object to delegation of power to agencies or to the agencies' exercise of combined functions under a delegation, even granting everything in his argument.

Here too, as with Lawson and Hamburger, the appeal to classical constitutionalism is self-defeating. The institutions of the classical constitution that Lawson and Hamburger admire, the classically separated powers that Waldron admires—these are the very institutions that have generated the grants of statutory authority and the statutory provisions combining functions in administrative agencies. By a considered, deliberate exercise in lawmaking, these separated institutions decided, each adding their distinctive mode of decision-making, that the combination of functions at the agency level was necessary in order to carry out the large-scale policy choices of the top-level institutions.

The Justices, to their credit, made this point long ago in the second round of the epic, defining litigation that goes by the name of *SEC v. Chenery Corp.*—what administrative lawyers call *"Chenery II."*[29] The Securities and Exchange Commission (SEC), through adjudication, formulated an administrative order and applied it to the parties at hand, rejecting their proposal for a corporate reorganization as inconsistent with a general statutory requirement of "fair and equitable" action. Justice Jackson, taking Waldron's part in dissent, protested vehemently against the "retroactivity" of the Commission's approach. In Jackson's view, rather than applying its order to the parties in the case at hand, the Commission ought to have first formulated a legislative-type rule applying solely prospectively, and only then proceeded to enforce it and adjudicate future violations. (This would have required letting the inequity in the case at hand go unredressed.) Jackson, in other words, argued for separation of functions at the agency level, not merely separation of powers at the level of Congress, the President, and the judiciary.

Waldron clearly wants this as well. But the *Chenery II* Court thought that Jackson's dissent, which only Justice Frankfurter joined, was overheated—inebriated by an excessive intake of principle. Although the Court agreed that "quasi-legislative promulgation" of prospective rules should occur "as much as possible," it rejected any "rigid requirement" to that effect. Instead, the Court offered a famously nuanced and levelheaded analysis of the circumstances under which separation of functions, and Waldron's preferred sequence of general rulemaking followed by specific application, might actually make impossible the execution of the very delegation with which the agency had been entrusted:

> [P]roblems may arise in a case which the administrative agency could not reasonably foresee, problems which must be solved despite the absence of a relevant general rule. Or the agency may not have had sufficient experience with a particular problem to warrant rigidifying its tentative judgment into a hard and fast rule. Or the problem may be so specialized and varying in nature as to be impossible of capture within the boundaries of a general rule. *In those situations, the agency must retain power to deal with the problems on a case-to-case basis if the administrative process is to be effective.* There is thus a very definite place for the case-by-case evolution of statutory standards. And the choice made between proceeding by general rule or by individual, ad hoc litigation is one that lies primarily in the informed discretion of the administrative agency.[30]

The sentence I have emphasized explains the problem with holding that separation of functions is required at the administrative level. At the higher level of statutory lawmaking, Congress, the President, and the judiciary have engaged in just the sort of reticulated, deliberative lawmaking process that Waldron wants; they have converged on a policy; and they have decided that the agency is best positioned to implement it. That decision—which must itself have unimpeachable credentials, on Waldron's view—will be thwarted if there must also be rigid separation of functions at the level of the agency, for all the practical reasons the Court gives. Where those circumstances obtain, two levels of separation is a pragmatically inconsistent arrangement, on Waldron's own premises.

The point is not that pragmatics override principle. Rather the separation of functions at the second, lower level has to give way, precisely *in order that* the principled, properly differentiated decisions reached at the higher level of statutory enactment and delegation may be given real life. In that sense, the administrative state must partially jettison the separation of administrative functions in order to carry out the larger purposes of the separation of powers. The form and the function of separation trade off against one another at higher and lower levels, and some sort of compromise—ideally an optimal compromise—must be effected between them. The Administrative Procedure Act (APA) and the rules of administrative law, which give agencies a great deal of latitude to combine functions, are best viewed as an effort to achieve an optimal compromise of this kind.

Justice Scalia and the Separation of Rulemaking from Interpretation

Chenery II, and the insights it contains about separated powers and combined functions, are also fatal for Justice Scalia's attempt, late in his career, to overturn the modern principle that courts defer to agencies' interpretation of their own rules. In order to understand the issues, some legal background is necessary. But amid the precedents and technicalities, the main issue is the combination of rulemaking and rule-interpretation—and, as we will see, the inextricably intertwined issue of agency power to choose between proceeding by rulemaking and by adjudication.

In a long line of precedents, starting with *Seminole Rock* in 1945 and reaffirmed in *Auer* in 1997 and *Perez v. Mortgage Bankers' Association* in 2015,[31] the Court has consistently said that the law, rightly understood, requires courts to defer to agencies' interpretations of their own rules. The rules at issue here are so-called binding "legislative rules," sometimes (although not necessarily, nor even typically) issued through the notice-and-comment procedures of Section 553 of the APA. In one salient sequence, the agency issues a legislative rule and then makes further policy adjustments by issuing guidance documents, which count as "interpretive" rules within the meaning of Section 553, and thus need not be promulgated or changed through notice-and-comment procedures. Such guidances have no force of law in their own right; they merely amount to a statement by the agency of its own understanding of the relevant binding law, in this case the legislative rule and the statute that rule implements.

The so-called *"Auer* doctrine" then addresses the effect of such interpretations in court. It says that courts will defer to the agency's interpretation of its own legislative rule, so long as the rule is ambiguous. The justifications for the rule are straightforward, and track the justifications often given for *Chevron*.[32] Within constitutional limits (which I will address shortly), Congress may allocate between courts and agencies the power to interpret ambiguous regulations. What allocation has Congress commanded? There is no clear general answer. The APA says that "courts shall decide all relevant questions of law," but this does not help us; what we are asking is precisely what the law says with respect to the interpretation of ambiguous regulations.[33] Thus the question is what general implicit background instruction to attribute to Congress. On grounds of agencies' relative expertise and political accountability, the best reconstruction—admittedly fictional—is that Congress would want agencies rather than courts to have the power to say what ambiguous regulations mean. In the overwhelming bulk of cases, the issues presented in such cases are technical and complex, and generalist judges have no comparative advantage at all.

Auer deference is subject to several exceptions and limitations. First, and most fundamentally, no deference will be afforded if the agency's interpretation is clearly incorrect. Courts always retain ultimate interpretive authority to police clear legal boundaries—albeit a far more limited authority than they would have had in Hughes's vision. Second, as the *Perez* court emphasized, arbitrariness review is always available to ensure that the agency has given adequate reasons for its choices, including both its interpretations and its policy choices. Finally, there is a principle—announced in *Gonzalez v. Oregon* in 2006[34]—that an agency will receive no deference for its interpretation if its earlier legislative rule simply "parrots" the statutory text. The thought here is complex, and not obviously correct or necessary. The thought is that *Auer* deference is somehow "stronger" even than *Chevron* deference—the deference an agency receives for its interpretations of the underlying statute itself. Accordingly, the argument continues, if the agency were able to parrot the language of the statute in a legislative rule, and then issue guidances interpreting *that* rule (as opposed to the underlying language of the statute), then the agency could leverage itself into a stronger form of deference. I will return to this issue shortly. In any event, the important point here is that *Auer* deference is the long-standing norm, subject to limitations and safeguards.

In the last years of his career, however, Justice Scalia mounted a campaign against *Auer* deference. His main argument was that it violates the separation of powers, root and branch. A subsidiary argument in a consequentialist vein was that *Auer* gives agencies an incentive to "delegate power to themselves" by creating bare-bones legislative rules that the agency then, by virtue of *Auer*, has increased leeway to adumbrate by interpretation through later guidances and adjudicative proceedings. Both arguments fail, or so I mean to argue.

Auer and the Separation of Powers

The separation-of-powers argument first appeared, in its full-blown form, in a concurrence in *Talk America v. Michigan Bell Telephone* in 2011 (a concurrence joined by no other Justice). Scalia wrote that it "seems contrary to fundamental principles of separation of powers to permit the person who promulgates a law to interpret it as well."[35] And in a separate opinion in *Decker v. Northwest Environmental Defense Center* in 2013 (also joined by no other Justice, although the Chief Justice, joined by Justice Alito, wrote separately to indicate discomfort with *Auer*), Scalia went further and affirmatively argued for abandoning *Auer* deference, writing that "[while] to clarify the statute is reasonable enough, there is surely no congressional implication that the agency can resolve ambiguities in its own regulations. For that would violate a fundamental principle of separation of powers—that the power to write a law and the power to interpret it cannot rest in the same hands."[36] Quoting Montesquieu, Justice Scalia insisted that when "legislative and executive powers are united in the same person . . . there can be no liberty,"[37] and added, "He who writes a law must not adjudge its violation."[38] Finally, in an important concurrence in *Perez v. Mortgage Bankers Association* in 2015, Justice Scalia reiterated his objections to *Auer* deference, maintaining that "there are weighty reasons to deny a lawgiver the power to write ambiguous laws and then be the judge of what the ambiguity means."[39]

Scalia's critique attracted support from Justice Thomas, in his own concurrence. Justice Alito, writing separately, also indicated a willingness to consider overruling *Auer*. Notably, however, neither the Chief Justice nor Justice Kennedy joined any of the concurrences in *Perez*. The opinion for the Court (written by Justice Sotomayor, and joined in full by the Chief Justice and Justices Kennedy, Ginsburg, Breyer, and Kagan) implicitly but unmistakably reaffirmed *Auer* deference, noting that such deference is subject to several checks and limits—principally that "even in cases where an agency's interpretation receives *Auer* deference, however, it is the court that ultimately decides whether a given regulation means what the agency says."[40] Most recently, a certiorari petition asked the Court to overturn *Auer*,[41] but was denied by a 7-1 vote, with Justice Thomas the lone dissenter.[42] In Justice Scalia's absence, it is not clear that any Justice besides Thomas hopes to overturn *Auer*. For now, despite attacks on *Auer* from the Court's flank, the center holds.[43]

But what of the merits? From the internal legal point of view, the separation-of-powers argument against *Auer* deference cannot be right, for several distinct reasons. First, Scalia becomes a victim of his own metaphors when he speaks of the agency "writing a law" and "resolv[ing] ambiguities." We need to be clear about what exactly is occurring, from the legal point of view, both when an agency issues a legislative rule (or for that matter an interpretive rule) and when it adjudicates cases under the rules. In any of these situations, the theory of American law—as we saw in Chapter 1—is that agencies are exercising *executive* power, nothing else.[44] When agencies create "legislative rules," they are acting within the bounds of statutory grants of authority, adding specification to statutory policy choices—a core executive task. When they "adjudicate," they are adding specification to statutes by elaborating their application to particular factual circumstances—a core executive task. In either case, in the theory of American administrative law, agencies are not exercising legislative or judicial powers, and there simply is no fusion of powers going on in the first place.

This is no novel understanding of my own. It is the understanding that generations of administrative lawyers have settled upon. The understanding was mentioned by none other than Justice Scalia in his *Talk America* concurrence, which acknowledged that "the adoption of a rule is an exercise of the executive rather than the legislative power."[45] If so, then the argument against *Auer* based on the separation of powers is a non-starter. And (as recounted in Chapter 1) the traditional understanding was most recently confirmed and explained by none other than Justice Scalia, speaking for the Court in *City of Arlington*, which observed that "[a]gencies make rules ('Private cattle may be grazed on public lands *X*, *Y*, and *Z* subject to certain conditions') and conduct adjudications ('This rancher's grazing permit is revoked for violation of the conditions') and have done so since the beginning of the Republic. These activities take 'legislative' and 'judicial' forms, but they are exercises of—indeed, under our constitutional structure they *must be* exercises of—the 'executive Power.'"[46] Accordingly the Supreme Court has repeatedly said that the combination of functions in agencies is not in itself a constitutional problem. Agencies combine functions, but not constitutional powers.

This understanding rests on a longstanding theory of the nature and scope of executive power—what has aptly been called the "completion" theory, in the context of presidential power.[47] When agencies make rules and interpret law in the course of executing their statutory grants of authority, they are carrying out or completing a legislative plan—"carrying [it] into execution," to adapt the words of the Constitution.[48] Nothing in that activity amounts to an exercise of legislative or judicial power, properly speaking. Of course there is a separate question here about the validity of the underlying grant of authority, which must contain an "intelligible principle" to avoid an invalid delegation of legislative authority.[49] But the constitutional critique of *Auer* is different from, and tangential to, the delegation issue; the former is meant to apply even when the grant of statutory authority is straightforwardly valid under the nondelegation doctrine.

The second and related problem with the critique of *Auer* on separation-of-powers grounds is that it sweeps far too broadly.[50] If the combination of lawmaking and law-interpreting functions in agencies really is constitutionally suspect as such, then there are much larger problems than *Auer* to discuss. The FCC, FTC, SEC, and a myriad of other agencies would seem to be constitutionally suspect as well; all of these agencies write binding rules, bring enforcement actions, and adjudicate violations. So there is a severe mismatch between the sweeping constitutional critique, on the one hand, and on the other the narrow context of *Auer*. If true, the critique actually amounts to an indictment not merely of *Auer* but indeed much of the contemporary administrative state, and its proponents should have the candor to argue for it on those terms. Scalia's critique of *Auer* was really a back-handed attempt to relitigate the New Deal.

Finally, and most fundamentally, the separation-of-powers critique of *Auer*, and of the combination of rulemaking and rule-interpreting functions, are pitched at the wrong level. As I urged when discussing Waldron, the separation of powers is fully satisfied so long as the principal institutions set out in the Constitution—Congress, President, and Judiciary—exercising their prescribed functions, devise and approve the scheme of agency authority that combines rulemaking and rule-interpreting power in the agency's hands. Whatever reasons that might make the constitutional separation of powers attractive in turn *support* that combination of functions. If the constitutional institutions, operating as they were set up to operate, have decided that such an arrangement is both valid and wise, then respect for the separation of powers counsels approval for the arrangement. Conversely, there is no constitutional rule that each and every subordinate body set up by the constitutional institutions must itself have the same internal structure as the Constitution of 1789, in some oddly fractal way.

Consequentialist Critiques of *Auer*

The consequentialist argument against *Auer* is not so clearly inconsistent with the structure of administrative law; as always with consequentialist arguments, its truth depends on the facts. Indeed it might be true to some extent or contain a useful warning about some variable, without being generally and abstractly true or false in all situations. I believe that the consequentialist critique of *Auer* is largely misguided but does contain a valuable caution. Let me explain.

The key premise of the argument is that *Auer* deference in effect enables agencies to "delegate" powers to themselves, by allowing them to create vague or general legislative rules that they will interpret in the future. Many of the steps in this somewhat attenuated chain of reasoning are vulnerable. There is a dubious premise, for example, that there is some important difference between *Chevron* deference and *Auer* deference. It has become widely recognized that the putative differences between "clear error" review and "substantial evidence" review are probably metaphysical, and that in reality judges operate in basically two modes—deferential or nondeferential.[51] Furthermore, as Cass Sunstein and I have written elsewhere, "[i]f an agency leaves a regulation ambiguous, it cannot be certain that a subsequent interpretation will be made by an administration with the same or similar values. For agencies, ambiguities are a threat at least as much as they are an opportunity."[52] The incentive arguments about *Auer* cut both ways.

However, I will focus on a different issue, one that is more fundamental. It is a simple confusion to suggest an agency could ever "delegate power to itself." Agencies just have whatever quantum of power they have, under relevant statutory grants of authority; whether they exercise that power through legislative rulemaking, guidances, or whatnot, the quantum of power itself is unaffected. Judges can always enforce the outer boundaries of the agency's grant of authority, however exercised. Indeed that was *precisely* Justice Scalia's response, writing for the Court in *City of Arlington*, to the concern that deferring to agencies on "jurisdictional" questions would allow agencies to expand their own powers, making them judges in their own cause. Wrote Scalia, "The fox-in-the-henhouse syndrome is to be avoided not by establishing an arbitrary and undefinable category of agency decision-making that is accorded no deference, but by taking seriously, and applying rigorously, in all cases, statutory limits on agencies' authority. Where Congress has established a clear line, the agency cannot go beyond it; and where Congress has established an ambiguous line, the agency can go no further than the ambiguity will fairly allow."[53]

What is really at stake in the *Auer* setting is not agency self-delegation of power, not the expansion of power, but rather *timing*—the timing of the exercise of whatever statutory power the agency otherwise has.[54] When agencies make valid legislative rules, those rules bind the agency itself as well as all the world. The more specific the rule, the less future discretion the agency has when interpreting the rule; the less specific the rule, the more future discretion the agency enjoys to flesh out the rule by means of guidances and adjudicative orders. Again, the overall quantum of statutory power is not expanded but instead *allocated* between present and future.

Put differently—and this is the way administrative law puts it—the agency's choice is to allocate its authority between more general rule-making now and more specific interpretation or adjudication later.[55] The more content the agency supplies through legislative rulemaking now, the less content it will have to supply (or indeed be able to supply) through issue-specific interpretation or case-specific adjudication later. It then becomes clear that the *Auer* issue that Scalia attempts to describe as an issue of self-delegation is really just the familiar administrative-law question of agency discretion to choose between policy-making forms or policy instruments.[56] And the law's answer—at least since *Chenery II* in 1947, and continuing throughout the modern era—has been that agency discretion in this regard is extremely broad.

Law's decision for broad agency discretion over the choice between rulemaking and adjudication does not rest on some sort of abdication by judges or surrender to statist pressure. It is based on good internal legal considerations, of the sort common-law judges are quite familiar with, that arise from trade-offs between rules and standards, and trade-offs between making decisions now or later. The famous passage from *Chenery II* that I earlier quoted against Waldron is apt here as well (and this is no accident; it is apt for the same reason):

Not every principle essential to the effective administration of a statute can or should be cast immediately into the mold of a general rule. Some principles must await their own development, while others must be adjusted to meet particular, unforeseeable situations. In performing its important functions in these respects, therefore, an administrative agency must be equipped to act either by general rule or by individual order. To insist upon one form of action to the exclusion of the other is to exalt form over necessity. . . . In other words, problems may arise in a case which the administrative agency could not reasonably foresee, problems which must be solved despite the absence of a relevant general rule. Or the agency may not have had sufficient experience with a particular problem to warrant rigidifying its tentative judgment into a hard and fast rule. Or the problem may be so specialized and varying in nature as to be impossible of capture within the boundaries of a general rule. In those situations, the agency must retain power to deal with the problems on a case-to-case basis if the administrative process is to be effective. There is thus a very definite place for the case-by-case evolution of statutory standards. And the choice made between proceeding by general rule or by individual, *ad hoc* litigation is one that lies primarily in the informed discretion of the administrative agency.[57]

This understanding of the real issue and the real stakes in *Auer* explains another puzzle of the caselaw: why problems of "retroactivity" come up in the *Auer* setting. In *Decker*, the Court's most significant recent encounter with the *Auer* doctrine, the majority identified "a reason to accord *Auer* deference to [the agency's] interpretation: there is no indication that its current view is a change from prior practice or a post hoc justification adopted in response to litigation."[58] Both halves of this backhanded reason implicate the holdings established in the *SEC v. Chenery* litigation. The second half, barring *post hoc* rationalization by agencies, is not unique to the *Auer* setting; rather it is a standard administrative-law principle established by *Chenery I*. The first half, the concern about "change from prior practice," is in substance a concern about the *de facto* retroactive effect of changes in agency interpretation. (*De facto* only, not *de jure*, because the underlying statute—the only positive source of law in the picture—has by hypothesis remained unchanged throughout.)

The concern about the retroactive effect of agency changes of course was the very concern raised in Justice Jackson's dissent in *Chenery II*—a concern that the majority acknowledged but did not treat as a trump card that would block agencies from ever changing their minds (without going through a new round of legislative rulemaking). Rather, observing that new judicial decisions always have retroactive effect, the majority took the sensible, pragmatic lawyers' view that *de facto* retroactivity may harm reliance interests but must also be balanced against the benefits of flexibility and learning on the part of agencies. The agency should take account of reliance interests in its choice of policy instruments—the choice between rulemaking on the one hand, and interpretation or adjudication on the other—and courts will review that choice for arbitrariness, although that review will be deferential. To the extent that the consequentialist argument against *Auer* goes further than this, it is an attempt to relitigate *Chenery II*, just as the broader separation-of-powers argument is an attempt to relitigate the New Deal.

Auer and Skidmore

It is sometimes suggested, as a kind of compromise, that even if *Auer* deference is not afforded to agency interpretations of their own regulations, courts may afford so-called *Skidmore* deference—granting agency interpretations "the power to persuade, if lacking power to control."[59] But there are a host of problems with this suggestion.

First, the *Skidmore* alternative seems to flinch from the logic of the very arguments the critics adduce to undermine *Auer*. After all, if agencies interpreting their own regulations are engaged in a kind of constitutionally illegitimate self-dealing that results from the fusion of lawmaking and law-interpreting power, why should their claims be given any sort of deference at all? The more consistent approach would be to treat such claims as tainted by their illegitimate origin, and to ignore them altogether.

A second problem with *Skidmore* deference is that it amounts to no more than the attention any minimally intelligent decision-maker would afford anyway to an entity with expert knowledge or experience of the subject. By analogy, the law says that medical decisions are (barring unusual circumstances) mine alone to make, but if I am at all sensible, I will consider what my doctor advises, granting her "the power to persuade" although not "the power to control." So too with courts. Even when courts have plenary authority to decide for themselves, if they are at all sensible they will take into account—for whatever they are worth—the expert views of agencies, legal scholars, or anyone else with an interest in the subject matter. It would be odd, to say the least, for a court to willfully refuse even to consider well-informed views. In this minimal sense, "*Skidmore* deference" has always been the law.

Ultimately, the Skidmore compromise does not engage the problem at hand, which is whether courts should recognize a stronger type of deference in this class of situations, and what implicit instructions about the allocation of interpretive authority should be attributed to

Congress. Since the 1940s, the same era when *Skidmore* was decided, the Court has consistently held and enforced the collective view—an abnegating view—that something more is warranted.[60] Where agency regulations are unclear or ambiguous, there is no affirmative reason for courts rather than agencies to decide what they mean. On what possible grounds could we think that a court is *better* positioned to do so? After all, the agency's advantages include not only (1) expertise and (2) political accountability but also (3) policy-making discretion and timing discretion in the choice between adjudication and rulemaking— which is, as we have seen, part and parcel of the *Auer* problem. And on the other hand, the negative criticisms of agency impartiality and of agency legitimacy launched by *Auer*'s opponents prove far too much, if they prove anything at all. They are in effect broadsides against the whole administrative state, not well-tailored objections to *Auer*.

Auer and Abnegation

Here is the overall situation. The general separation-of-powers argument against the *Auer* doctrine fails on multiple grounds: first, because agencies *always* exercise *only* executive power (unless they simply transgress the limits of their authorizing statutes), and thus do not actually combine otherwise separated legislative lawmaking powers with judicial law-interpreting powers; second, because the argument would sweep far too broadly, condemning all agency combination of functions and thus more or less undoing modern administrative law; third and most fundamentally, because the combination of functions the critics protest is itself the offspring of the separation of powers, through the operation of the top-level institutions of the Constitution of 1789. If that system is a good one, so is the combination of functions at the lower level of agencies; conversely, if the combination of functions in agencies is bad, then the critics' real complaint is with the constitutional system itself.

The consequentialist argument for *Auer* misstates the issues by focusing on "agency self-delegation," on agencies' putative attempts to expand their own powers—concerns that are constrained, here as elsewhere, by judicial review to ensure that agencies stay within the boundaries of their statutory grants, as Justice Scalia wrote for the

Court in *City of Arlington*. Rather the issue is the *timing* of the exercise of agency powers, and the allocation of those powers between rulemaking now or interpretation later. This is the choice examined in *Chenery II* and essentially committed to agency discretion by the Court (then and in many later cases), subject to deferential review for arbitrariness. The *de facto* retroactivity of agency changes of course is a legitimate concern, but not a trump; it is a consideration, a harm to reliance interests, a cost. The agency must balance that cost against the benefits of maintaining its flexibility and ability to update policy as circumstances change, subject again to deferential judicial review if the agency's weighing of these factors is arbitrary.

So the critiques of *Auer* deference fail, in a way that illuminates the main thesis. Administrative law has abnegated to agencies the power to interpret the agency's own rules, for good internal legal reasons. To be sure, the doctrine does take account of the consequentialist concerns raised by *Auer*'s critics; none of this is to say that *Auer* deference is unconstrained. The constraints include (deferential) judicial review for clear mistake, and for statutory authorization under *Chevron*; the "no parroting" principle of *Gonzalez v. Oregon*; (deferential) judicial review of the agency's choice between rulemaking and adjudication and its balancing of retroactivity costs and benefits, both under *Chenery II*; and of course—as the *Perez* decision emphasized—the omnipresent backstop of (deferential) arbitrariness review, as everywhere in administrative law. *Perez* observed that under current law, an agency interpretation might be arbitrary and capricious because it defeats reliance interests without adequate explanation.[61] Indeed, interpretations that are inconsistent over time, or that create "unfair surprise," may be disqualified from receiving *Auer* deference at all.[62] But the doctrine, very sensibly, does not accept that there is some general and intrinsic problem with deference to agencies on the interpretation of their own rules.

Desacralized Separation of Powers

The *Auer* issue is a case study in abnegation. We have seen that law itself—interpreted with Dworkinian integrity, relying on both fit and justification—has made an important decision to defer to agencies on the interpretation of their own regulations. That decision arises from the working-out, in a different setting, of the logic underlying *Chevron*— illustrating once again that abnegation arises from lawyer's and judges' commitment to rational consistency, to the law working itself pure.

Auer is, however, merely a special case of a more general point about the administrative state and the separation of powers. Law has decided to allow the combination of lawmaking, law-interpreting, and adjudicative functions in the same set of administrative hands, where there are good reasons to do so—reasons evaluated by the classical constitutional institutions themselves, in the exercise of their constitutional powers. Law's abnegation is generated from within.

Put most broadly, constitutional law has come to see, over time, that the separation of powers is not to be treated as an idol the way Waldron and Scalia would have it. Not every subordinate institution within the system must have the same internal structure as the Constitution itself. There is no requirement of fractal separation of powers, all the way down.

Rather, for the excellent internal legal reasons on display in *Chenery II*, the classical ideal of separated powers is just one decision-making structure among others; it is to be optimized, traded off against a myriad of other goods. The classical separation of powers is then demoted, as it were, to just another consideration that agencies themselves have the principal responsibility for taking into account, subject only to loose judicial oversight. Law oversees the agencies to see that they take a plausible stab at balancing the relevant considerations, accounting for the costs as well as the benefits of departing from the separation of powers. But for the most part, putting aside this loose oversight, law has abnegated to the agencies authority over the separation of powers itself.

3

Deference and Due Process

Since procedural decisions should be made to serve the substantive
task, it follows that expertness in matters of substance [is] relevant to
the exercise of procedural discretion.

> —Louis Jaffe, *Judicial Control of Administrative
> Action* 567 (1965).

Using modern due process analysis, the Agency, in the second step
of its *Chevron* analysis, carefully weighed the risks and benefits of
informal hearing procedures . . . determining that these procedures
would not violate the Due Process Clause of the Constitution.

> —Environmental Protection Agency, *Amendments to Streamline
> the National Pollutant Discharge Elimination System Program
> Regulations: Round Two*, 65 Fed. Reg. 30,886, 30,898 (2000),
> appeal dismissed, *Dominion Energy Bracton Point LLC v. Johnson*,
> 443 F.3d 12 (2006).

ADMINISTRATIVE PROCEDURE is shaped and constrained not only by
the separation of powers but by constitutional rights, especially the
procedural rights that have traditionally been read into the Due Process Clause of the Fifth Amendment.[1] Such constitutional rights are a
critical test case for the abnegation thesis. Here if anywhere, we would
expect judges to hold the line against the march of law's logic, stopping short of abnegation.

Nominally and superficially speaking, that is indeed what we observe. In the textbooks, procedural due process is a strictly judicial enterprise.[2] As the story runs, the Court in *Mathews v. Eldridge*[3] settled on a balancing test for determining what process is due, while in *Cleveland Board of Education v. Loudermill*[4] the Court finally decided that while the political branches may determine substantive entitlements, it is for courts to decide independently what process the Constitution requires. The notion that procedural due process might be committed primarily to the discretion of the agencies themselves is almost entirely absent from the academic literature.

I will claim, however, that procedural due process actually provides a clear example of abnegation. The facts on the ground are very different than the academic wisdom suggests. Thanks to converging strands of caselaw after *Mathews*—partly involving due process, partly involving post-*Chevron* cases on agency interpretation of procedural provisions, and partly involving the long shadow of *Vermont Yankee v. NRDC*[5] and its latest incarnation, *Perez v. Mortgage Bankers Association*[6]—agencies themselves are now the primary front-line expositors and appliers of the *Mathews* test. Administrative constitutionalism has already come to the Due Process Clause.[7]

In the second epigraph to the chapter, the Environmental Protection Agency, referring to itself in the third person, solemnly determined that it had correctly applied the *Mathews* factors to decide how much procedure to afford in a class of permit decisions.[8] (The epigraph also shows how closely the due process issues are entangled with questions of *Chevron* deference, when agencies are interpreting procedural provisions in organic statutes. I will disentangle all that later.) Similar examples are legion, arising from all sectors of the administrative state. The Nuclear Regulatory Commission applied *Mathews* to formulate rules of procedure for licensing of plant operators.[9] The Bureau of Alcohol, Tobacco, and Firearms applied *Mathews* to decide whether it should use formal hearings in the denial or revocation of "certificates of label approval" for alcohol.[10] The Treasury Department applied *Mathews* to decide how much procedure to afford when deciding whether to revoke certificates of surety upon complaint from agencies.[11] The Centers for Disease Control even applied *Mathews* in a proposed rule to determine procedures for quarantine of travelers suspected of carrying a communicable disease, although the rule was never made final.[12] There are examples from the Department of Labor,[13] from the immigration agencies,[14] from the Labor Board,[15] the FEC,[16] HUD,[17] and on and on—anywhere and everywhere. Descriptively, agencies are the first to apply the marginalist cost-benefit approach to due process.

The courts, for their part, have no settled theoretical approach to such decisions but behave fairly consistently in practice. Some agency applications of *Mathews* are apparently never reviewed in court at all, leaving the agency as both the first and last body to apply the test. When cases do reach court, the law in action is deferential. Nominally speaking, the conventional wisdom is that courts are supposed to apply *Mathews* independently, and some cases do just that. Others emphasize language in *Mathews* that requires deference to legislative or administrative judgments about what process is due in a given domain—a strand whose relationship to the standard framework of procedural due process is undertheorized, to say the least. Another line of cases slices the same pie differently, saying that where deference is appropriate, *Mathews* does not apply in the first place—thereby preserving the nominal independence of the test, but only by contracting its domain. Finally, there are many cases that apply *Mathews* without any express or acknowledged deference, but in a fashion that can only be described as cursory, implicitly crediting agency assertions unless they are patently unreasonable. Overall, whatever form deference may take, the caselaw reviews agency determinations about due process with a light hand.

That judicial posture of deference is exactly right, or so I will argue. Rather than decide for themselves "what process is due," courts should ask only whether the agency offered a rational justification for providing whatever process it did choose to provide. Although courts should continue to apply the reigning *Mathews* calculus, according to which the process that is due is a function of the (marginal) risks and costs of error and of procedural safeguards, courts should not *independently* assess what the *Mathews* calculus requires in the circumstances. Rather they should defer to reasonable agency decisions about the design of procedural arrangements, reviewing the agency's choices for arbitrariness, but not correctness. Although the *Mathews* calculus will supply the governing legal norm, courts will relegate themselves to the institutional margins, reviewing agencies' execution of the *Mathews* calculus rather than performing it themselves. This approach extends to all procedural due process contexts what Justice Kennedy has recently advocated in the setting of immigration: so long as the agency offers a "facially legitimate and bona fide reason" for its procedural choices, "courts will neither look behind the exercise of that discretion, nor test it by balancing its justification against the constitutional interests of citizens."[18]

A Dworkinian Theory of Due Process Abnegation

Viewed from one angle, the theory is radical; from another, it attempts to make coherent sense of a number of converging strands of recent caselaw, and is in that sense conventional. The theory is radical insofar as it implies a greatly reduced role for courts in overseeing agency procedural choices under the rubric of procedural due process. In a Dworkinian spirit, however, the theory is firmly embedded in unfolding precedent. It attempts to combine justification, the best account of the principles underlying the precedents, with fit, a coherentist account of the law's path in recent decades. Dworkinism tends to be associated with the expansion of Law's Empire, but that is a strictly contingent association, stemming in part from Dworkin's own proclivities. Fit-and-justification may just as well counsel abnegation of authority by law in favor of administrative bodies; I will suggest that it does exactly that in this setting.

On the dimension of fit, surrounding developments in the law since *Mathews* was decided in 1976 support a reduced due process role for courts. Those developments include (1) the "very basic tenet of administrative law that agencies should be free to fashion their own rules of procedure," announced by the Supreme Court in *Vermont Yankee*,[19] two years after *Mathews*, and recently reaffirmed in *Perez v. Mortgage Bankers Association*;[20] (2) the watershed of *Chevron*,[21] decided in 1984, and its key premises that on grounds of both expertise and accountability, agencies are better positioned than courts to interpret governing statutes; (3) the growing body of caselaw that affords agencies *Chevron* deference even on procedural provisions in organic statutes—a body of caselaw that has witnessed agencies taking charge of the *Mathews* calculus and that squarely rejects due process counterarguments; and (4) the Court's recent emphatic pronouncement that under *Chevron*, agencies may even be entrusted with power to determine the scope of their own jurisdiction. Last but certainly not least, (5) a number of post-*Mathews* due process cases explicitly or implicitly expand upon *Mathews*'s own cryptic suggestion that "in assessing what process is due in this case, substantial weight must be given to the good-faith judgments of the individuals charged by Congress"[22] with administering the relevant statutes. Although in principle courts do not defer to agencies on the application of the *Mathews* calculus, this body of caselaw shows that sometimes deference of that sort does occur—and I believe for good reason.

On the dimension of justification, I suggest that these converging developments in the caselaw after *Mathews* rest on a master principle, the one identified by Louis Jaffe in the first epigraph: for many of the same reasons that agencies are better positioned than courts to interpret the procedural provisions contained in their organic statutes, agencies are also better positioned than courts to assess the marginal costs and benefits of additional increments of procedure for program beneficiaries and regulated actors, as *Mathews* requires. The traditional lawyer's instinct is to say that procedural questions are for courts, especially when the relevant procedure is in some sense constitutionally mandated. But these instinctive commitments no longer reflect the governing premises on which the law operates. Rather the law now takes into account the interdependence of procedure and substance, and understands that agency choice of procedures is an exercise in *system design*, which must allocate risks of error and determine the marginal benefits and costs of decision-making in light of administrative goals. Generalist courts, which observe the system only episodically, should play a subsidiary reviewing role, asking only whether the agency's procedural choices are rationally defensible.

The *Mathews* Calculus

Procedural due process had a long history before *Mathews* was decided in 1976, and I will advert to that history where relevant. Under the

nominally prevailing current doctrine, however, there are three analytic steps in any procedural due process challenge to administrative
action. In some presentations, some of the following steps may be expressed differently, subdivided or put in a different order; but the law
ends up in much the same place anyway.

First, the court must identify a protected interest in "life, liberty or
property." There is a separate, elaborate body of law that addresses the
problem of protected interests,[23] but I will bracket this set of questions,
which were not relevant in *Mathews* and are not my topic here. There
is one large qualification to this bracketing, however: I will have to
address protected interests to identify one very large red herring
dragged across the path of the law—the idea that due process claimants must "take the bitter with the sweet," once urged by then-Justice
Rehnquist.[24]

Second, the court must ask whether there has been a "deprivation"
of a protected interest. Here too there is a body of law detailing what
counts as a "deprivation" (or alternatively: which deprivations are constitutionally actionable). The major line is between intentional and
negligent government action inflicting harm on protected interests;
negligent action, even if tortious, does not amount to a deprivation (or
a constitutionally actionable one).[25]

Third, given the deprivation of a protected interest, the court must
decide what process is due. Here there is a critical distinction between
agency action that is legislative in character (rulemaking), and agency
action that is court-like (adjudication). An adjudicative hearing is not
constitutionally required for legislative action by agencies, meaning
action that applies in a generalized fashion across regulated actors,
rather than applying on the basis of particular features of specific parties.[26] For general rulemaking, legislative process is all the process that
the Constitution affords, although of course the Administrative Procedure Act (APA) may require more.

As to adjudicative action by agencies, the basic requirement of due
process is "some kind of hearing."[27] The elements of the required
hearing vary with circumstances and are highly contextual. In some
cases, a traditional formal judicial-type hearing on the record will be
required; in others, an informal paper hearing, without argument or
testimony, may well be sufficient. The timing of hearings also varies;

due process does not necessarily require a pre-deprivation hearing,[28] although often it does. Finally, due process requires an impartial decision-maker, but the Court takes a narrow view of what counts as impartiality; pecuniary interest in the decision at hand is disqualifying,[29] but there is no general due process prohibition on institutions that combine legislative, executive, and adjudicative functions[30] and thus "judge in their own cause."

In an attempt to bring some sort of conceptual order to all this circumstantialism, *Mathews* announced a marginalist, cost-benefit approach to determining what process is due. *Mathews* involved payments under Social Security to a putatively disabled beneficiary; it was acknowledged by all concerned that the claimant asserted a protected property entitlement, in the form of "new property"—an entitlement to public benefits. The contested questions were what process was due in order to protect that claimed entitlement, and when the relevant process was due. In particular, the question was whether the claimant was entitled to an oral evidentiary hearing in the agency before benefits were terminated, or whether the agency could provide only a "paper hearing" before deprivation. Under the agency procedures in place, the claimant could submit written testimony and evidence; an agency official would then consider all the evidence, including medical reports on the claimant's disability, and then decide whether to terminate benefits. Post-termination, the claimant could obtain a full formal hearing on the record, first before an administrative law judge and an agency appeal board, and ultimately before a federal court.

A somewhat similar case decided in 1970, *Goldberg v. Kelly*,[31] had announced a procedural due process entitlement to pre-termination evidentiary hearings when welfare benefits were at issue. The *Mathews* Court, however, both distinguished *Goldberg v. Kelly* and moved to clarify the governing framework. The Court announced a simple marginalist calculus of marginal error costs and decision costs—essentially the same one underlying the Hand formula in negligence law,[32] and the free-speech balancing test of *Dennis v. United States*.[33] Under the *Mathews* calculus, "identification of the specific dictates of due process generally requires consideration of three distinct factors: First, the private interest that will be affected by the official action; second, the risk of an erroneous deprivation of such interest through the procedures used, and the probable value, if any, of additional or substitute proce-dural safeguards; and finally, the Government's interest, including the function involved and the fiscal and administrative burdens that the additional or substitute procedural requirement would entail."[34] Under the calculus, there were two key grounds for distinguishing *Goldberg v. Kelly*. The first was that the private interest affected was weightier in the case of welfare benefits than in the case of disability benefits. Welfare beneficiaries are by definition living on the edge of subsistence, and thus have a powerful interest in full procedure before benefits are terminated. Disability benefits, by contrast, were unrelated to need, and thus beneficiaries could on average more easily tolerate a tempo-rary erroneous deprivation. The second was the different character of the evidence in disability cases and welfare cases. The former involved medical reports that could be adequately examined in paper hearings, the latter involved facts about the life circumstances of claimants that would more often require personal participation by the claimants.[35]

The *Mathews* calculus came in for criticism right away. Predictably, some questioned the very notion of "erroneous deprivation" or "accu-racy" embodied in the calculus, or questioned its consequentialist character, or at a minimum questioned whether the Court had ne-glected important consequentialist considerations, such as litigants' appraisal of the legitimacy of the process itself.[36] I believe most of these objections misguided, but will bracket those questions here, excluding them from the topic. My enterprise is not to critique *Mathews*, but to show that even assuming its validity, it is consistent with a far greater degree of deference to administrative discretion than has been realized to date—especially once subsequent developments in the law are taken into account.

Legal Norms and Decision-Making Competence

A critical analytic distinction for my purposes is the distinction be-tween legal norms, on the one hand, and the allocation of decision-making competence ("who decides"), on the other. There is a crucial logical slip in *Mathews*: to announce a legal norm, even a constitu-tional norm, is to say nothing at all about which institution is best positioned to implement and apply that norm. *Mathews*'s marginal cost-benefit calculus is not necessarily a rule of decision for judges, although the *Mathews* Court assumes—for the most part, but not always, as we will see—that judges should apply it independently. There is no conceptual barrier to saying that the marginalist calculus is the legal norm, but that application of that legal norm should be committed primarily or even wholly to the agency's discretion.

This analytic point is not to be confused with two other, entirely distinct questions: (1) Whether a (total or partial) commitment of decision-making competence to agencies in due process cases would comport with the larger fabric and development of public law; (2) Whether it would be a good idea, all things considered. So far I have said nothing on either question, although I will do so shortly. All I mean to point out here is that one cannot, as a logical matter, derive an answer to the institutional-allocation question from the bare specification of the legal norm. It is perfectly possible to identify a procedural constraint, even a constitutional constraint, yet to entrust application of that constraint to a body other than courts. As we will see, the *Mathews* Court seemed to conflate these two issues—until it did not.

Rules of Decision vs. Standards of Review

The rule I suggest commits the marginalist *Mathews* calculus to agencies, subject to arbitrariness review by courts. Under this description, the *Mathews* calculus is itself the constitutional norm, and the suggestion is that courts should read the Constitution as committing to agencies the primary responsibility for implementing that norm. This description fits with the Court's current understanding of the so-called "political question doctrine"—the current interpretation of that doctrine being that constitutional norms, rightly understood, might sometimes themselves be entrusted or committed to the decision-making competence of nonjudicial institutions.[37] Under this description, the *Mathews* calculus supplies a rule of decision for the agency.

In contrast to the agency's rule of decision is the court's standard of review. While agencies would have a constitutional obligation to actually apply the *Mathews* calculus when formulating their procedural rules to implement statutory delegations, the role of the courts will be to ensure that agencies have rationally considered the factors that are relevant under the *Mathews* calculus and have given an adequate explanation for their application of those factors. The court's task is not to decide what the correct application of the factors is, but whether the agency's application was rationally defensible and defended, or instead arbitrary.

This sounds as though I am adapting to constitutional purposes the body of caselaw interpreting the APA's "arbitrary and capricious" test; that caselaw instructs reviewing courts to determine whether agencies have considered the relevant factors and adequately explained their choices.[38] Although the comparison is valid, the influence actually runs in the other direction. The idea that judges should review agency decision-making under an "arbitrary and capricious" standard of review was originally a due process test,[39] one that predates the APA. When the APA was drafted, the "arbitrary and capricious" language was lifted from the extant due process caselaw and adapted as a statutory standard of review.

In another sense, however, the administrative-law analogy is exactly correct. Agencies already cite and apply the *Mathews* factors when designing procedures to implement statutory delegations. When they do so, they are thinking and talking about the right things. In administrative-law terms, the role of the *Mathews* calculus is to supply "relevant factors"[40] that the agency must consider and address, in order to survive arbitrariness review of the agency's procedural choices.

Finally, let me clear away the possibility of so-called "*Skidmore* deference," under which courts—although deciding independently—ask whether the agency's views have "power to persuade, if lacking power to control."[41] The proposal I offer goes a large step beyond that. As discussed in Chapter 2, *Skidmore* just describes the attitude of any minimally sensible decision-maker, who listens to any relevant arguments of well-informed parties when deciding what to do, for whatever those arguments may be worth. In that sense, the current regime already builds in *Skidmore* deference; courts always listen to the views of agency counsel about what procedures are best. The problem is that, under the current regime, courts still make the ultimate decision for themselves, on an all-things-considered basis. (In theory, anyway; we

will see that the caselaw is actually conflicted.) In the regime I propose, by contrast, courts will *review* rather than *decide;* they will confine themselves to asking whether the agency's proffered justifications
are arbitrary, or instead reasonable.

Fit

So far I have merely stated and clarified the claim. Now let us turn
to the considerations that support it, as well as reasonable concerns about it. At the outset, let me be clear about what I take as
fixed, and what as variable. I will begin with the dimension of fit, and
turn to justification later—although of course the aim is to achieve
reflective equilibrium across the two dimensions, so inevitably I
will constantly glance at justification while talking about fit, and
vice versa.

I will take the *Mathews* calculus as a fixed point, and also assume the
validity of broader developments in administrative and constitutional
law after *Mathews.* The result is emphatically not a blank-slate theory
of procedural due process, but rather an embedded theory: conditional on
accepting the broad outlines of current law, what conception of procedural due process does best on dimensions of both fit and justification?
This need not imply, of course, slavish adherence to every decision of
every district court. A good embedded theory has some critical bite,
tacking back and forth between the legal materials and their best justifications. But the basic structure of the argument will be respectful
of extant law. I aim to show that *Mathews*'s core idea, the calculus of
procedure, can be respected while allocating front-line responsibility
for implementing that calculus to agencies rather than courts, and
that such an approach actually makes the most sense of post-*Mathews*
developments in the surrounding legal terrain. Those developments
have emphasized the interdependence of procedural choices and
policy-making, such that the very reasons that have pushed courts
toward deference on legal, factual, and policy judgments also support
deference on procedural judgments, even when protected entitlements
are involved.

The Due Process Mess

The problem with procedural due process is that there is great confusion at the level of theory, combined with a fair and growing degree of consistency at the level of practice. The two main axes of theoretical confusion are (1) whether courts should independently apply the *Mathews* calculus; and (2) when does the *Mathews* calculus apply at all. As I will explain, "deference" may or may not be invoked as to either question. The result is an appalling mess, an Augean stable that it would take a Hercules to clean out. And none of our judges is a Hercules. Happily, however, there is increasing consistency in practice. The arc of due process law bends toward abnegation.

"Good-Faith Judgments": Deference under *Mathews*

I will begin with *Mathews* itself, which was more ambiguous than is usually realized. To be sure, *Mathews* implicitly assumed, for the most part, that courts should apply the process calculus independently, without deference to the agency's initial determination. But in a cryptic passage toward the end of the opinion, the Court took another tack: "In assessing what process is due in this case, substantial weight must be given to the good-faith judgments of the individuals charged by Congress with the administration of social welfare programs that the procedures they have provided assure fair consideration of the entitlement claims of individuals. . . . This is especially so where, as here, the prescribed procedures not only provide the claimant with an effective process for asserting his claim prior to any administrative action, but also assure a right to an evidentiary hearing, as well as to subsequent judicial review, before the denial of his claim becomes final."[42] The passage is not discussed in many casebooks, perhaps because it seems out of step with the rest of *Mathews*. It illustrates that there is no necessary connection between *Mathews*'s due process calculus and the implicit assumption of the commentators that procedural due process must entail the allocation of primary decisional responsibility to courts. In another passage, *Mathews* gave something of a clue for a rationale that might underpin deference, observing that "procedural due process rules are shaped by the risk of error inherent in the truth-finding process as applied to the generality of cases, not the rare exceptions."[43] This means that *procedural rules must always be designed as a system*, in light of the overall goals of the administrative program at issue. This implies a leading role for agencies in procedural design, and a subsidiary role for courts, or so I will argue.

Deference after *Mathews*

The *Mathews* opinion thus took no wholly consistent position on whether courts should independently apply the procedural calculus. Later cases are theoretically inconsistent as well. In some cases the Court has described *Mathews* as an "intrusive" test and contrasted it with a deferential approach.[44] Yet a number of cases, both from the Supreme Court and the lower courts, have explicitly or implicitly deferred to agencies in roughly the sort of way I recommend, assessing the rationality of the agency's procedural choices rather than implementing the *Mathews* test directly.

Supreme Court Caselaw. A leading example of the deferential approach is *Schweiker v. McClure*,[45] decided in 1982 and written by Justice Powell, the author of *Mathews* itself. The case involved a network of statutory provisions and administrative regulations providing that certain hearing officers, administering Medicare benefits, be appointed by the Medicare carriers themselves, rather than being independent administrative law judges or other government officials. The Court upheld the provisions and regulations, in part on the basis of deference to the procedural judgments of legislature and agency: "[D]ue Process is flexible and calls for such procedural protections as the particular situation demands. We have considered appellees' claims in light of the strong presumption in favor of the validity of congressional action and consistently with this Court's recognition of 'congressional solicitude for fair procedure. . . .' Appellees simply have not shown that the procedures prescribed by Congress *and the Secretary* are not fair or that different or additional procedures would reduce the risk of erroneous deprivation of [benefits]."[46] Notable here are the Court's highly circumstantial description of due process, which naturally empha-sizes the factual and policy elements of the enterprise of designing procedural rules, and its attribution to Congress—and derivatively to the Secretary—of "solicitude for fair procedure."

Shortly, I will amplify on the last point, by way of analogy to John Hart Ely's process-based theory of constitutional judicial review. There is no general reason to think that either Congress or agencies acting under statutory grants systematically desire to afford as little process as possible to either claimants in benefits cases or even to regulated entities in other contexts. In benefits cases, the very fact that Congress or the agency has created the program in the first place suggests that it attaches positive weight to beneficiaries' welfare; and many benefits-administering agencies have voluntarily bound them-selves to provide more rulemaking procedure than the APA requires of them.[47] In regulatory cases, agencies themselves have an interest in providing a generally accurate system of administrative adjudica-tion. Absent some special grounds for suspicion that the agency has crafted a procedural system on distorted or biased grounds, courts have no reason to substitute their judgments for those of the primary decision-makers.

Schweiker v. McClure is not an outlier. In other cases, the Court has invoked deference in a range of settings. Another leading example involves veterans' benefits.[48] A statute enacted in the mid-nineteenth century limited to $10 the fees that veterans could pay to lawyers for assistance in administrative proceedings to obtain veterans' benefits.[49] The avowed aim of the statute was paternalistic; Congress feared that veterans would be exploited by unscrupulous lawyers, and the overall benefits system was intended to be a nonadversarial means of trans-ferring resources to veterans.[50] A set of would-be beneficiaries claimed that the limit on lawyer's fees violated due process, because it effec-tively barred them from retaining private counsel.[51]

The Court rejected the claim, based in large part on two important principles. The first was the premise that "deference to congressional judgment must be afforded even though the claim is that a statute Con-gress has enacted effects a denial of . . . procedural due process. . . ."[52] The second was *Mathews*'s own admonition that procedural due pro-cess requires an exercise in system design: "the very nature of the due process inquiry indicates that the fundamental fairness of a particular procedure does not turn on the result obtained in any individual case; rather, 'procedural due process rules are shaped by the risk of error inherent in the truth-finding process as applied to the generality of cases, not the rare exceptions.' "[53] The second principle supports the first, or so I will suggest when we come to justification.

The residual problem is that these cases do not actually explain when and why deference should or should not be afforded. Nor has the Court explicitly repudiated the pervasive assumption, taught as elementary in the hornbooks, that the *Mathews* calculus is to be applied independently by the courts.[54] The unsatisfactory situation is that the nominally prevailing approach is sometimes explicitly contradicted, but never explicitly repudiated.

Lower-Court Caselaw. Lower courts, for their part, sometimes review agencies' procedural choices deferentially, reciting the passage from *Mathews* about the good-faith judgments of administrators. A humdrum example is *Wilson v. SEC*.[55] Wilson, an investment adviser, was penalized in a Securities and Exchange Commission (SEC) proceeding and complained that the Commission had violated due process by presenting a witness who was examined and cross-examined by telephone. The court, deferring to the Commission's good-faith judgment, reviewed the Commission's procedural determinations under an "arbitrary and capricious" standard and upheld them. The Commission had given valid reasons for using the telephone procedure, rather than face-to-face confrontation, and that was enough.[56] Similar examples are strewn through the federal reports.[57]

"Far Less Intrusive"—Deference in Contrast to *Mathews*

There is another line of cases that wields deference in a somewhat different way, albeit with similar practical effects. In this line of cases, deference is taken as a reason not to apply the *Mathews* framework at all. On this conception, *Mathews* is taken to be a nondeferential approach, and the key inquiry is into the toggle-switch conditions that determine whether the *Mathews* framework governs, or instead some alternative deferential framework.

A leading example is *Medina v. California*,[58] which determined
that the *Mathews* framework would not govern the allocation of burdens of proof in procedures for determining competency in state criminal courts.[59] The Court's historical review of the origins of *Mathews*
implied, without quite saying, that *Mathews* applies only to "administrative law" or "administrative procedures."[60] In the case of procedures
ancillary to the criminal-justice system, however, it was appropriate to
apply a historically inflected test of fundamental fairness developed
in an earlier case, *Patterson v. New York*.[61] The key difference between the two tests was deference: "[B]ecause the States have consid-
erable expertise in matters of criminal procedure and the criminal
process is grounded in centuries of common-law tradition, it is appropriate to exercise substantial deference to legislative judgments in
this area. The analytical approach endorsed in *Patterson* is thus far less
intrusive than that approved in *Mathews*."[62] But it is not as though the
Court has spoken with one voice, over time, on this issue either. *Medina v. California* had to confine to their facts—"without disturbing
the[ir] holdings"—several earlier cases[63] that had applied the *Mathews*
framework as the governing test, even in proceedings ancillary to the
criminal process, such as motions to suppress evidence and capital sen-
tencing.[64] The core problem, of course, is that the boundary between
administrative procedure and criminal procedure is surprisingly ill-
defined—an insight of recent scholarship in public law that has cross-
fertilized the two subfields.[65]

Inconsistent Law-on-the-Books

So there are at least three lines of cases in the picture. One takes
Mathews as the touchstone test of due process, at least in the sense
that no scope conditions for the application of *Mathews* are mentioned,
and then applies the test independently, without deference to legislative or administrative judgments. A second line applies the *Mathews*
approach with deference built in, but these cases too say nothing to
limit the scope of the *Mathews* approach. The third is explicit about
scope conditions, but those conditions are themselves spongy around
the edges ("administrative procedure"). Under the third approach, def-

erence is not built into *Mathews*, but is instead given as a reason not to apply the *Mathews* test at all.

Analytically, the source of confusion is that the issues are multidimensional. A court must decide both (1) when *Mathews* applies and (2) whether the *Mathews* test should be applied according to the court's independent judgment, as a standard of decision, or instead deferentially, as a standard of review. Any particular answer to (1) need not imply any particular answer to (2), and vice versa. And indeed the three approaches we have identified give disparate answers. The first and third approaches agree that *Mathews* should not be cast as a deferential standard of review. The second and third approaches agree that courts should not necessarily exercise independent judgment about what process is due. The first and second, however, seemingly agree that *Mathews* always applies. These three propositions (that *Mathews* always applies, that it should not build in deference, and that courts should not necessarily exercise independent judgment about what process is due) cannot all be true simultaneously, although any two of them can. If the three approaches were persons voting over a multidimensional agenda, a Condorcet paradox of inconsistent aggregation would arise, although each approach is consistent on its own terms.

All this obviously poses, at a minimum, a conventional problem of judicial housekeeping: the doctrine needs to be put into some sort of order. One might even be grandiose and suggest that the current mess is bad enough to warrant concern from the standpoint of the rule of law. More importantly for my purposes, it also underscores that my proposal here is not as radical a departure from the caselaw as might be imagined. At a minimum, the nominal *Mathews* approach of independent judicial assessment is not to be taken strictly at face value.

The Red Herring of *Arnett v. Kennedy*

Unfortunately, we are not yet done clarifying the problem and straightening up the mess. The caselaw about the *Mathews* procedural calculus is entangled with, or obscured by, another defunct line of caselaw. The red herring was dragged across law's path in 1974, two years before *Mathews*, by Justice Rehnquist, writing a plurality opinion in *Arnett*

v. Kennedy, which said that for due process purposes, substantive entitlements are themselves conditioned on and limited by the statutory
procedures provided to enforce them.[66] The Court has since repudiated
Arnett, but it lives on as a bogeyman, an anti-model. Some believe *Arnett* to be related to the questions examined here, but it actually is not,
or so I will argue. Despite appearances, *Arnett* has nothing to do with
the question whether courts or agencies should have primary responsibility for applying the *Mathews* calculus. Let me explain.

The claimant in *Arnett* was a civil servant discharged for cause, as
the relevant statute required, but without being afforded a full adversary
hearing before termination. The claimant argued that the for-cause
limitation created a protected (property) interest and that the procedures afforded before termination did not provide due process. Justice
Rehnquist undertook to kill the burgeoning due process caselaw in its
crib, by building the procedures into the definition of the protected
entitlement itself:

> Here [the claimant] did have a statutory expectancy that he not be
> removed other than for [cause]. But the very section of the statute
> which granted him that right, a right which had previously existed
> only by virtue of administrative regulation, expressly provided also
> for the procedure by which "cause" was to be determined, and ex-
> pressly omitted the procedural guarantees which [the claimant] in-
> sists are mandated by the Constitution. Only by bifurcating the very
> sentence of the Act of Congress which conferred upon [the claimant]
> the right not to be removed save for cause could it be said that he had
> an expectancy of that substantive right without the procedural limi-
> tations which Congress attached to it. . . . *Where the grant of a sub-
> stantive right is inextricably intertwined with the limitations on the
> procedures which are to be employed in determining that right, a
> litigant in the position of [the claimant] must take the bitter with
> the sweet.*[67]

Although the logic has seemed compelling to some,[68] to others
Rehnquist seemed to offer a trivial *non sequitur*. So what if the protected interest and the limited procedure are laid out in adjacent statutory clauses? If the Constitution determines procedure, but allows
legislatures to determine substance, then one clause may be valid while

the other is not. As Justice Powell put it in a concurrence in *Arnett*, "[T]he right to procedural due process . . . is conferred, not by legislative grace, but by constitutional guarantee. While the legislature may elect not to confer a property interest in federal employment, it may not constitutionally authorize the deprivation of such an interest, once conferred, without appropriate procedural safeguards. As our cases have consistently recognized, the adequacy of statutory procedures for deprivation of a statutorily created property interest must be analyzed in constitutional terms."[69] Although a few subsequent cases seemed to adopt the approach of the *Arnett* plurality,[70] Powell's view eventually won out. In *Cleveland Board of Education v. Loudermill*,[71] the Court emphatically announced that "the Due Process Clause provides that certain substantive rights—life, liberty, and property—cannot be deprived except pursuant to constitutionally adequate procedures. The categories of substance and procedure are distinct. Were the rule otherwise, the Clause would be reduced to a mere tautology. 'Property' cannot be defined by the procedures provided for its deprivation any more than can life or liberty. The right to due process 'is conferred, not by legislative grace, but by constitutional guarantee.' "[72]

This sequence, although seemingly clarifying, produces its own set of confusions. All that *Loudermill* settles is that the Constitution, not statute, is the paramount source of law on the question what process is due. As has been true at least since *Marbury v. Madison*, however, a persistent occupational hazard of (some) lawyers is to skip lightly from the paramount status of the Constitution to the fallacious inference that courts must decide everything for themselves. The "bitter with the sweet" approach of *Arnett* was a radical attack on due process rights, an attempt to define them away right at the outset. Rejecting that approach, commentators have overcompensated, assuming that anything short of full, independent judicial assessment of the *Mathews* factors would amount to a return to *Arnett v. Kennedy*.[73] But this is wrong, analytically wrong.

Not one word in *Loudermill* denies or even addresses the possibility that the constitutional rule itself might permit or require courts to defer to agencies on the question of what process is due. *Loudermill* speaks rather narrowly to a sources-of-law question, but the deference issue is about two further interconnected questions: *what* constitutional law requires and *who decides* what the procedural regime will be. A regime in which courts allow agencies to design procedures, subject to arbitrariness review, does not define protected interests out of existence. It recognizes them and then goes on to ask what institutional regime, what allocation of authority to design procedures, will best accommodate that interest as part of a larger system of interests that must be balanced, reconciled, and—at some resource frontier, assuming agencies do not have infinite time and infinite budgets—traded off against one another?

Ironically, this approach may actually capture most of what Justice Rehnquist was worried about. Buried at the core of the *Arnett* plurality was a pragmatic kernel: the plurality referred to the challenged scheme, in which tenured civil servants would receive some, but not full, procedure pre-termination as a "legislative compromise."[74] The underlying concern was to protect an administrative space in which competing aims and values could be traded off against one another. There are two ways of clearing such a space: by a conceptual fusion of entitlements with process that necessarily defines away all constitutional constraint (the *Arnett* plurality's approach) or instead the creation of a zone of deference in the application of a constitutional standard. The rejection of the first approach says nothing at all about the validity of the second. And my suggestion of the second approach does not turn in any way on accepting the first.

Converging Precedent

I turn now from theoretical confusion to the relatively consistent practice of the courts. There are three streams of precedent in adjacent areas of law that fit nicely with a deferential conception of procedural due process. All three are post-*Mathews* developments. Together with the deferential strands of the due process caselaw itself, they suggest that independent judicial assessment of agency procedures is an increasingly marginal phenomenon—marginal in both the colloquial and technical senses. Abnegation is now the norm, in due process as elsewhere.

Agency Authority over Procedure: Vermont Yankee *and* Perez

The first major development, two years after *Mathews,* was the Court's emphatic reassertion in *Vermont Yankee* of the "very basic tenet of administrative law that agencies should be free to fashion their own rules of procedure."[75] On the basis of that principle, the Court eliminated an entire body of caselaw from the Court of Appeals for the District of Columbia Circuit that had forced or encouraged agencies to engage in "hybrid rulemaking"—offering more procedure than organic statutes and the Administrative Procedure Act required for informal rulemaking, although less than would be required under full, formal trial-type procedures.[76]

We have to be careful here to distinguish the holding of *Vermont Yankee* from its reasoning, which swept far more broadly. There are really two *Vermont Yankee* decisions. One is *Vermont Yankee* writ small, as a technical legal holding, and one is *Vermont Yankee* writ large, as a larger set of institutional commitments and principles that may be applied beyond and outside that legal holding.

Strictly speaking, of course, *Vermont Yankee* writ small merely held that courts have no *common-law* authority to require agencies to use more or different procedures than those specified in the APA. It did nothing at all to curtail judicial authority over the *constitutional* law of procedural due process. The Court carefully bracketed "constitutional constraints" as a separate source of procedural requirements[77]— arguably an unnecessary bracketing in any event, as the subject before the Court was procedural requirements in rulemaking, which is subject to minimal constitutional requirements anyway.[78] As a technical matter, writ small, *Vermont Yankee* has nothing to do with constitutional due process.

Yet the institutional rationale of *Vermont Yankee*—the writ-large significance of the decision—is not so easily cabined. The Court's basic insight, and its basic argument for deference, was the interdependence of substance and procedure. In other words, two sets of choices that seem distinct—(1) the choice of administrative procedures and (2) the choice of rules through substantive administrative lawmaking—are in fact one unitary enterprise. The Court's very first description of the sin of hybrid rulemaking was that it amounted to courts "engrafting

their own notions of proper procedures on agencies entrusted with substantive functions."[79] And *Vermont Yankee*'s rationale for the master
principle that agencies, rather than courts, should choose agency procedures was that

> administrative agencies and administrators will be familiar with the
> industries which they regulate and *will be in a better position than
> federal courts or Congress itself to design procedural rules adapted
> to the peculiarities of the industry and the tasks of the agency in-
> volved.* . . . [T]his Court has for more than four decades emphasized
> that the formulation of procedures was basically to be left within the
> discretion of the agencies to which Congress had confided the respon-
> sibility for substantive judgments. . . . Absent compelling constitu-
> tional constraints or extremely compelling circumstances, the
> administrative agencies should be free to fashion their own rules of
> procedure and to pursue methods of inquiry capable of permitting
> them to discharge their multitudinous duties.[80]

Throughout *Vermont Yankee*, this point was brigaded with a seemingly distinct point about resource allocation.[81] Agencies have limited
resources, and judicial proceduralization intrudes on the agency's authority to set priorities and allocate limited resources in ways that best
ensure the overall achievement of its specified goals.[82] Indeed, in
Heckler v. Chaney,[83] the Court (once again through Rehnquist) described this as the master rationale of *Vermont Yankee*.[84]

But resource allocation on the one hand, and the interdependence
of substance and procedure on the other, are really the same point, just
viewed from different angles. The agency enterprise, rightly understood, is optimal policy-making under resource constraints—an exercise in which the content of rules (whether created through rulemaking
or adjudication) and the procedures for arriving at that content are both
interdependent variables in the constrained optimization problem.
Because of this interdependence, the agency's informational advantage
("expertise") as to the content of rules spills over, as it were, to the procedures for determining what those rules should be.

In emphasizing the interdependence of substance and procedure, I
do not wish to be misunderstood as reviving in a different guise the
fusion of procedure with substantive entitlements attempted in *Arnett*

v. Kennedy. That approach attempts a complete *conceptual* fusion of substance and procedure, whereas *Vermont Yankee* (and *Heckler*) make a very different type of claim. According to that claim, it is not that procedure and substance are conceptually fused; we can disentangle procedural and substantive decisions at a conceptual level. Rather the point is that one cannot sensibly make choices about one without simultaneously making choices about the other. A producer of wheat must decide, in an interdependent fashion, both what variety to plant (substance) and how and when to plant it (procedure); yet we need not think that the variety and the methods of planting just are the same thing. So too with the producer of administrative policy.

Vermont Yankee is by now an old case, and for many years scholars awaited its second coming.[85] The wait is over. In *Perez v. Mortgage Bankers Association*,[86] discussed in Chapter 2, the Court brusquely eliminated a new and different body of D.C. Circuit caselaw on administrative procedure, one that purported to bar agencies from changing "definitive" interpretations except through notice-and-comment procedures.[87] The Court's admonition was stern:

> Time and again, we have reiterated that the APA "sets forth the full extent of judicial authority to review executive agency action for procedural correctness." Beyond the APA's minimum requirements, courts lack authority "to impose upon [an] agency its own notion of which procedures are 'best' or most likely to further some vague, undefined public good." To do otherwise would violate "the very basic tenet of administrative law that agencies should be free to fashion their own rules of procedure." These foundational principles apply with equal force to the APA's procedures for rulemaking. . . . Agencies are free to grant additional procedural rights in the exercise of their discretion, but reviewing courts are generally not free to impose them if the agencies have not chosen to grant them.[88]

It is striking that although due process is of course an independent source of "judicial authority to review executive agency action for procedural correctness," the sweeping language of *Perez* omits all mention of due process. There is a logic to the omission: the "foundational principle" *Perez* underscores is essentially an anti-judicial principle, a constraint on judicial authority to impose additional procedures on executive actors. I will return to this point shortly.

Chevron *and Procedure*

More recent developments have also underscored the interdependence of substance and procedure. A critical question for administrative law involves the allocation of authority between agency and court to interpret procedural provisions in agencies' organic statutes and in related provisions in the APA itself. The Supreme Court has not yet squarely settled the question. But in the lower courts, unless and until overturned, a consensus in favor of abnegation has emerged. The consensus holds that agencies have broad authority to interpret gaps and ambiguities in statutory procedural provisions, including in adjudication, subject only to deferential judicial review.[89]

The leading case is *Dominion Energy Brayton Point LLC v. Johnson*,[90] in which the Court of Appeals for the First Circuit, reversing its earlier approach, held that a requirement of "public hearing" in the Clean Water Act did not oblige the Environmental Protection Agency (EPA) to offer more than a paper hearing, on the basis of written submissions, when deciding upon requests for a variance from permit requirements. Holding that *Chevron* provided the correct framework, the court described the statutory language as ambiguous.[91] In conducting the *Chevron* analysis, the court emphasized that it was asking only whether the agency's procedural choices were "reasonable" and found that *EPA had itself reasonably balanced the* Mathews *factors* when deciding whether to afford the regulated party additional procedure.[92] Here the court did not clearly distinguish the reasonableness of the agency's interpretation, at the second step of *Chevron*, from the question whether the agency's decisional process was reasonable, or instead "arbitrary and capricious."[93] In this, the court did no worse than the Supreme Court, which has frequently and sometimes deliberately conflated the two inquiries as well.[94]

Dominion Energy's deferential approach to the interpretation of statutory procedural clauses supplies an analogy, an exportable model, for the deferential approach to procedural due process. Agencies' procedural choices should be reviewed to determine whether agencies have considered the *Mathews* factors and offered minimally acceptable reasons for their optimizing interdependent choices—no more. The near-universal consensus among the courts of appeal is now that *Chevron* deference applies to agencies' interpretation of statutory procedures—a position that in effect places front-line authority for applying the *Mathews* calculus in agencies rather than courts, as occurred in *Dominion Energy* itself.

Chevron *and "Jurisdiction"*

The last converging strand involves a legal rule that is (now) firmly settled, eminently logical, and yet odious to the traditional legal mind: agencies receive judicial deference on the statutory boundaries of their own authority—what traditional lawyers call their "jurisdiction."[95] The relevance of this is indirect, but important nonetheless. Stock arguments against deference to agencies' procedural choices invoke the risk of agency self-dealing, the risk that a legal rule putting agencies in charge (within rational limits) of their own procedures would in effect make agencies "judges in their own cause." Traditional legalists made exactly the same self-dealing argument to show that agencies could not enjoy deference on the limits of their own jurisdiction. The Court, however, rejected the argument on grounds that apply to the procedural setting as well. Law itself has partly abnegated its authority over both agency jurisdiction and agency procedure, for similar reasons.

Recall, from Chapter 1, *Crowell v. Benson*'s admonition that unless courts review *de novo* the facts on which agency jurisdiction depends, the result "would be to sap the judicial power as it exists under the federal Constitution, and to establish a government of a bureaucratic character alien to our system."[96] To be sure, the category of "jurisdictional fact" rather quickly faded into the twilight reserved for doctrines that are only half-alive. But a related notion floated around the margins of the *Chevron* doctrine after 1984—the notion that there was some sort of exception to *Chevron* for "jurisdictional questions."[97] Along these lines, the traditional legal mind has always felt—although the feeling is protean and assumes ever-shifting doctrinal forms—that courts must determine for themselves *de novo* what the boundaries of agency jurisdiction are, including the facts that determine those boundaries.

As we also saw in Chapter 1, in *City of Arlington v. FCC*, decided in 2013, the Court swept away the whole idea that agency "jurisdiction" is an exceptional category. In what is perhaps the most relentlessly logical majority opinion in the *U.S. Reports*, Justice Scalia even denied that any identifiable category of "jurisdictional" questions exists or ever existed. Under any organic statute, the logic runs, there are N statutory prerequisites to the agency's exercise of coercive legal authority over regulated parties. Absent any one of these statutory prerequisites, the agency lacks legal power to proceed. There is no basis for singling out some particular subset of those prerequisites and labeling them "jurisdictional." *Chevron* deference must extend to all the prerequisites, or to none. The only question is whether the agency's assertion of statutory authority is or is not "reasonable."[98]

The same applies in parallel to agency choice of procedures. Courts should police agencies to ensure that (1) clear procedural provisions in statutes are honored, while agencies have discretion to interpret ambiguities (as in *Dominion Energy*); and (2) agencies have remained within reasonable bounds in their application of *Mathews*'s marginalist analysis of procedure. The former constraint does for agency choice of procedures, under *Mathews* and the constitutional guarantee of procedural due process, exactly what *City of Arlington* does for agency assertions of statutory authority, while the latter constraint adds a layer of judicial review that goes beyond what is available in purely statutory cases about agency procedure.

Here is the larger picture. We have these three adjacent areas of precedent, none of which directly involves procedural due process (although *Dominion Energy* sits right on the line). In all three areas, after *Mathews*, the underlying rationales and principles embody a judicial willingness to carve out space for greater agency discretion over procedural choices. It is time to circle back to the main issue and apply those principles directly to procedural due process itself.

Justification

Let me now turn from fit to justification, bearing in mind that we will always be tacking back and forth between the two. The converging strands of caselaw after *Mathews* are not unreasoned. They rest on a set of institutional principles—principles that, rightly understood and interpreted in their best light, limit the reach of law's empire.

Procedure, Substance, and Expertise

The leading critique of *Dominion Energy* correctly remarks that "issues involving procedural provisions are distinct from substantive issues."[99] Again, however, although the two are indeed conceptually and analytically distinct, the problem is that they are pragmatically interdependent in the larger institutional system of agency decision-making. In *Dominion Energy* itself, it is not clear how the most well-motivated agency could think coherently about the substantive questions in some given array of regulatory variance decisions without *also*, and simultaneously, thinking about how much time and resources to invest in determining whether to grant a variance in particular cases. The decision over how much procedure to afford, with some resulting costs of decision-making and of error, is just a decision about the allocation of limited agency resources—a decision about optimization under constraints.

For reasons of this sort, Louis Jaffe, in the epigraph with which I began the chapter, observed that expertise as to substance is impossible to cabin and separate cleanly from procedural discretion. Substance spills over into procedure, obliterating the traditional legalism that while agencies may understand the substantive problems involved, courts are experts at procedure. The two cannot be separated, pragmatically speaking, because the design of a procedural system for agency decision-making will itself determine, at least in part, whether, how, and when the agency will achieve its substantive goals, and what trade-offs agencies will make when multiple substantive goals interact. In a world of limited resources, agencies must allocate resources. The same point in effect underlies *Vermont Yankee* and the post-*Chevron* cases on the interpretation of procedural provisions in organic statutes.

Although those cases nominally involve sub-constitutional questions, and are thus nominally consistent with fully independent judicial application of *Mathews*, their underlying premises are not so easily confined.

Part of the problem here is that traditional legalism elides the distinction between systemic and case-specific thinking, and the problems of resource allocation that inevitably arise when agencies must think in aggregate long-run terms. In any given case, it is true, *ex post*, from the standpoint of a reviewing institution like a court, that we can imagine arriving at the given substantive decision by different procedures, or arriving at a different substantive decision with the same procedures. But that case-specific and *ex post* standpoint is not the agency's own standpoint. The agency's problem is always *ex ante* and aggregated; its problem is to design and operate a procedural system over an array of cases, deciding at several margins simultaneously where and how to invest its limited resources in deciding what policies and legal rules to adopt. That sort of optimizing cannot be substance-independent; the agency will have to decide which sorts of errors are more costly, how many resources it can invest in, which sorts of decision-making, and which sorts of proceedings or cases will yield the greatest return-on-investment for its policy goals. All procedure is aggregate procedure, usually over an array of similar problems or cases, or at a minimum in the sense that investments in more procedure in any one area will entail less procedure in a different area, given constraints on the agency's resources. The traditional legal mind has difficulty transcending the particularity of litigated cases, but agencies operate on an aggregate basis.

Systemic Procedure and the Marginal Benefits of Judicial Review

Thus *Mathews* itself correctly emphasizes,[100] as do later cases,[101] that the correct perspective in matters of due process is systemic. Every procedural decision that agencies make implicitly amounts to, and presupposes, a view about the design and operation of the overall system. But *Mathews* did not fully appreciate the implications of its own systemic logic. Despite the Court's aside that the "good-faith judgments"[102] of administrators must be respected, the pervasive assumption of the opinion was that courts should apply the calculus independently. If procedural decisions are not only pragmatically intertwined with substantive ones, but also inevitably and necessarily aggregative and systemic, then the right question is whether courts or agencies are better positioned to design the agency's overall procedural system. More precisely still, the question is marginalist: given that agencies will inevitably be forced to take some view or other about the design of procedural systems, what *marginal* contribution do the judges make when reviewing those decisions?

It has seemed obvious to increasing numbers of judges themselves—the judges who have fashioned the post-*Mathews* caselaw on agency procedural discretion over the past two generations—that agencies are better positioned to design procedural systems. Federal judges get snapshots of agency procedure in particular cases; the limited institutional memory of a federal circuit does not provide the overall perspective that agency officials enjoy. The federal judicial system is not set up, not equipped, to engage in a sustained course of synoptic institutional engineering. The limits of the generalist, case-specific, and episodic perspective of the federal judicial system are exacerbated by a world in which the underlying problems become increasingly complex; the design of procedures for nuclear plant operator licenses is a very different problem than, say, the design of procedures for carriage licenses.

This is not to say that the judicial system is helpless or that it makes no marginal contribution at all. Shortly I will suggest that the judges should retain the sort of role they play in other areas of administrative law, by examining the reasons agencies give for their procedural choices, and thereby providing agencies with an *ex ante* incentive to proceed on the basis of defensible reasons. But I do mean to say that judges should recognize—and increasingly have recognized, under various but converging strands of caselaw—the possibility that their limited information, episodic perspective, and time constraints together imply that the marginal benefits of judicial intervention in procedural design may be low or even negative, as the intensity of intervention increases.

A Process-Failure Approach

Another angle of vision comes most directly from constitutional theory rather than administrative law. The process-failure literature stemming from John Hart Ely proposes a judicial role limited to reinforcing democratic representation, rather than the substitution of judicial value judgments for those of the political branches.[103] The Elyian judge asks, in brief, whether there has been some political self-dealing that chokes off the channels of political change, and whether some sort of majoritarian bias is in evidence.[104] Absent either condition, the Elyian judge will stay her hand.

On this perspective, rather than plunging into procedural design themselves, courts should stop, look, listen, and then ask a logically antecedent question: is there any reason to think that the relevant agency will have systematically skewed incentives or make systematically distorted judgments when applying the *Mathews* calculus, such that the agency will systematically over-weight or under-weight particular factors? If there is no reason to think that the agency has systematically distorted incentives or is prone to systematic distortions of judgment, then there is no reason for judges to displace agency choices about the marginal costs and benefits of additional (or different) procedure in the execution of the agency's program. Agencies may of course make random errors, but so too may judges—especially generalist judges deciding on the value of procedures under programs they only dimly understand.

Agency Motivations and Judgments: Some Mistakes

At this point one tends to encounter a number of sweeping generalities about agency motivations and judgments:

1. Agencies want to offer as little procedure as possible, perhaps because they are "mission-oriented."
2. Agencies are "political," so procedural judgments are politicized rather than "impartial."
3. Courts are experts in "procedure," agencies are not.
4. In a variant of (3), lawyers are experts in procedure, agency technocrats are not.

Of course it is possible to mix and match these generalizations—combining (1) with (2), or (2) with (3), or smushing all of them together.

The main thing to say about such judgments is "not really." Some are demonstrably false, some merely overblown. Obviously there are oceans of literature on the motivations and judgments of both agencies and courts, in both legal theory and political science. It is hard to generalize, which is my point; because it is hard to generalize, courts should not use an approach that implicitly rests on crude stereotypes or on systematic distrust of agencies' procedural choices. Let me offer a few comments on each of these flawed generalizations in turn.

(1) It is not the case that agencies want to offer as little procedure as possible.[105] In rulemaking, where *Vermont Yankee* first squashed judicial requirements of "hybrid" procedure, agencies frequently offer more procedure than the notice-and-comment requirements of Section 553 of the APA demand, even as judicially interpreted.[106] Agencies may offer cross-examination of staff, oral presentations, or other components of formal trial-type hearings. In adjudication the same is true,[107] even after the *Vermont Yankee* rule was explicitly extended to informal adjudication in 1990.[108] Even when statutes do not require a formal "hearing on the record" sufficient to trigger the APA procedures for trial-type adjudication, the bare-bones procedure for informal adjudication in APA Section 555 is often voluntarily supplemented by the agencies themselves.[109]

So it is a misconception that agencies will never offer more procedure than they are legally required to offer. There are any number of reasons why agencies often go beyond their legal obligations; again, the point is that it is very hard to generalize. Sometimes they do so to appease constituencies, stakeholders, or regulated parties who wish to be heard (or who wish to show to *their* own constituents and stakeholders that they have been heard); sometimes they do so to make a full record for judicial review; sometimes—more frequently than cynics believe—agencies may simply think, on *Mathews*-type grounds, that the issue at hand warrants more process than the legally mandated minimum. But one of the major reasons agencies go beyond the legal minimum is that precisely *when and to the extent that agencies are mission-oriented, they will have an interest in accuracy,* and will sometimes provide extra procedure in order to ensure accuracy (at least in an aggregate sense). Accuracy often appears on both sides of the ledger, both the side of the agency and of the regulated entity; promoting accuracy is sometimes a common interest.[110]

The SEC, for example, has little interest in inaccurate administrative adjudication of civil penalties.[111] Errors in its own internal adjudication are costly, in part because erroneous decisions are more likely to be challenged in court on evidentiary grounds, and in part because erroneous imposition of penalties actually dilutes deterrence. If penalties were imposed randomly, there would be no deterrence of regulated parties, and the agency's mission of efficient regulation would actually suffer; hence to some degree, at least, the agency and regulated parties have a joint interest in accuracy. Agencies will, of course, never be willing to invest as much in any given case as regulated parties might like, yet that does not or at least need not show any distortion of incentives or judgments on the agencies' part. What it shows is that agencies have to balance more considerations than do single-minded parties. Judges sometimes overlook this by focusing on the particulars of the case at hand; they observe, correctly, that some extra increment of procedure would have increased accuracy in that case, forgetting that under resource constraints more procedure here means less procedure there.

(2) Of course there is a sense in which all agencies are "political." There is also a sense in which all courts are "political"—as the ever-growing pile of evidence on ideological and strategic judicial voting demonstrates. There is another sense, however, in which neither agencies nor courts are "political," not pejoratively anyway. The universal testimony of both agency officials and judges is that cases are rarely if ever decided, nor rules made, on grounds that are political in the core sense of "telephone justice"—that some powerful person X favors the interests of person Y for corrupt or ideological reasons. On the other hand, the universal testimony of both agency officials and judges is that agencies *do* act "politically" in the quite appropriate sense that agencies adopt the value premises held by democratically elected officials who are influential with the agency, as overseers, stakeholders, appointers of

agency heads, or hierarchical superiors. Such premises must come
from somewhere, and if they do not come from agencies (derivatively),
they will come from the judges themselves, which will be no less
"political."

All that said, my main point, here and throughout, is that generalizations about agencies are treacherous in the extreme, and that legal
rules must always take account one way or another of agency hetero-
geneity. The idea that agencies are "political" is a particularly mean-
ingless generalization. It elides the differences between independent
agencies and executive agencies, which may or may not both be
"political," but are at least political in different ways, with respect to
different constituencies;[112] between or among agencies whose members are chosen according to strict statutory requirements of partisan
balance, multimember agencies without partisan balance requirements,
and single-head agencies; and on and on. As I will discuss shortly,
rationality review of agencies' procedural choices is the most flexible
and natural way to flush out "political" motivations, somehow defined, if those are taken to be something that need to be flushed out.
Whether they should be so taken is a separate question. There is a live
debate in administrative law about whether rationality review does
or should allow agencies to make choices on "political" grounds, with
varying definitions of "political" flying about.[113] I need not engage
that debate, because it cuts across the category of procedural choices
that I examine here.

(3)–(4) The traditional lawyer's conceit about procedure—that the legal
profession has some sort of peculiar expertise in the design of procedural rules—is mystifying, in several senses. First, the *basis* for the
conceit is mystifying; every profession designs procedures for the conduct of its business, economists and doctors and corporate managers
and public administrators no less than lawyers. Indeed the drafters of
the APA themselves recognized the existence of a distinctive category
of "business procedures" that agencies might adopt in certain circumstances.[114] Second, the *relevance* of the conceit is mystifying. Lawyers
work *within* agencies as well as on the bench, or at the bar. If lawyers
are experts in procedural design, why should the judgments of one set
of lawyers, the ones to be found in courts, trump the earlier judgments

of another set, the ones who designed the agency procedures in the first place? And, finally, the *effects* of the conceit may well be mystifying in a Benthamite sense, insofar as the conceit deters law's subjects from questioning whether judges are well-positioned to design agency procedures, or even to make a marginal contribution to the enterprise of design.

Flushing Out Agency Motivations and Judgments

None of this is to say that agencies will never act from bad motivations or from distorted judgments. I certainly do not want to overclaim, or to be understood as suggesting, that the crude generalizations I have criticized should be replaced by crude generalizations in the opposite direction. What I do mean to say is that no large generalizations are possible. Precisely *because* that is true, procedural due process should rest on a posture of judicial agnosticism about agency motivations, accompanied by the same presumption of regularity that is generally taken as the baseline for evaluating administrative action. That presumption may be rebutted by a showing, in the circumstances, that agencies have not offered rational grounds for their procedural choices.

Put differently, I suggest that even in the domain of procedural due process, courts should use one of law's standard methods for flushing out undesirable agency motivations or distorted agency judgments: requiring agencies to provide valid reasons for their choices. Agencies acting on the basis of undesirable motives or distorted judgments will, all else equal, find it more costly to provide reasons that plausibly justify their choices, and the worse their motives or judgments, the costlier it will be. That approach allows the problem of agency motivations and judgments to be approached in a standard-like way rather than a rule-like way, without sweeping generalizations, but with sensitivity to the particular statutes, programs, and circumstances at issue.

When courts apply *Mathews* independently, however, not reviewing the agency's choices but making the choices themselves, they are in effect making extreme assumptions about agency motivations, or judgments, or both. They are assuming, quite invisibly, that agencies are systematically not to be trusted and that courts must step in to decide on sensible agency procedures *de novo*. The result is a kind of irrebuttable presumption of distrust. An approach to *Mathews* that makes it a standard of review for courts and a rule of decision for agencies, rather than a rule of decision for courts, would avoid making such sweeping assumptions. It would embody a more nuanced *rebuttable* presumption of agency regularity, assuming that agencies' front-line experience and superior information about the substance of relevant programs counts for something, and that courts may use ordinary review of agency reason-giving to flush out marginal cases of bad agency motivation or distorted judgments.

The Fox and the Henhouse

Finally, let me return to the question of agency self-dealing, a concern often invoked with the aid of the maxim *nemo iudex in sua causa*—"no man should be judge in his own cause." This is a standard reflex for lawyers who critique judicial deference to agencies' procedural choices; such deference makes the agencies judges in their own causes, does it not? For reasons both general and particular, however, I think this reflex ought to be resisted if at all possible.

The general reason is that even the most casual overview of constitutional law shows that there is just no general principle against making institutions judges in their own cause; state and national constitutions, including our own, frequently make institutions the final arbiters of their own composition, compensation, or power.[115] Legislators determine the boundaries and composition of their own constituencies, decide who counts as a validly seated member of the legislature, and set their own salaries. The President may pardon friends, family, and subordinates, and quite arguably even himself, while the Vice President may quite arguably preside at his own impeachment. Judges determine the constitutionality of provisions that set their own salary, sometimes by hearing class action suits composed of all judges—thus quite literally sitting as judges in their own cause. (All this occurs under cover of a judicially created doctrine, the "rule of necessity." Why exactly it is necessary that judges be able to decide such matters is not altogether clear.) The final culprit is judicial review itself, which as Jeremy Waldron points out in effect makes the Supreme Court the final legal arbiter of its own constitutional power.[116]

So constitutional law not infrequently makes officers or institutions the judges of their own compliance with the Constitution itself. The Court has recognized, in other words, that it is perfectly intelligible to say *both* that (1) the Constitution creates a legal norm that constrains some institutional actor; *and* that (2) the Constitution commits to that very actor the determination whether the norm has been complied with. Perhaps the most dramatic example involves the procedural rules to be used in a federal impeachment trial in the Senate, where—the Court has said—the Senate itself enjoys unreviewable authority to determine whether the constitutional rules have been followed.[117] The approach to procedural due process that I propose does not go so far as that; it sees the constitutional rule as committing the procedural calculus to executive discretion, but only subject to judicial review for arbitrariness.

So much for the general background of constitutional law, which simply cannot be successfully understood through the lens of the *nemo iudex* maxim. The particular reason involves administrative agencies and their decisions, both procedural and substantive, in adjudication. The pure baseline position—the imagined world of the *nemo iudex* maxim, a world that may or may not have ever existed—cannot be invoked as a guiding principle with respect to particular issues in administrative law, because our whole administrative law emphatically rejects that baseline position. As recounted in Chapter 2, the architects of the administrative state, acting with eyes open, severely compromised the *nemo iudex* principle by combining in the hands of agencies the classical functions of lawmaking, law-execution, and adjudication, at least at the agency-head level. (At lower levels, as we saw, the APA creates a separation of functions between administrative law judges and prosecutorial or investigative staff within agencies.) They did so in order to obtain other overbalancing goods, especially public checks on *private* self-dealing; vigorous liberty-promoting activity by agencies; and a faster rate of policy adjustment in an ever-changing modern economy. The upshot is that invocation of the *nemo iudex* maxim, either in an administrative-law setting or in public law generally, is simplistic. Neither the written Constitution, nor constitutional law, nor administrative law can be successfully understood through the lens of that maxim.

Thus in *City of Arlington*, as I explained before, the Court rejected the concern over agency self-dealing by reasserting judicial authority to police clear statutory violations by agencies: "The fox-in-the-henhouse syndrome is to be avoided not by establishing an arbitrary and undefinable category of agency decisionmaking that is accorded no deference, but by taking seriously, and applying rigorously, in all cases, statutory limits on agencies' authority. Where Congress has established a clear line, the agency cannot go beyond it; and where Congress has established an ambiguous line, the agency can go no further than the ambiguity will fairly allow."[118] The check on putative agency self-dealing is the residual authority of courts to enforce very clear statutory texts. Short of that, however, there is to be no separate, free-floating judicial oversight.

Judicial Abnegation and Administrative Due Process

In areas of law abutting procedural due process, law has abnegated a great deal of its authority over the choice of procedures to be used in agency decision-making. Not all of its authority, to be sure; courts still enforce clear commands about procedure inscribed into organic statutes and apply the general procedural rules of the APA. But courts have increasingly come to see procedure as a matter committed to agency discretion, subject only to statutory floors. In due process law itself, courts often review agencies' application of the *Mathews* calculus, rather than simply apply the calculus for themselves.

This increasing abnegation of judicial authority rests on a set of principles, in the form of an essentially economic and institutional insight. Judges have come to realize that agencies, even or especially when pursuing the mission that Congress has assigned to them, engage in a form of constrained optimization. Under resource constraints, agencies must design procedures with a view to substance, and vice versa. Hence procedure and substance, whether or not conceptually distinct, are pragmatically inextricable, and agencies must calibrate both margins simultaneously. Agency authority over substance, explicitly or implicitly delegated by Congress and justified by agency expertise, necessarily implies authority over procedure as well.

The abnegation is only partial because judges retain authority to review agency procedural decisions for rationality. Agencies may not arbitrarily set procedures, but they enjoy a margin of reasonable discretion in applying the *Mathews* cost-benefit calculus. The judges, in other words, have opted for a regime of partial administrative constitutionalism, because the judges themselves have realized, from *within* law, that agency procedural decisions are decisions of policy and institutional design, not subject to full legalization. On Dworkinian grounds, I suggest that this regime fits well with converging strands of caselaw and is normatively sensible. Law's empire, here as elsewhere, has voluntarily contracted its frontiers.

4

Rationally Arbitrary Decisions

The sense in which I am using the term ["uncertainty"] is that in which the prospect of a European war is uncertain, or the price of copper and the rate of interest twenty years hence, or the obsolescence of a new invention, or the position of private wealth-owners in the social system in 1970. About these matters there is no scientific basis on which to form any calculable probability whatever. We simply do not know. Nevertheless, the necessity for action and for decision compels us as practical men to do our best to overlook this awkward fact and to behave exactly as we should if we had behind us a good Benthamite calculation of a series of prospective advantages and disadvantages, each multiplied by its appropriate probability, waiting to be summed.

—John Maynard Keynes, "The General Theory of Employment,"
51 *Quarterly Journal of Economics* 209, 214 (1937).

I NOW CONTINUE the story of abnegation—a narrative combining fit and justification—into administrative-law proper, derived from the Administrative Procedure Act itself rather than under the Constitution (as in Chapters 1 through 3). This chapter and Chapter 5, in combination with the appendix, will offer an overview of judicial review of agency action that inquires into rationality—a critical topic in a world in which agencies enjoy broad grants of statutory authority, and enjoy *Chevron* deference even on the scope of their own authority, so that statutory constraints on agency power are severely attenuated.

In this chapter, I will examine a problem of great and increasing importance for the administrative state: how does law cope with genuine *uncertainty?* How should law do so? I will suggest that agencies frequently and increasingly face decisions under unavoidable uncertainty—often called "Knightian uncertainty," after the great University of Chicago economist Frank Knight.[1] In this framework, agencies take decisions under either (1) certainty; (2) risk, involving calculable probabilities; (3) Knightian or genuine uncertainty, in which the possible outcomes are known but probabilities cannot be attached to them (more precisely, although probabilities can always be generated, those probabilities have no epistemic foundation beneath them or warrant backing them); or (4) ignorance, in which the possible outcomes and their probabilities are both indeterminate.[2]

The significance of uncertainty for the law of rational agency decision-making cannot be overstated. Increasingly, agencies operate at a policymaking frontier where settled science and expert consensus have run out. When agencies do face serious uncertainty of this sort, reasons themselves sometimes run out as well. Agencies may have excellent reason to make some decision or other, yet the actual decision will necessarily amount to a leap in the dark. In that sense, their decisions will inevitably be arbitrary, yet rationally so. Agencies will make *rationally arbitrary decisions.*

I will also suggest the circumstances of uncertainty do and should sharply limit judicial review. Where uncertainty prevails, reasons run out, and an insatiable judicial demand for reasons merely inflicts harm on the legal system. The combination of arbitrary agency decision-making at the uncertainty frontier with deferential judicial review is horrifying to the traditional legal mind, which craves fully reason-based decision-making by government, enforced by law. In fact, however, law maturing over time has rejected that traditional stance, for good legal reasons. The result is legal tolerance for arbitrariness, the ultimate abnegation of law's pretensions.

A Dworkinian Defense of Arbitrary
Decision-Making by Agencies

As always, my argument is embedded in precedent. Courts not only should, but for the most part in fact do, adopt a modest and deferential posture in such cases, allowing agencies to rationally make arbitrary choices. The presence of uncertainty is good and sufficient reason for law's abnegation.

Uncertainty is a special case of the thin theory of rationality review, which I will explain in full in Chapter 5. But it is also a critical case. If uncertainty justifies a modest judicial posture, and such a posture in fact amounts to the central tendency of the law, and if it is furthermore true that uncertainty is an ever-increasing phenomenon in the administrative state, then there is a kind of engine of abnegation built into rationality review itself.

I believe this is exactly what we observe, interpretively speaking. Here as throughout, my claim combines fit with justification in Dworkinian fashion. As I will explain, both here and in the next, continuous chapter, Chapter 5, the Supreme Court has been clear and emphatic that lower courts are to respect the limitations of rationality under conditions of uncertainty, and that lower courts must not impose upon agencies burdens of reasoned explanation that they cannot bear, given the problems they face. Decisions from *Baltimore Gas & Electric v. NRDC*[3] to *FCC v. Fox*[4] and *EPA v. EME Homer*[5] have underscored this theme. The episodic lower-court decisions that do not respect it are deviations from law's central tendency, unfolding over time.

Decision-Making under Uncertainty:
By Agencies and by Courts

Let me begin by clarifying the problems and providing some initial examples, to motivate the discussion. In the modern administrative state, the problem of uncertainty occurs at two different levels. At the first level, agencies exercise delegated statutory authority to regulate, yet their regulatory decisions with some frequency must be taken under genuine uncertainty. At the second level, courts review agency decisions taken under uncertainty and must apply general administrative-law requirements of rational decision-making. At this level, the question is not what the correct decision under uncertainty would be, but rather whether the agency has approached the decision in a rational way.

I will focus on the second level, asking how courts do and should review agency decisions under uncertainty. Here are some recent, and real, examples of the relevant problems:

- The Secretary of the Interior, acting through the Fish and Wildlife Service, must decide whether to list the flat-tailed horned lizard as a "threatened" species under the Endangered Species Act. The problem is that the methodology previously used to estimate the number of lizards in a given area has been exposed as worthless, and newer methods are not yet operational. In short, no one has any rational basis for estimating how many lizards there are. What should the Secretary do? What should the court say the Secretary may, may not, or must do?

- The Department of Energy wants to open a "biosafety level 3" facility, handling pathogens like the SARS virus, at the Lawrence Livermore National Laboratory. How serious is the possibility that the pathogens will escape, either because of accident or terrorist attack? How much analysis, or what kind of analysis, should courts require the Department to conduct before allowing the facility to be built?

- The Nuclear Regulatory Commission has to decide whether to license nuclear power plants. One of the issues in that decision is whether spent nuclear fuels stored at such plants pose a threat to health or to the environment. The time-scales involved beggar the imagination, as some of the materials involved have half-lives running into hundreds of thousands of years. How should the Commission assess the possible harms? Should reviewing courts require the agency to use "cautious" or "conservative" assumptions about those harms?

- The Securities and Exchange Commission must decide whether fixed indexed annuities should count as "annuities" within the meaning of the federal securities laws. Statutes require the Commission to consider the effects of its decision on "efficiency" and "competition." The Commission believes that the worst possible state of affairs is legal uncertainty about whether fixed indexed annuities count as "annuities"; either decision on that question will promote competition. But the question remains: which way should it decide?

As we will see, the Supreme Court has understood its proper role in such cases quite intelligently, and with surprising consistency. The Court has been very clear that agencies are to enjoy the broadest possible latitude to make predictive judgments under uncertainty, judgments that cannot be proven correct or incorrect, and that necessarily embody irreducible choices—what I will call rationally arbitrary decisions. Moreover, we will also see that the Court has understood very clearly that in the presence of uncertainty, "conservative" assumptions have no necessary priority or superiority.

Lower courts, however, sometimes misconceive their role in such cases, in part because they make conceptual mistakes about what it means to make rational decisions under uncertainty. Procedurally, judges sometimes demand reasons that cannot be given. Under conditions of genuine uncertainty, reasons run out and a relentless demand for further reason-giving becomes pathological. There is a category of agency decisions is which *it is rational to be arbitrary,* in the sense that no first-order reason can be given for agency choice within a certain domain, yet some choice or other is inescapable, legally mandatory, or both.

Substantively, lower courts sometimes err by assuming that uncertainty demands worst-case reasoning. Courts that make this mistake assume, in other words, that under uncertainty some version of maximin, or (more generally) highly "conservative," assumptions are the only rational course. On the contrary, in the face of uncertainty a rational decision-maker may set the α-value—the parameter that captures pessimism or optimism—anywhere within a range defined by the worst-case and best-case scenarios; and courts should defer to agency choices about how pessimistic to be. There is an inescapable element of arbitrariness in the choice of an α-parameter, yet courts cannot improve the situation by demanding of agencies reasons that they cannot give, or by requiring agencies to use maximally pessimistic assumptions—itself an arbitrarily chosen criterion.

There is a proper role for courts in ensuring that agencies have adequately invested resources in information-gathering, which may resolve uncertainty, perhaps by transforming it into risk or even certainty. Yet the procedural and substantive problems I have identified may recur at the meta-level, for in some cases the value of further investments in information-gathering will itself be genuinely uncertain. If so, courts should defer to agencies' second-order choices about informational investments on the same grounds that justify deference to agencies' first-order choices under uncertainty.

Uncertainty, Rationality, and Law

I will begin with some legal background. In American administrative law at the federal level, requirements of administrative rationality flow from several sources, principally the Due Process Clause of the Fifth Amendment and the Administrative Procedure Act (APA). In many of the cases and areas I will discuss, furthermore, the National Environmental Policy Act (NEPA) indirectly strengthens these requirements by mandating consideration of environmental values that might otherwise be excessively discounted. The due process rationality requirement is minimal and, in administrative law, has largely been superseded by the more demanding requirements of the APA and by framework statutes like NEPA.

The Administrative Procedure Act. As relevant here, the APA provides that agencies (1) must act within the bounds of their delegated statutory mandates; (2) must supply "substantial evidence," or at least a reasoned evidentiary basis for their factual findings; and, most crucially for my purposes, (3) must offer reasons for their policy choices, reasons that connect the facts found to the choices made. My focus is on the last of these three obligations, although they are interconnected.

Under Section 706(2)(A) of the APA, courts "shall" set aside agency action that is "arbitrary [and] capricious."[6] The conventional antonym of "arbitrary and capricious" is "rational"; as the Court of Appeals for the District of Columbia Circuit puts it, "[t]he 'arbitrary and capricious' standard deems the agency action presumptively valid provided the action meets a minimum rationality standard."[7] Hence courts applying the arbitrary and capricious test review the rationality of agency decisions.

The traditional and highly deferential approach, under the constitutional law of due process, equated rationality review of agency decision-making with rational-basis review of legislation.[8] Starting with *Citizens to Preserve Overton Park v. Volpe*[9] in 1971, however, a vast and baroque caselaw elaborated the requirements of rational agency decision-making under the APA, and in 1983, in *Motor Vehicle Manufacturers Association v. State Farm (State Farm)*, the Court specifically held that rationality review of agencies under Section 706(2)(A) should be more demanding than rational-basis review.[10] In a common formulation of rationality review, courts must either take a "hard look" at the rationality of agency decision-making, or at least ensure that agencies themselves have taken a "hard look" at the relevant problems. "Hard look review" is taken to encompass multiple quasi-procedural obligations that, taken together, ensure agency rationality.[11] Chapter 5 will advance the claim that "hard look review" is a misnomer that does not accurately describe the central tendencies of the law. For now, I will refer generically to rationality review.

Statutory Authorization. In order to isolate the issue of rational policymaking, I will assume throughout that the agency's delegated statutory authority allows it to make a range of decisions under uncertainty. Under the prevailing legal framework constructed in two famous administrative-law decisions, *Chevron U.S.A., Inc. v. Natural Resources Defense Council, Inc.*,[12] and *United States v. Mead Corp.*,[13] agencies making rules or engaged in formal adjudication will usually be taken to have statutory discretion whenever the relevant statutes are silent or ambiguous—and in the regulatory state, that is the usual state of affairs.

There is of course no legal requirement that this be so. In matters where the Constitution does not apply, Congress may specify exactly what the agency is to do, under conditions of uncertainty or otherwise. Statutes may require agencies to use worst-case ("maximin") assumptions under uncertainty, or not; they may require agencies to collect a certain amount of information, or not; everything is up to Congress. But instructions of that sort are not the ordinary case in administrative law. The ordinary case is that agencies acting under uncertainty possess discretion, because the relevant statutes do not clearly specify, one way or another, what the agency must or may or may not do. And that is the sort of case I will assume to obtain, for purposes of discussion here.

Current Doctrine. Assuming that the agency possesses statutory discretion, what does rationality review require under conditions of genuine uncertainty? Some courts, especially the lower courts, are chronically hazy about the differences among risk, uncertainty, and ignorance, and as a consequence use loose terminology that confuses the issues. In a recent decision, *New York v. Nuclear Regulatory Commission,* the Court of Appeals for the District of Columbia Circuit—the nation's premier administrative-law tribunal—went so far as to use language incautiously suggesting that an agency assessing the environmental consequences of its action must articulate an expected-harm analysis that "examine[s] both the probability of a given harm occurring and the consequences of that harm if it does occur."[14] This was to ignore the genuine uncertainties spectacularly on display in the case before the court; at issue was the longstanding problem of how to dispose of spent nuclear fuel, a substance that remains potentially harmful, by the court's own account, for "time spans seemingly beyond human comprehension."[15] No human actor, in my view, has any epistemic justification for attaching probabilities to events that may or may not occur eons in the future. Yet there is probably less here than meets the eye. I do not think we need to impute to the D.C. Circuit some sort of principled Bayesian view that uncertainty does not exist or presents no distinctive problems. Rather, the judicial grasp of the distinction between risk and Knightian uncertainty is shaky.

A number of general and well-settled administrative-law principles are useful for structuring rationality review in situations of uncertainty. One is that reviewing courts are to be at their "most deferential" when agencies make "predictions, within [their] area[s] of special expertise, at the frontiers of science."[16] Another principle is that when experts disagree, agencies are entitled to rely upon the reasonable opinions of their own qualified internal experts.[17] As we will see, courts violate these principles with some frequency, not because the judges do not think the principles applicable, but because judges make conceptual mistakes about what counts as rational decision-making under uncertainty.

I will argue, for example, that the best reading of these settled principles implies that courts should defer to agencies in situations of brute uncertainty, in which well-defined facts about the world relevant to the decision cannot be ascertained (at acceptable cost); strategic uncertainty, in which interdependent choices create multiple equilibria; and model uncertainty, in which the very analytic framework to be used to assess uncertain choices is itself unclear. Furthermore, the principles imply that agencies are under no obligation to make "cautious" or "worst-case" assumptions under uncertainty, contrary to a meme that is surprisingly persistent in the lower courts.

As we will see, however, the Supreme Court to its credit has rejected the meme on at least two occasions, in *Baltimore Gas & Electric* and in *Robertson v. Methow Valley Citizens Council.*[18] More generally, the Court has displayed broad tolerance for agency decision-making under uncertainty, and has frequently rebuked lower courts that afford agencies insufficient leeway. And that is as it should be. In all of these situations, law not only does but should leave room for rationally arbitrary decisions—decisions such that no first-order reason can be given for a decision one way as opposed to another, within a certain domain, even if there is excellent reason for making a decision within that domain.

The National Environmental Policy Act. NEPA is an environmental statute that cuts across all areas of public law.[19] Its basic requirement—a procedural rather than substantive obligation—is that federal agencies must consider whether any of their actions will have significant effects on the environment. If the agency performs an "environmental assessment" and believes that the action will have no significant effects, it may file a finding saying so; courts will uphold the finding so long as the agency has taken a "hard look" at the issues and has offered "convincing reasons" in support of its finding, a standard that more or less duplicates ordinary APA rationality review. If the agency cannot meet that test, the agency becomes obliged to do a more extensive review called an "environmental impact statement" that considers all potentially relevant environmental risks and harms.[20]

For my purposes here, the interesting feature of this legal framework—NEPA combined with the APA—is that it authorizes courts to require agencies to invest in further information-gathering about environmental problems. In the theory of rational decision-making, under either uncertainty or risk, one question is what it is rational to decide *given* some set of information; a distinct and logically prior question is how much information it is rational to gather before making a decision. As we will see, uncertainty may enter the picture either at the first level (what to do) or at the second level (how much information to collect before deciding what to do).

At the level of judicial review of agency action, hard questions arise about how much information courts may or should require agencies to collect. I will suggest that under administrative-law principles and NEPA principles rightly understood, the existence of an uncertain problem implies that, sometimes, the very question whether collecting further information will be cost-justified is itself uncertain. In cases like that, courts must leave room for agencies to make rationally arbitrary decisions about when to cut off the process of information-gathering.

When Reasons Run Out

I turn now to one sort of mistake that courts can commit when agencies face decisions under genuine uncertainty. I bracket for the time being the question whether the situation genuinely is one of uncertainty, or instead whether further cost-justified investments in information-gathering might resolve the uncertainty, transforming it into risk or certainty. I will take up that question later; for now, I will assume that the uncertainty is stipulated to be genuine by all concerned, including the reviewing judges, and that all cost-justified information has already been gathered. I will also assume, for the time being, that agencies are acting in good faith to maximize overall welfare. Later I will ask what courts should do if they worry that agencies are invoking "uncertainty" in a pretextual fashion, to shield decisions made on illegitimate grounds.

The mistake at issue in some of the cases, I suggest, is the belief that it is always possible for agencies to give first-order reasons for their choices. By a first-order reason, I mean a reason that justifies the choice relative to other choices within the agency's feasible set. A second-order reason is a reason to make *some choice or other* within the feasible set, even if no first-order reason can be given. In situations of uncertainty, agencies will often have perfectly valid second-order reasons even when no first-order reason is possible. In other words, there is a domain of agency decisions that are necessarily and unavoidably arbitrary, in a first-order sense. Reviewing courts must not press their demands for reasons and reasoned decision-making beyond the point at which the possibility of reason is exhausted.

Brute Uncertainty

One type of uncertainty, brute uncertainty, arises from the sheer cost of acquiring facts about the world.[21] The flat-tailed horned lizard is "a small, cryptically colored iguanid . . . that is restricted to flats and valleys of the western Sonoran desert."[22] The Secretary of the Interior has a statutory obligation to decide, in light of the "best available" scientific data, whether to list the lizard as a "threatened" species. The details are unnecessary, but the statute constrains the Secretary's ability to wait until more information comes to light; it requires a decision now.

How many flat-tailed horned lizards are there? No one knows, and for the time being the knowledge cannot be obtained. In litigation between the Secretary and environmental groups, "both parties acknowledge[d] that the formerly common 'scat count' method of estimating lizard population size has been discredited,"[23] destroying the evidentiary basis for extant assessments. On the other hand, a newer method, in which lizards are captured, marked, and perhaps recaptured (with the rate of recapture of marked lizards conveying information about population size), has not yet yielded reliable information. The number of lizards is an unknown that is known to be unknowable, at least in the short run.

How then should the Secretary decide whether to list the lizard as a threatened species? How should a reviewing court decide whether the Secretary's decision is arbitrary and capricious, or instead rational? For convenience, let us suppose that the Secretary may find the number of lizards to be "high" or "low." In the actual case, the Secretary in effect chose "high"; he made a finding that lizard populations remained viable throughout the lizard's extant range. The appellate court rejected that conclusion, holding that "if the science on population size and trends is underdeveloped and unclear, the Secretary cannot reasonably infer that the absence of evidence of population decline equates to evidence of persistence. . . . We thus conclude that the administrative record does not support the Secretary's determination that lizard populations persist throughout most of the species' current range."[24]

The problem with the court's conclusion is that the administrative record failed to support the opposite conclusion either. A counterfactual finding by the Secretary, that the lizard populations did not remain viable in the lizard's range, would have been equally unfounded. Judge Noonan, dissenting, got it right. "It's anybody's guess," he wrote, "whether the lizards are multiplying or declining. In a guessing contest one might defer to the government umpire."[25]

By way of fancying up Judge Noonan's point, the agency was presented with a choice it had second-order reasons to make—indeed a second-order obligation to make—but no possible first-order grounds for making one way or another. I say a "choice" rather than a "finding" because the facts of the matter were, for the actors involved, epistemically unattainable. The Secretary had to decide in which direction to take a leap of faith, and it is a kind of pathological hyper-rationalism to demand that the Secretary give reasons for taking it in one direction rather than the other.

Default Reasoning

A natural reaction to the lizards case, and to uncertainty generally, is to use some sort of default reasoning.[26] If we do not know how many lizards there are, perhaps we should err on the side of caution. The problem is that there are many ways to interpret that injunction. The

Secretary might decide that the Type I error, listing the lizard as threatened when it really is not, is less costly than the Type II error, failing to list the lizard as threatened when it really is, so that "caution" requires an aggressive listing strategy. On the other hand, the Secretary might decide that erring on the side of "caution" means not listing species as threatened if there is a very real possibility—how real none can say—that they are not. There are multiple substantive, problem-relevant default positions that the Secretary might invoke.

Given this, Judge Noonan suggests a different form of default-based reasoning. The environmental petitioners—in effect the plaintiffs—are challenging the Secretary's finding. The Administrative Procedure Act is quite clear that the burden of proof lies upon them to show that the finding is arbitrary.[27] If the facts that would enable such a showing are unattainable, then the Secretary wins in virtue of the legal default, even if the Secretary could not prove his position correct either, were the positions reversed. A tie goes to the "government umpire."

The view I am suggesting cheerfully concedes that the Secretary's finding is arbitrary at the first order. But that is a point about arbitrariness in a decision-theoretic sense, not about "arbitrariness" in the legal sense. In legal terms, I mean to argue that decisions in which first-order reasons have run out should not count as "arbitrary" within the meaning of the Administrative Procedure Act. It is not *legally* arbitrary to make an unavoidable decision, resting on valid second-order reasons, even if the decision is arbitrary in a first-order sense.

Strategic Uncertainty

Let me now turn from brute uncertainty—about epistemically unattainable facts that in some sense lie out there—to a different form of uncertainty, arising from the strategic interdependence of actors' choices. This is the province of game theory rather than decision theory. Game theory is rife with multiple equilibria, especially in indefinitely repeated games but also more generally.[28] Some games have no unique solution in pure strategies, so that rational parties will at least partly randomize their behavior; some games have no unique solution even with mixed strategies. And players of the game may have insufficient experience with the behavior of other players to form epistemically well-grounded beliefs about what those others are able or likely to do, giving rise to genuine strategic uncertainty.

One domain in which strategic uncertainty constantly arises is the counterterrorism problem. Should the Department of Energy create a level-3 biohazard research facility at Lawrence Livermore National Laboratory? How should reviewing courts evaluate the rationality of the Department's decision? One problem is that pathogens might escape by accident; another is that the facility might become the target of a terrorist attack. There is a fair amount of accumulated experience with such facilities elsewhere, and a fair sense of how to construct and operate such facilities so as to minimize the possibility of accidents. But the proposed Lawrence Livermore facility had some unique features. At the time of construction it was the only level-3 facility to occupy the same complex as a nuclear weapons research facility, and it was built after 9/11, raising difficult questions about counterterrorism risks—stemming either from domestic or international sources.

The Department decided in favor of building the facility. Petitioners challenged the decision under NEPA and the APA, arguing that the Department had not given adequate consideration to terrorism risks and the resulting harms to people and the environment, should pathogens escape. In making its assessment, the Department relied upon a model developed by the Army to assess the risks of releases of pathogens after a natural disaster or mechanical accident. The model suggested that the maximum credible harms from a release were modest and that the chance of a release in the first place, although impossible to quantify, was remote. Plaintiffs' experts, however, argued that such a model was inapposite to the problem, which involved the risk of deliberate attacks by terrorists. The difference between disaster or accident risks on the one hand and terrorism risks on the other was, in this case, also a form of model uncertainty; the very framework for assessing the problem was itself contested by the parties.[29]

The plaintiffs' view might or might not be correct. The issue is genuinely uncertain, in part because it has a strategic dimension. Terrorists would presumably be able to know or guess something about what model the Department was using; after all, the court's decision explaining the issues is a matter of public record. The consequence is that the Department's choice of a model would itself endogenously affect the risk being modeled—the bite of strategic uncertainty. Supposing that the model shows that the possibility of a terrorist attack is low, we might imagine that the model is self-undermining, because its use suggests that the Department is complacent, and thus gives terrorists increased incentives to focus on Lawrence Livermore relative to other possible targets. We might instead imagine that the model is self-confirming, because it shows terrorists that the expected benefit (from their point of view) of an attack on the facility are in fact low. Absent more information about the terrorists' likely response, a question that is essentially a guessing game, it is irreducibly unclear whether the Department's model raises, reduces, or has no effect upon the chance of a terrorist incident at the facility. In circumstances of strategic uncertainty, reasons run out, within the broad boundaries set by the agency's statutory authority.

The court upheld the Department's decision to build the facility, principally on the ground that if experts disagree about the proper model to be applied to a problem, the agency is entitled to rely upon the model favored by its own experts.[30] That holding was, in effect, Judge Noonan's reasoning from the lizards case, albeit applied to strategic rather than brute uncertainty. Under the irreducible uncertainty created by strategic indeterminacy, there is no reason to favor one model or another, at least within the broad boundaries of professionally respectable opinion.

I am extrapolating or embellishing a bit. The court's actual opinion merely adverted to the model uncertainty and the controversy among experts, and then awarded victory to the agency, without explaining the deep sources of the uncertainty that caused the controversy. Whatever the adequacy of the court's explanation, however, I believe that it had the right instincts and reached the correct outcome. The question whether it is sensible to build a biohazard facility at Lawrence Livermore was a decision at the frontier where the knowable passes into the unknowable, and where agencies may or may not take a leap of faith, depending upon how robust their appetite for risk may be. Once such a frontier has been reached, courts that demand further reasons are asking for the impossible.

Recognizing When Reasons Have Run Out

Finally, there is the question how reviewing courts are supposed to know that they (or more accurately the agency) face a decision of the type in which it is rational to be arbitrary. Such situations do not come labeled by God; and if the agency has a comparative informational advantage over the reviewing court, how is the court supposed to make the logically antecedent determination that a case for rationally arbitrary decision-making has even arisen?

In the nature of things, it is impossible to be sure, but there are a number of rules of thumb the reviewing court might use. First, a hallmark of problems calling for a rationally arbitrary decision is a kind of *mirror-image reversibility.* If the agency chooses A over B, and the court overturns that decision as arbitrary, it will also be the case that the agency's choice of B over A could be overturned on exactly the same ground. Indeed, *any choice the agency makes could be overturned for lack of first-order reasons.* Recognizing this, the reviewing court should realize that the agency may be facing a situation in which no non-arbitrary choice is feasible.

A stylized example may be drawn from the case of the fixed indexed annuities. The SEC had to decide whether such instruments should count as "annuities" under the federal securities laws and had a statutory obligation to consider the effects of its decision on "competition" and "efficiency." For present purposes, let us suppose the Commission rationally believes that a decision *either way* will promote competition and efficiency by reducing legal uncertainty for regulated firms; whichever substantive decision is best, a decision either way will be better than an ongoing muddle. Yet it is also irreducibly uncertain *which* first-order decision will do more than the other to promote competition and efficiency.

In such a situation, whether or not the Commission chooses to count fixed indexed annuities as "annuities," it ought to decide one way or another. Yet the problem is that a reviewing court may overturn *either* decision on the ground that reducing legal uncertainty is not a sufficient rationale to explain why the Commission chose one way rather than the other. After all (the fallacious reasoning runs) the Commission could have reduced legal uncertainty by making the other decision, too. The court's failure to recognize that the problem is subject to mirror-image reversibility ensures the worst possible outcome, by perpetuating legal uncertainty.

A second rule of thumb is that problems calling for a rationally arbitrary decision will often produce intractable disagreement among experts, as it did in the case of the biosafety facility at Lawrence Livermore. Expertise will certainly be necessary to reach the uncertainty frontier at which rationally arbitrary decisions lie, but expertise will be finally unable to prescribe a unique choice among the feasible options. This is hardly a watertight inference, because disagreement among experts may arise for other reasons as well, but the existence of such disagreement is some positive evidence that the uncertainty frontier has been reached.

Finally, the court might ask the agency for a clear statement that a problem calling for a rationally arbitrary decision has arisen. The possibility that the agency will claim falsely, or pretextually, that such a case has arisen is a real one—I take up such issues later—but the clear statement will serve as a kind of reputational bond. Agencies in a repeat-play relationship with reviewing courts will be reluctant to take the risk of making a false claim that might later be exposed.

Optimism, Pessimism, and Uncertainty

I turn now to a related problem—a particularly important special case of reasons running out. Under genuine uncertainty, what assumptions should decision-makers use? In particular, how optimistic or pessimistic should they be? There is a pervasive folk meme to the effect that under uncertainty, worst-case assumptions have a kind of priority. "Err on the side of caution"; "better safe than sorry"; the proverbs are legion.

One problem is that the advice to err on the side of caution will sometimes or often be indeterminate. The "Dismal Theorem" shows that given certain assumptions about the distribution of the risks of climate change—the existence of a fat tail—catastrophic harms of staggering magnitude are a real possibility and should overwhelm other considerations, dominating the decision problem.[31] But this does not necessarily mean that we should immediately curtail economic activity in a bid to avert catastrophic climate change. There might equally be a Dismal Theorem about the catastrophic fat-tail risks of doing *that*.[32] Perhaps the resulting contraction of the economy might become so severe as to cause global conflicts that radically reduce standards of living or even wipe out the human population. The example generalizes. A chronic problem with maximin strategies for coping with uncertainty is that worst-case scenarios often lie on all sides of the problem. Where that is true, the idea of taking "precautions" may be indeterminate.[33]

Yet there is also a second, analytically distinct problem. Even where a precautionary approach is conceptually determinate, it is just not the case that under uncertainty, only maximally pessimistic assumptions are rational. In the standard Arrow-Hurwicz framework,[34] rational decision-making under uncertainty may be based upon the worst case, the best case, or a weighted combination of the two extremes.[35] Maximin, which attempts to choose the outcome with the best worst-case payoff, is not the uniquely rational approach. Equally rational is maximax, which attempts to choose the outcome with the best best-case payoff.[36] A standard generalization of Arrow-Hurwicz, the α-maximin framework, models decision-makers as choosing a parameter that may range from maximal pessimism to maximal optimism. There is no basis in the theory of decision-making for courts to single out one extreme on this spectrum—the maximally pessimistic extreme—and elevate it into a sort of universal fallback requirement for situations of uncertainty.

Is there a general basis in law for such a fallback requirement? Particular statutes might, of course, enforce caution in particular settings; but does administrative law generally require courts to enforce "conservative" assumptions on agencies? In 1978 the Council on Environmental Quality (CEQ), an executive body charged with promulgating regulations to enforce NEPA, specifically required agencies to address "worst-case" scenarios in their environmental impact statements (EIS), if relevant information about possible environmental harms was nonexistent or too costly to obtain.[37] The consequence was that agencies were obliged, or felt obliged, to address a suite of highly speculative and implausible scenarios.[38] In 1986 the Council rescinded its worst-case requirement and replaced it. "The regulation now requires agencies to get incomplete or unavailable information in an EIS when getting it does not come at an exorbitant cost and it is 'relevant to reasonably foreseeable significant adverse impacts.' If the information cannot be obtained because it is too expensive or the means to obtain it are not known, then the CEQ regulations require an agency to state this fact, along with a summary of the relevance of the information, and a summary of the existing credible evidence on the matter."[39] The Supreme Court upheld the change in *Robertson v. Methow Valley Citizens Council*, observing that the worst-case requirement threatened to "distort the decisionmaking process by overemphasizing highly speculative harms," thereby diverting agencies' limited time and cognitive resources from consideration of more substantial environmental risks.[40]

I conclude that (1) neither law nor canons of rationality generally require that agencies choose "safe" or "cautious" assumptions under uncertainty, and that (2) in some cases the very idea of making "cautious" assumptions is indeterminate anyway—where, for example, there are fat-tail risks on both sides of the decision-making ledger. Hence there is no basis for courts to foist a requirement of conservatism upon agencies through judicial implementation of rationality review under the APA, or NEPA either. Yet sometimes lower courts seem to bridle when agencies make anything but pessimistic assumptions under conditions of uncertainty, despite the admonition in the Supreme Court's *Methow Valley* decision. I will confine myself to one recent example, out of the many that decorate the pages of the law reports.

The example also comes from the law of endangered species. Yellowstone grizzly bears were listed as a "threatened" species in 1975, but their numbers have since increased to the point where the Fish and Wildlife Service attempted to delist them.[41] In the delisting decision, a key question was whether the bears would be threatened by declines in the prevalence of whitebark pine, a tree that provides them with an important source of food. All parties acknowledged the potential for such a threat, in part because of climate change, which has spurred the growth of parasites and diseases that kill the whitebark pine, and in part because of a well-documented correlation between reductions in whitebark pine on the one hand and grizzly mortality on the other.

But the agency discounted the seriousness of the overall threat to the grizzlies, on several grounds: grizzlies are notoriously flexible and adaptable about their sources of food (if whitebark pine fails, more picnic baskets will be stolen); whitebark pine has always been a highly variable resource, one that the bears have proven they can go without; and other populations of grizzlies have flourished despite the loss of whitebark pine. Overall, the agency concluded, "the specific amount of decline in the whitebark pine distribution and the rate of this decline are difficult to predict with certainty. The specific response of grizzly bears to declines in whitebark cone production is even more uncertain."[42]

The court, however, declared the agency's position arbitrary, citing the lizards case discussed earlier. "It may be that scientists will compile data demonstrating grizzly population stability in the face of whitebark pine declines. Such information, however, simply is not in the record before us. The lack of any data showing a population decline due to whitebark pine loss is not enough."[43] But of course the whole point was that there was no information in the record either way, and (we are assuming for now) there was no cost-justified procedure for obtaining such information. The court's reasoning in effect required the agency to make a conservative or pessimistic assumption about the admittedly uncertain consequences of whitebark pine losses, whereas the agency had chosen an optimistic assumption. The former has no analytic or legal priority over the latter, so the court ought to have left the agency's decision in place.

It is certainly fair play for policymakers to criticize agencies for excessive optimism, or excessive pessimism for that matter. Policymakers, such as the President and legislators, are entitled to set α-parameters as they see fit in particular domains, through executive orders or through legislation. Statutes sometimes, though infrequently, require agencies to make cautious substantive assumptions in the face of uncertainty. Procedurally, I have mentioned the prior NEPA regulations that required agencies to analyze worst-case scenarios. But none of this implies that, under current law, courts have any basis for reading a *de facto* requirement of maximin decision-making into the general rationality requirements of administrative law. There is no systematic reason to think that courts are better positioned than agencies to set α-parameters, and no general reason to think that agencies will malfunction in doing so, in ways that courts are able to oversee or correct. Rationality in the decision-theoretic sense does not require pessimism; nor should rationality in the legal sense.

Part of the judicial intuition, rarely articulated, must be that the choice of an α-parameter seems essentially arbitrary. Why should the agency set the parameter here rather than there, without explanation? Yet that does not explain why courts seem to gravitate toward maximin, as opposed to maximax or any number of other decision-rules compatible with the Arrow-Hurwicz result. That further tic of judicial behavior seems to occur because maximin resonates with pessimistic folk wisdom ("better safe than sorry"), and thus supplies an apparently neutral and prudent benchmark criterion. But it is not neutral, nor is it necessarily any more prudent than the alternatives; after all there is also folk wisdom about the value of optimism ("nothing ventured, nothing gained").

Nor should the agency be tasked with explaining the inexplicable. It is tempting to say that the agency's minimum obligation is to give reasons for setting the α-parameter here rather than there. But in decision-making under genuine uncertainty agencies operate at the frontiers of reason; agencies no less than firms or entrepreneurs will act more or less boldly depending upon what Keynes called their "animal spirits." Over time public opinion and policymaking officials will judge whether agencies have acted with excessive optimism or pessimism; in the meantime, courts should leave the decision with the agency.

If this posture of judicial self-denial and toleration of rational arbitrariness seems implausible, even unattainable, the Supreme Court itself has given us a laudable counterexample. In a 1983 decision, *Baltimore Gas & Electric v. Natural Resources Defense Council*,[44] the question was whether the Nuclear Regulatory Commission could allow nuclear plants to be licensed on the optimistic assumption that there would be "zero release" of spent nuclear fuel from on-site storage facilities. Despite the radical uncertainty surrounding the long-term environmental and health effects of storing nuclear fuel, the Court said emphatically that it was for the Commission to make the sort of "policy judgment" embodied in the zero-release assumption, and that there was nothing arbitrary or irrational about the Commission's approach.[45] There are various ways of cabining or narrowing the Court's reasoning, but the spirit of the decision is clear enough: judges are perfectly capable of recognizing that under uncertainty, pessimism has no rational or legal priority, assuming as always that relevant statutes are silent or ambiguous.

Optimal Information-Gathering

So far we have been bracketing questions about information-gathering. Such questions arguably lie at the heart of NEPA and the APA as well, insofar as those statutes require agencies to follow rational procedures for information-gathering, both with respect to environmental effects and more generally. But what does that mean exactly? Under uncertainty, what does optimal information-gathering look like?

A standard line in the economics of information is that decision-makers should invest in gathering information just up to the point at which the (increasing) marginal costs of doing so equal the expected marginal benefits of further information.[46] If there is no cost to reversing a decision once made, then there is no need to wait; any current decision may be undone if later information suggests the agency erred. But if there is some positive cost to reversing decisions once made, then waiting for new information has an option value, which increases with the cost of reversal.[47] The greater the option value, the greater the benefit of further information-gathering before the agency decides.

That approach may be adequate for stable, familiar, relatively simple environments. In environments of that sort, decision-makers can form epistemically justified probability distributions over the (expected) value of future information. Searching for consumer goods in a mall, I have a clear idea of the expected value of the information I will turn up by going to one more store. But many of the problems agencies face are not like that at all. Where the environment is so unfamiliar, or so complex, that the marginal benefit of acquiring further information is itself genuinely uncertain, there may be prohibitive costs to gathering the information needed to form an epistemically justified probability distribution over the value of information.[48] An infinite regress looms: the decision-maker must decide how much to invest in gathering information about the marginal benefit of further information-gathering, and so on.[49]

As to firms in competitive markets, it has been observed that "the choice of a profit-maximizing information structure itself requires information, and it is not apparent how the aspiring profit-maximizer acquires this information or what guarantees that he does not pay an excessive price for it."[50] The same point holds, with appropriate modifications, for agencies maximizing social welfare. Uncertainty may afflict not only the agency's first-order decision but also its second-order decisions[51] about how much information to collect. Critically, there is just no nonarbitrary solution to this infinite regress; it is a special type of optimal search problem in which any stopping rule is arbitrary, within the boundaries of the relevant uncertainty.[52] At the frontiers of knowledge, what agencies do is "like going into a big forest to pick mushrooms. One may explore the possibilities in a certain limited region, but at some point one must stop the explorations and start picking because further explorations as to the possibility of finding more and better mushrooms by walking a little bit further would defeat the purpose of the hike. One must decide to stop the explorations on an intuitive basis, i.e., without actually investigating whether further exploration would have yielded better results."[53]

The role of courts in reviewing the rationality of agency information-gathering should be sensitive to these considerations. In ordinary NEPA cases, for example, courts may be able to identify cases in which agencies have failed to make cost-justified investments in information-gathering (I will give an example shortly). "Ordinary" means that agencies and courts have made decisions about similar problems, in similar environments, with sufficient frequency that the expected value of additional increments of information is rationally calculable. But in the sort of decision-making environments mentioned earlier— counterterrorism, nuclear fuel, endangered species problems at the frontier of biological and ecological understanding—courts ought to stay their hand; agencies must have leeway to stop collecting information at a given point, even or especially when the location of that point cannot be justified on grounds that appear rational in a first-order sense. In informationally uncertain environments, "[a]t some point, the individual must assert in some noncalculating way how he will use resources to establish what he wants: He must, in effect, take a stab in the dark. . . ."[54]

In the case of the Yellowstone grizzlies, described earlier, the court seems to have misconceived its role, in effect requiring the agency to give reasons for the choice of a stopping rule in an informationally uncertain environment. "The [Fish and Wildlife] Service," wrote the court, "must rationally explain why the uncertainty regarding the impact of whitebark pine loss on the grizzly counsels in favor of delisting now, rather than, for example, more study. Otherwise we might as well be deferring to a coin flip."[55] Under genuine uncertainty, however, no such reasons may be forthcoming; the choice of a stopping point will necessarily be arbitrary in a first-order sense, although some stopping point there must be. Halting the search for further information somewhere or other is not arbitrary at all, so that there are perfectly good second-order reasons for the agency's behavior. (It is a separate question whether, upon halting its information-gathering process, the agency should or should not decide to delist the grizzlies; I addressed that issue earlier.) Because the shadow of infinite regress looms, courts should let agencies take a "stab in the dark," at least when there is no evidence in the record suggesting that the uncertainty can be dispelled at low cost.

I do not argue for utter judicial abdication, because the qualification I have offered is a real one: agencies do sometimes fail to make cost-justified investments in information that would dispel uncertainty. An example comes from a case about the Glacier Bay National Park and Preserve in Alaska, *National Parks & Conservation Association v. Babbitt.*[56] The issue, under NEPA, was whether the National Park Service had to prepare a full environmental impact statement (EIS) in order to assess the possible harms—to endangered and threatened species, to air quality, and on other margins—of increasing the number of cruise ships allowed into the bay. Putting aside the particulars of the case, the court got off on the wrong foot by announcing the general principle that "[p]reparation of an [environmental impact statement] is mandated where uncertainty may be resolved by further collection of data."[57] It is always true that uncertainty might be resolved by further collection of data. Then again, it might not. The dilemma is precisely that where there is genuine uncertainty at the second- or higher-order level, it is uncertain whether first-order uncertainty will be resolved by further collection of information, and it is thus analytically unclear whether to pay the price of doing so.

Nonetheless, on the facts of the case at hand, the court was justified in requiring the Park Service to prepare an EIS. The details are unnecessary; suffice it to say that the record itself conclusively demonstrated that there existed low-cost studies that the agency could do to dispel the uncertainty.[58] In other words, the case was an example of *first-order uncertainty without second-order uncertainty*. In the mushroom problem described earlier, if the hikers could, by paying a penny, be given a map of the locale with mushroom clusters marked on it, there would be a cost-justified step they could take to dispel the first-order uncertainty; thus there would be no uncertainty at the second order. The Park Service in the Glacier Bay case was in the same position, and its refusal to undertake the relevant studies was genuinely irrational. The court was correct to force its hand. It is tempting to think that the value of the map must itself be uncertain before we examine its contents, so that the infinite regress of information-gathering *always* obtains. I think this is false, however. We may have sufficient extrinsic knowledge of the map-maker's credentials and abilities, or sufficient experience with the map-maker's track record on other occasions, to be confident that the map will contain useful information, even without inspection. The infinite regress of information-gathering is a possibility, but not a necessity.

Rationally Arbitrary Decisions

My larger theme has been that, in the presence of uncertainty, administrative law does and should make space for agency decision-making that is rationally arbitrary. Two distinctions are critical: first, the difference between "arbitrariness" in the decision-theoretic sense and in the legal sense; second, the difference between the normative and positive theory of decision-making under uncertainty. In light of these distinctions, my claims are that (1) some decisions are rationally arbitrary in the decision-theoretic sense, but do not and should not count as "arbitrary and capricious" within the terms of the Administrative Procedure Act; (2) rationally arbitrary decisions are sometimes normatively proper, whether or not people (or agencies) actually make them. I will distill these claims, consider what courts may do if they are concerned that agencies are invoking uncertainty pretextually, and then return to the interpretive question about how courts actually do approach these problems.

Uncertainty: An Institutional Solution

Sometimes agencies have excellent second-order reasons to make a decision on a certain topic, including an important set of cases in which law mandates a decision now rather than later. Yet even when such excellent reasons exist, it may also be the case that no first-order reasons can be given for making the relevant decision one way or another, or even for adopting optimistic or pessimistic assumptions to factor into the decision; genuine, Knightian uncertainty presents cases of that sort. In such cases, law must not adopt a cramped and erroneous conception of rationality, one that requires agencies to do the impossible by giving reasons as to matters where reason has exhausted its powers.

The logic may also apply to decisions about whether to collect further information before making a substantive decision—that is, to decisions about optimal stopping under uncertainty. Sometimes, there is an infinite regress of uncertainty about how much information to collect before deciding how much information to collect, and so on. Where that occurs, there is no alternative but to cease collecting information at some arbitrary point, and to take a "stab in the dark."

The Administrative Procedure Act does not recognize any category of decisions that are "arbitrary and capricious" yet also legally permissible; under the terms of the Act, courts "shall . . . hold unlawful and set aside" agency action that is "arbitrary."[59] It does not follow, however, that any decisions that are rationally arbitrary, in the decision-theory sense, must also *count as* arbitrary in the legal sense. Courts may and should instead conclude that rationally arbitrary decisions count as adequately reasoned for purposes of administrative law, when and insofar as those decisions rest on second-order reasons that are themselves valid, even when first-order reasons have run out.

Under this approach, courts would defer to some agency choices under uncertainty that do not even purport to be based on first-order reasons. The dilemma of decision-making under genuine uncertainty would be resolved *institutionally,* by allocating the power of arbitrary decision-making across branches of government, rather than through first-order reason. Courts seem uncomfortable with this sort of purely institutional solution, for reasons I will also discuss. But if there is no valid normative basis for that reaction, the judicial discomfort is merely a bad habit that the legal system should ignore or suppress, rather than indulge.

Uncertainty, Pretext, and Inconsistency

A valid concern for law, and a concern that some judges probably hold, is that agencies will invoke "uncertainty" pretextually or inconsistently, using it to justify choices made covertly on illegitimate grounds—political favoritism, ideological bias, simple shirking, or the like. Perhaps agencies will claim that the situation is one of uncertainty when it is really one of risk; perhaps the agency is too lazy to calculate the relevant risks or fears that doing so would produce uncongenial results and make them too obvious to reviewing courts. Likewise for particular assumptions under uncertainty. Perhaps the agency will adopt optimistic assumptions if the population of an endangered species is uncertain, just because the agency has an ideological distaste for the endangered species laws; perhaps agencies will be inconsistent across cases, adopting either optimistic or pessimistic assumptions as necessary to promote the agency's political objectives.

Although these concerns are valid, they are not particularly tied to agency claims of uncertainty. Pretext and inconsistency are general problems with agency decision-making, whether under uncertainty, risk, or for that matter certainty. If an agency claims that a given decision is justified by an ordinary risk analysis, such that the relevant project has asserted probabilities of asserted payoffs, the agency may actually be motivated by political favoritism or ideological bias. Perhaps the agency is even describing the situation as one of risk when the situation is actually one of uncertainty, to give a false patina of scientific determinacy to its decision. The problem of the "science charade"[60] is orthogonal to the distinction between risk and uncertainty.

So the pretext concern sweeps very broadly, well beyond the domain of uncertainty and well beyond any of the methods for decision-making under uncertainty that were mentioned earlier. Suppose the agency claims to have flipped a coin and reached result X, where X is ideologically congenial to the agency but Y would not be. The court may be worried that the agency is lying, and that it never really randomized at all. (If so, the court might demand that the coin-flip happen in the court's presence.) But the agency could be lying in lots of other cases as well, having nothing to do with randomization or uncertainty; it could be lying about its motives for making up a new policy or for granting a waiver from an old rule. The usual methods for "flushing out" an agency's real motives involve techniques like mandating that the agency make decisions on a formal record; mandating that the agency respond specifically to comments even if there is no formal record; allowing cross-questioning of agency experts; and checking the fit between the agency's findings and its conclusions. These methods may be applied as well, or as poorly, to agency decisions in situations of uncertainty as to other types of decisions.

So too with inconsistency. It is a stock problem in administrative law whether and to what extent agencies have an obligation of consistency, across cases or rules, in the reasons they give and the legal interpretations they offer.[61] There is nothing unique to uncertainty in such cases. If and to the extent that agencies have an obligation of consistency across cases and decisions, then that obligation should extend to the choice of assumptions for uncertainty, but the issue is a far broader one.

Agencies at the Uncertainty Frontier

So far I have said nothing at all about the empirical incidence of uncertainty, or of litigated cases involving uncertainty. On one view, which is certainly possible and which cannot be refuted on *a priori* grounds, cases of genuine uncertainty are rare in the field of agency decision-making. Agencies mostly encounter problems of risk, to which quantifiable probabilities can be attached, and to which quantified cost-benefit can be applied, or so the argument would run.

The view advanced here is different. Agencies frequently encounter novel problems at the frontiers of scientific and technical knowledge, such that even expert probability assessments are unreliable and real uncertainty is pervasive. The ordinary problems of risk assessment and regulation, involving calculable probabilities and known risks, have a diminishing market share over time, as agencies handle easy problems and move on to more difficult ones. When agencies face regulatory choices premised on guesses about the effects of climate change,[62] or the chances of a novel type of domestic terror attack,[63] or the future of a species whose number is simply unknown,[64] or the effects of a novel regulatory constraint on shareholder voting,[65] they face choices in which any probability assessments lack respectable epistemic foundations; they face genuine uncertainty. A sensible theory of rationality review has to take account of the pervasive presence of uncertainty in the administrative state.

In the 1960s and 1970s, federal agencies faced a policy landscape in which there were lots of easy decisions to be made; rivers were so polluted that they were catching on fire.[66] The landscape no longer looks like that, in either the literal or figurative sense. Many of the easy problems have been addressed (not all), and some increasing fraction of what agencies do lies at or beyond the scientific frontier, where all problems are hard. The arc of the administrative state bends toward uncertainty.

But the increasing importance of uncertainty inevitably encourages deference. Given pervasive uncertainty, courts have sensibly relaxed their requirements of first-order reason-giving. As agencies approach the uncertainty frontier, there will be more and more cases in which relentless judicial demands for first-order reasons are pathological and damaging, forcing agency decision-makers to make up reasons they may or may not actually believe, and that will chronically fail to actually justify their decisions—leaving open the possibility of costly judicial remands for further rounds of reason-giving, and so on *ad infinitum*. It is damaging when courts overturn agency decisions for lack of first-order reasons when such reasons cannot actually be supplied, and where the opposite decision by the agency could have been overturned on the very same grounds. The judicial decision is then a sort of deadweight loss that cannot even in principle improve the decision, but can only force the agency to cough up an epistemically unjustified rationale for what is essentially an arbitrary decision, and rationally so.

In the current circumstances of the administrative state, then, it is imperative that law should recognize a category of rationally arbitrary agency decisions. Happily, judicial hyper-rationalism that craves fully specified reasoning is very much the exception, not the rule. As I will detail in Chapter 5 and its appendix, there is a powerful body of precedent, within administrative law itself, in support of a more capacious and enlightened view, under which the rule of law will rest satisfied with second-order reasons, at least where first-order reasons run out. We have seen that the Supreme Court has several times admonished lower courts for imposing excessive constraints on agency decision-making under uncertainty, recognizing that agency action at the frontiers of knowledge is not to be reviewed as stringently as agency action comfortably within the frontiers. Structurally, the Court and its Justices are as much lawmakers as they are reviewers of decisions made by others, and this may instill within them a somewhat more sympathetic understanding of the dilemmas that face decision-makers under conditions of uncertainty. It is not inconceivable that the Court would someday acknowledge the existence of a category of decisions that are rationally arbitrary—and thus not arbitrary at all, in the law's sense anyway.

As things currently stand, the best view of the law of agency rationality (a Dworkinian and interpretive view, combining fit and justification) runs this way: at the level of the Supreme Court the law has decided to abnegate authority to agencies under conditions of uncertainty, and rightly so. The same is largely true of lower courts, but the Supreme Court's message has not been received in full by its subordinates. Some lower courts—especially panels of the D.C. Circuit— sometimes demand the unobtainable, overturning agency decisions for lack of first-order reasons that could not be supplied no matter how the agency had decided. Such decisions are holdovers, excreta of the traditional legal mind, which are not central to law as it now stands, and which will in an event disappear as the law increasingly works pure its own abnegation. Chapter 5 will expand on this claim.

5

Thin Rationality Review

THIS CHAPTER OFFERS two connected claims: "Hard look review" neither is the law nor should be the law, in light of the surrounding texture of developments since the enactment of the Administrative Procedure Act (APA) and since the *State Farm* decision in 1983. If true, those two claims go a long way toward completing the Dworkinian and interpretive case for law's abnegation. Recall that the *Crowell* framework largely failed to anticipate the rise in large-scale administrative rulemaking, and that the APA—as originally understood anyway— imposed few procedural obligations on agencies in rulemaking. One of the major "surrogate safeguards" supposed to provide a kind of substitute legal oversight was the "hard look" doctrine, developed by lower-court judges in the 1960s and 1970s in order to strengthen judicial oversight of agencies, especially when making rules, and then— so the lore goes—confirmed by the Supreme Court in 1983. But it is just lore.

If "hard look" does not provide an account that fits and justifies the current law, so that courts are deferring to agencies on their legal interpretations (*Chevron*), on the procedures they use for decision-making (Chapter 3), and on the rationality of their policy choices (Chapters 4 and 5), law's empire is shrunken indeed. As against "hard look," I will propose a much less demanding and intrusive interpretation of the "arbitrary and capricious" standard in Section 706(2)(A): thin rationality review. That interpretation puts the extant law in its best possible light, given the modern theory of rational decision-making.

The argument has both prescriptive and descriptive components, related in Dworkinian fashion by tacking between justification and fit. Here, as throughout, the argument is thoroughly Dworkinian in spirit, although it implies a modest and chastened role for courts, one that would have been thoroughly uncongenial to Dworkin's vision of courts as the "heartland of Law's Empire." It is Dworkinian because it does not interpret the APA on a blank slate, in light of some extra-legal theory that is imposed on the legal materials from without. Rather it attempts to respect the Supreme Court's strong and consistent message since 1983—law's abnegation should extend to arbitrariness review, just as it has extended to review of agency legal interpretations and agency procedural choices—and to put the Court's commitments in their best light, with the aid of the theory of rational decision-making. (The appendix to this chapter provides the doctrinal details about those commitments, as reflected in caselaw.)

The Prescriptive Thesis

Prescriptively, rationality is a much *thinner* notion than some commentators seem to think, and rational decision-making requires far less from agencies than lawyers tend to realize. Courts, especially lower courts, have sometimes adopted an excessively intrusive approach because, acting in the best of faith, they have misunderstood what rationality requires. In particular, they have failed to grasp a crucial twist: under a robust range of conditions, *rational agencies may have good reason to decide in a manner that is inaccurate, nonrational, or arbitrary.*

Although this claim is seemingly paradoxical or internally inconsistent, it simply rests on an appreciation of the limits of reason, especially in administrative policy-making. Agency decision-making is nonideal decision-making; what would be rational under ideal conditions is rarely a relevant question for agencies. Rather agencies make decisions under constraints of scarce time, information, and resources. Those constraints imply that agencies will frequently have excellent reasons to depart from idealized first-order conceptions of administrative rationality. The chapter is thus structured around a series of limitations to agency rationality, and argues for an approach to rationality review that takes these limitations seriously—thin rationality review.

In a simplistic and idealized conception of administrative rationality, which is rarely articulated in explicit terms but which implicitly underlies many judicial decisions, rational agencies should attempt to choose the best policy among the feasible options, after considering all relevant statutory factors and policy variables. This conception turns out to be riddled with legal mistakes, conceptual slips, and institutional problems. Under the best reading of the "arbitrary and capricious" test, agencies have no legal obligation to consider all policy variables that strike the judges as arguably relevant; agencies often have good reason to choose policies that do not necessarily represent the best feasible option; agencies may choose policies that the agency has not compared to other feasible options; and agencies may choose policies that do not even produce net benefits in the case at hand. Generalizing the claims of Chapter 4, agencies often have good second-order reasons to depart from the simplistic first-order conception of rationality, under certain conditions.

All this is negative critique, but the positive conception is straightforward. In contrast to thick rationality review, the thin version posits that *agencies are (merely) obliged to make decisions on the basis of reasons.* Second- or higher-order reasons may, in appropriate cases, satisfy that obligation. What is excluded by the "arbitrary and capricious" standard is genuinely ungrounded agency decision-making, in the sense that the agency cannot justify its action even as a response to the limits of reason. While truly capricious decision-making in this sense is no doubt uncommon, it does exist; the caselaw contains examples.[1]

The Descriptive Thesis

So much for prescription. Descriptively, thin rationality review fits the bulk of the caselaw but not all of it. One might never guess this from reading administrative-law textbooks, which typically suggest that *State Farm* inaugurated an era of stringent judicial review of agency decision-making for rationality. As we will see, that suggestion is flat wrong at the level of the Supreme Court. At that level, agencies almost never lose. Indeed the facts show that *State Farm* itself is an outlier (see the appendix to this chapter). Starting in October Term 1982, when *State Farm* was decided, the Court has passed on the merits of arbitrariness challenges sixty-four times. Of those, agencies have lost arbitrary and capricious challenges only five times—a remarkable win rate of 92 percent.[2]

At the level of doctrine and announced principles, many of the modern cases feature strong rebukes of lower courts for excessive interference, or specifically disavow idealized conceptions of rationality review developed by lower courts. Over against *State Farm* there stands a long line of decidedly deferential decisions running from *Baltimore Gas & Electric v. NRDC*[3] in 1983 to *FCC v. Fox*[4] and *EPA v. EME Homer City*[5] in recent years. (The exceptions like *Judulang v. Holder*[6] stand out and are more easily recalled precisely because they are rare.) This line of precedent embodies an approach to rationality review that is more aware of, and tolerant of, the inescapable limits of rationality when agencies make decisions under uncertainty—the chronic condition of decision-making in the administrative state. *State Farm* is not representative of the law; beloved of law professors and frequently cited in rote fashion by judges, it nonetheless lies well outside the mainstream of the Supreme Court's precedent.

Of course there are many possible explanations for these data, which we will examine in detail. Selection effects must be accounted for, both at the stage of the selection of cases for litigation and at the stage of selection of cases for review by the Supreme Court. Agencies' won-loss record in arbitrariness challenges before the Court of Appeals for the District of Columbia Circuit is somewhat less impressive, although the data are sketchy. At a minimum, however, administrative lawyers need to reassess, perhaps dramatically, the folk wisdom about the era of "hard look review." Forced to pick one case to encapsulate the Court's approach to rationality review, the best choice would be the powerfully deferential opinion in *Baltimore Gas*, decided in the same Term as *State Farm*. Plausibly, rather than living in the era of "hard look review" or the *State Farm* era, we live in the era of *Baltimore Gas*.

Taken together, the descriptive and prescriptive sections offer a unified account of rationality review. The caselaw and the theory march in tandem to a surprising extent, although with notable exceptions and outliers. To some substantial degree, judicial practice already embodies the thin approach to rationality review that theory recommends—an approach that is far more flexible, accommodating, and intelligent about agency rationality and its inescapable limitations than is the "hard look" approach. Here as elsewhere, law's abnegation rests on internal legal reasons.

The Real World of *State Farm*

There are really two versions of *State Farm*. One is the opinion itself, which is rather narrower than many commentators have made it out to be. Another is the broader aura of the decision. Commentators generally suspicious of agency rationality have puffed up *State Farm* into a synecdoche for "hard look review," contributing to a pervasive but latent culture of academic skepticism toward agency explanations and agency decision-making. Just as there are two versions of *Marbury v. Madison*—the rather narrow decision itself, and the inflated and heavily symbolic *Marbury v. Madison* that the Court so routinely invokes as a symbol of judicial supremacy—and two versions of *Vermont Yankee*, writ small and writ large, so too *State Farm* as doctrine coexists uneasily with *"State Farm"* as symbol.

My target is the latter, not the former. *State Farm* itself is in important respects less demanding than the lawyers' culture of "hard look" suggests. The decision is clear, for example, that judges have no warrant to require agencies to consider and discuss any policy alternative that the judges happen to believe is relevant to the problem at hand.[7] And the Supreme Court has been careful, over time, about policing the boundaries and maintaining the limits of *State Farm*. But the problem is that lower courts and (especially) commentators have sometimes been less careful. Over-reading *State Farm*, they have applied it as though it demands a kind of unbounded, ideal rationality from agencies, insensitive to the costs of information and decision-making. Thin rationality review, by contrast, emphasizes that agencies are constrained by limited resources, information, and time, and asks what (nonideal) reasons agencies may have for acting inaccurately, nonrationally, or arbitrarily, in light of those limits. While *"State Farm"* as symbol is not the law, there is nothing in *State Farm* itself that is inherently incompatible with thin rationality review.

Some Facts about the Law

What does the real world of arbitrary and capricious review look like? A descriptive survey is impressionistic, but suggestive. In both the Supreme Court and the courts of appeals, there is a distribution of cases, with important cases in the tails. Nevertheless, the outliers should not be allowed to blur the overall picture. There are, of course, instances of aggressive and intensive review under the arbitrary and capricious framework; but in the Supreme Court at least, agencies almost always win. If the task for appellate courts is to practice what the Supreme Court both preaches and practices, the message is to apply a thin form of rationality review. In the run of cases, arbitrary and capricious review entails a predictably and sensibly deferential review of agency policy judgments.

The Supreme Court. Starting with the 1982–1983 Term, when *State Farm* was decided, the Court has passed on the merits of arbitrariness challenges sixty-four times. The agency lost on arbitrariness grounds in only five of these cases, for a win rate of 92 percent. (There are some minor coding issues around the edges; with enough work, one can reduce the win rate to fifty-three wins out of sixty-one cases, or a win rate of 87 percent. But the thrust of the point is the same, whatever the metrics chosen, arbitrariness review by the Supreme Court is extremely deferential. The details are in the appendix to this chapter.) Clearing the "hard look" hurdle in the Supreme Court is hardly a heroic task. What should we make of the fact that the Court deems agency decisions arbitrary only 8 percent of the time?

To make headway on this problem, consider first the cases in which the agency's decision was struck down as arbitrary. To be sure, these cases are outliers, but like all exceptions, they are important data points for understanding the rule. Two of these cases, *Massachusetts v. EPA*[8] and *Morgan Stanley Capital Group, Inc. v. Public Utility Dist. No. 1,*[9] actually involve agency decisions not to act at all. Famously, *Massachusetts v. EPA* overturned EPA's decision not to decide whether greenhouse gases constituted "pollution" pursuant to the Clean Air Act.[10] But this was hardly a run of the mill "hard look" case. While agency decisions not to act—at least decisions not to engage in rule-making—may be subject to "hard look review,"[11] in practice, agency failures to act tend to reach the Supreme Court in a posture of near-complete failure by the agency to carry out its statutory obligations on a given issue.[12] When the agency loses in such cases, the Court is saying in effect that the agency must do *something*, but that is a far cry from intensive "hard look review" of an ultimate agency decision. When the agency has decided which of several policy options to pursue, the Supreme Court almost never strikes down that judgment as arbitrary. It is when the agency has said, "We will do nothing," that the Supreme Court is willing to step in. Whether or not the action-inaction dichotomy cuts much ice conceptually, it is noteworthy that half of the Court's arbitrariness cases in which the agency loses involve agency refusals to act.

So the few cases in which the agency loses before the Court feature either refusals to act altogether or the adoption of a decision rule that is entirely unrelated to any statutorily relevant factor, and in that sense genuinely is capricious.[13] The main point, however, is that the rare cases must not be allowed to take up too much space in the collective memory of the profession. As a first rough approximation, agencies *always* win arbitrariness challenges in the Supreme Court.

And to be clear, the distribution of these cases is diverse. Six of the cases involve challenges to Environmental Protection Agency actions, including enforcement orders, permit decisions, and notice-and-comment rules. Two cases review Board of Immigration proceedings. Five cases review decisions of the Federal Communications Commission, including rate-setting, enforcement actions, and several informal rule-makings: no action was held to be arbitrary and capricious. The agency represented most in the sample of Supreme Court challenges is the Department of Health and Human Services, which saw thirteen challenges before the Court; in all but one, the agency's action was upheld as not arbitrary and capricious. The other cases involve a smorgasbord of agencies, including the National Labor Relations Board (three enforcement orders upheld as not arbitrary and capricious), the Department of the Interior, the Department of Commerce, the Securities and Exchange Commission, and the Merit Systems Protection Board. The agencies at issue are quite heterogeneous, and the cases include a mix of actions from informal rulemaking, formal adjudication, enforcement actions, licensing and permit decisions, rate-setting, and so on. In case after case, no matter what the agency and no matter what the action, the most likely outcome, by an overwhelming margin, is for the Court to uphold the action as not arbitrary and capricious. Nor does there seem to be much partisan disagreement about the thinness of review. The cases upholding agency action include majority opinions by Justices Scalia, Rehnquist, Roberts, Souter, Stevens, Ginsburg, Thomas, White, Breyer, Powell, Kennedy, Blackmun, Alito, Kagan, and O'Connor. In short, all of the Justices are well represented in the thin rationality review camp.

Courts of Appeals. In the courts of appeals, the record of arbitrary and capricious is more mixed. There are quite a few empirical studies of judicial review of agency action—broadly defined—in the courts of appeals, but few of arbitrary and capricious review specifically. Miles and Sunstein remarked in 2008 at the "sparse empirical literature . . . on the actual operation of the hard look doctrine," noting additionally that "[t]here is no systematic evidence on the rate of invalidation under hard look review."[14] In reviewing empirical studies across multiple judicial review doctrines, Richard J. Pierce Jr., noted in 2011 that only Miles and Sunstein had examined agency success rates in the courts of appeals under *State Farm*.[15]

Miles and Sunstein conclude that agencies win 64 percent of court of appeals cases reviewing their decisions for arbitrariness. Their data set includes "all published appellate rulings from 1996 to 2006 involving review of decisions of the EPA and review of NLRB decisions either for arbitrariness or for lack of substantial evidence."[16] The authors sensibly limited their analysis to decisions reviewing those two agencies because the issues at stake mapped easily onto political worldview—the primary focus of the article. But if one looks at the distribution of actual cases, just under 85 percent of the cases they study are NLRB cases.[17] The NLRB is an important agency, but as students of administrative law will quickly recognize, the Board makes policy in a way that is almost unique in the universe of administrative agencies, proceeding to formulate rules of general applicability through adjudication rather than rulemaking. Moreover, as the authors note, the NLRB's decisions—when they do anything at all—tend to be more consistently "liberal" by traditional metrics, making them targets of whatever conservative judicial politics might exist.[18]

Thus, the 64 percent figure is somewhat misleading. Judges voted to overturn far more consequential EPA decisions on arbitrariness grounds in barely more than 1/4 of the cases.[19] EPA decisions are upheld against arbitrariness challenge nearly 80 percent of the time. This is, of course, a partial sample of the arbitrary and capricious universe— NLRB and EPA decisions from 1996 to 2006—but there is little in the data to suggest that "hard look" is being used as an elaborate or onerous form of review.

More recently, however, there have been several notable cases in which courts of appeals have adopted a form of "hard look review" that is consistent with neither the Supreme Court's principles and practice nor even past lower-court approaches. In *Business Roundtable v. SEC*,[20] the D.C. Circuit struck down SEC rule 14a-11, which required public companies to provide shareholders with information about, and their ability to vote for, shareholder-nominated candidates for the board of directors. The court concluded that the SEC's rule was arbitrary and capricious: "Because the agency failed to make tough choices about which of the competing estimates is most plausible, [or] to hazard a guess as to which is correct, we believe it neglected its statutory obligation to assess the economic consequences of its rule."[21] So far, the modal response to *Business Roundtable* among administrative lawyers has been a mix of surprise and dismay.[22] Importantly, some have taken the case to stand for the proposition that an agency rule is arbitrary and capricious if it is not supported by careful and rigorous cost-benefit analysis, including a detailed statement of any potential costs or benefits that cannot be quantified and a clear statement about how competing estimates of costs were resolved. So interpreted, the case stands for an ambitious form of arbitrariness review that requires cost-benefit analysis to the extent possible, unless statutorily precluded.[23]

Unusual cases tend to grip the mind. But *Business Roundtable* and a set of other related or similar cases[24] are outliers. The days of systematically aggressive "hard look review," as in the D.C. Circuit's decisions from the 1970s and early 1980s, are mostly behind us—thanks in part to the Supreme Court, which sat down heavily on the D.C. Circuit in both *Vermont Yankee*[25]and *Baltimore Gas*,[26] and which recently overturned another procedural innovation from the D.C. Circuit in *Perez v. Mortgage Bankers Association*,[27] discussed in Chapter 2.

Selection Effects? Like all studies of judicial decisions, observed arbitrariness cases are the result of a complex set of anticipated behaviors by agencies and courts. If agencies believe that judicial review will be aggressive, then strategic agencies may be more conservative in their policy choices, adopting decisions that are very well justified by the available evidence. As a consequence, agencies might usually win in litigation, making it appear that courts are applying a highly deferential standard. By the same token, if agencies believe judicial review will be modest, they might be more aggressive in their decisions, stretching policies just to the edge of justifiability and beyond. If so, agencies might lose more frequently in litigation, making it appear that courts are adopting a stringent form of review. These are familiar dynamics and travel under the rubric of *selection effects*.

Selection effects are not a challenge to the prescriptive vision of arbitrariness review; but they are a potential problem for the descriptive account of arbitrariness review as already thinner than the commentators realize. Suppose the courts apply a form of thin rationality review. If agencies recognize this, they might begin to relax the rigor with which they justify their own decision-making. Courts, applying the same standard of thin rationality review, would suddenly strike down more agency actions, not because the court has adopted more aggressive review but because the agency has weakened its decision-making. Similarly, suppose the courts are engaging in an ambitious thick form of rationality review. Agencies, recognizing this practice, may begin to beef up their decision-making process and justify their conclusions with more elaborate and careful consideration. As a result, courts—again, applying the same thick form of rationality review—

would uphold many more agency decisions, making it appear that there was a new, easy bar to clear, over which agencies virtually never trip. Furthermore, when agencies lose in the courts of appeals, the Solicitor General (SG) often acts as a gatekeeper, whose consent agencies must win in order to file a certiorari petition in the Supreme Court. If the SG files petitions only when the agency's case is strong, agencies might have a better win rate in the Supreme Court than in the lower courts, as indeed they do.

All these possibilities are intrinsically speculative. That said, there is some indirect evidence. David Zaring performed a meta-analysis of existing data and also added new data on judicial review of agency fact-finding.[28] Zaring finds that no matter what standard of review was being utilized ("hard look," *Chevron*, or substantial evidence) and no matter what aspect of the decision was being reviewed (policy, law, or fact) agency win rates are surprisingly stable. Almost uniformly, agencies win in litigation about 70 percent of the time. Neither the standard of review nor the aspect of the underlying decision being challenged seems to matter much at all. To be sure, selection effects might be operating offstage in all these settings, including in the lower courts, but at a certain point that abstract possibility ceases to impress. The important point for our purposes is that no matter what linguistic formulation courts invoke when engaging in rationality review, courts do not seem to be engaging in "hard look" analysis—or at least it requires major epicycles about selection effects to save the "hard look" story. Agencies usually win, and rather than requiring anything like a searching "hard look" inquiry, the resulting distribution of agency wins is far more consistent with a thin form of rationality review.

Another type of indirect evidence involves the putative problem of "ossification." The myth of rigorous *State Farm* review has long been accompanied by several mini-myths, part of the inherited generational wisdom about the costs of intensive judicial review of agency policymaking. Chief among these is the problem of agency ossification: consistent agency losses in litigation coupled with fear of judicial review resulted in agency paralysis. Informal rulemaking began taking years, if not decades; rulemaking records grew exponentially as agencies were forced to address every possible concern with respect to every possible issue in every rulemaking no matter how large or small. The *State Farm* version of "hard look review" made it increasingly difficult for agencies to do their jobs, or so we have been taught.

If true, agency ossification would be some empirical evidence in favor of the strong version of *State Farm* review. Like rigorous *State Farm* review itself, however, the ossification phenomenon is long on anecdote and short on data. In fact, recent studies of agency rulemaking find virtually no evidence of the ossification thesis. EPA rules go from start to finish in an average of a year and a half.[29] In one exhaustive study of the unified regulatory agenda, Anne O'Connell concludes that the costs of rulemaking are certainly not so high as to prohibit substantial rulemaking activity.[30] And, in another comprehensive survey of agency regulatory activity, Yackee and Yackee conclude that agencies are able to get out large numbers of rules fairly quickly.[31]

If there is little evidence of actual ossification, why has the idea of ossification had so much influence? In part, it is because the few outlier examples are high profile and therefore highly visible; but for that very reason, one cannot accurately generalize from those cases to the remainder of the distribution of rulemakings. There is a simpler explanation as well. If one believes that *State Farm* entails searching "hard look review," then it simply stands to reason, as a matter of nearly inimitable logic, that ossification will result. Once that misguided assumption is relaxed, the fact that there is little evidence of ossification makes perfect sense. Arbitrariness review is like a legal phantom: it can scare, but it rarely hurts. So long as agencies comply with some minimal rationality requirements, they usually win in litigation.

The possibility of strong selection effects complicates the descriptive claim about agencies' overwhelming won-loss record in the Supreme Court, and *a fortiori* their impressive, but not overwhelming, won-loss record in the courts of appeals. However, the selection effects hypothesis is speculative, and there is indirect evidence that it is at most a weak force—evidence both from Zaring's global comparison of standards of review and from the ossification studies. And what the Court *says* is even more important than the won-loss record. Justices of all types—unlike some lower-court judges—show a deep appreciation for the constraints under which agencies act, high tolerance for agency action under uncertainty, and a willingness to allow agencies to adopt strategies of second-order rationality that permit inaccurate, nonrational, or arbitrary action in particular cases. Or so I will now attempt to illustrate.

Prescription: Thin Rationality Review

What if anything might justify this pattern of deferential rationality review? What would put it in the best possible light? There is a theory implicit, and sometimes explicit, in the bulk of the Court's caselaw: thin rationality review. The theory has both a negative and a positive dimension.

On the negative dimension, here are many things that rationality review does *not* require and that the Court has generally disavowed, despite contrary assumptions or arguments scattered through the lower-court caselaw and especially the commentary. Judges may not require agencies to conduct quantified cost-benefit analysis, even presumptively; may not always require agencies to conduct comparative policy evaluation, obliging agencies to show that the chosen policy is superior to feasible alternatives, or superior to the agency's own past choices; may not require agencies to have valid first-order reasons for all their choices; may not force agencies to opt for "conservative" assumptions in the face of uncertainty; need not require a "rational connection between the facts found and the choices made,"[32] depending upon how exactly that critical idea is understood; need not require agencies to be able to explain or convey their reasons, to the satisfaction of a panel of generalist judges; and may not lard rationality review with quasi-procedural obligations.

On the positive dimension, a simple affirmative formulation of thin rationality review runs this way: agencies must act based on reasons, where the set of admissible reasons includes second-order reasons to act inaccurately, nonrationally, or arbitrarily. That formulation seems paradoxical, but the paradox is illusory. Neither the theory of rational decision-making nor the caselaw requires agencies to exercise a kind of unbounded ideal rationality. I will examine some contexts and problems to flesh out this claim.

"Relevant Factors"

To begin with, there is a recurring confusion that stems not from *State Farm*, but from the original framework for rationality review laid down in *Overton Park*. Chief among the latter's innovations was the idea that agencies must consider "the relevant factors," and also avoid "clear error[s] of judgment."[33] The injunction to consider the "relevant factors" has fostered nontrivial confusion, because the source of those factors is not obvious. Is *Overton Park* saying, for example, that judges should identify policy factors in the problem at issue, policy factors that seem relevant to them, and then require agencies to consider those factors?

Not at all; indeed the Court has specifically repudiated that procedure, both in *State Farm* itself[34] and in subsequent cases.[35] Understood in the larger framework of judicial review of agency action, the function of the "relevant factors" inquiry is simply to ensure that the agency has given due consideration to any factors *made relevant by the authorizing statute itself*, and to ensure that the agency has not considered any factors the statute rules off-limits. Absent constitutional problems, Congress enjoys the power by statute to set the agency's deliberative agenda, either in positive or negative terms, and the "relevant factors" inquiry ensures that agencies respect Congress's choices.

Given that the relevant factors inquiry is really one of statutory interpretation, it is subject to the rules of statutory interpretation that always govern in administrative law. One of those is the *Chevron* doctrine, under which agencies rather than courts enjoy the authority to fill in statutory gaps and ambiguities. The Court has made it very plain that *Chevron* applies to the interpretive question about what factors the statute makes relevant.[36] And, two Terms ago the Court also explained that *Chevron* applies to agency interpretations of their own jurisdiction as well.[37] In particular, where statutes are silent or ambiguous, agencies rather than courts enjoy discretion to decide what the relevant factors may be and whether to consider those factors.

They also enjoy discretion to decide *when* to consider those factors. The Court has also been very clear that agencies need not consider all logically relevant policy factors at once, but may instead parcel them out into different proceedings, considering problems by parts and proceeding one step at a time.[38] Relatedly, agencies may in adjudication single out one or a few defendants from the mass of similarly situated firms in order to create a test case or to examine the relevant questions case by case—even if from the defendant's point of view the selection is entirely arbitrary.[39]

This relaxed approach makes eminent good sense. The precondition for *Chevron* to apply is a "step zero" analysis, which asks whether Congress has delegated law-interpreting authority to agencies rather than courts.[40] The animating objectives of *Chevron*—political accountability and expertise—both suggest that Congress's default intention is that agencies rather than courts should determine which policy factors count as "relevant," and which factors should be considered in which proceeding, absent clear statutory indication to the contrary or some special reason to think that the question is so important that it is not fit for agency resolution.[41] As to any reasonably complex policy problem, an indefinitely large number of policy factors are potentially relevant, or can be claimed to be relevant by litigants who will benefit from delaying agency action. Generalist judges who attempt to sift the wheat from the chaff will run every risk of becoming confused, absent explicit statutory guidance, and will inevitably end up making *de facto* policy choices that should lie within the province of relatively more responsive and better-informed agencies.

So an agency that otherwise enjoys delegated interpretive authority, under *Chevron* "step zero," also enjoys the authority to decide which factors count as "relevant" for purposes of *Overton Park*—provided, of course, that the underlying statute is silent or ambiguous. Where statutes are clear, however, either mandating or prohibiting consideration of relevant factors, then courts must enforce their terms. In other words, the ordinary *Chevron* inquiry governs. For our purposes here, the important point is that rationality review neither requires nor even permits generalist judges to decide, on their own initiative, that a given factor that happens to strike them as important is a legally "relevant factor" under *Overton Park*. Absent clear statutory instruction, or an issue of extraordinary political and economic significance, policy relevance is a matter for agency determination.

Cost-Benefit Analysis—Quantified and Otherwise

With the advent of *Business Roundtable,* some have begun to suggest that cost-benefit analysis is a necessary component of rational decision-making, so that a requirement of cost-benefit analysis should be read into arbitrary and capricious review. How can a decision be rational if it is unjustified by the attendant costs and benefits?[42] Legally, there are two related but distinct ideas. As to the interpretation of agency organic statutes, one view holds that congressional silence or ambiguity should be read to require cost-benefit analysis, quantified where possible.[43] In a related view, unless statutes clearly prohibit the consideration of costs, arbitrariness review should be understood to require that agencies supply quantified cost-benefit analysis, wherever quantification is possible.[44]

These claims hover somewhere between confused and mistaken. There is a thin tautological sense in which rationality requires that decision-makers do what is better, as opposed to what is worse. But rationality certainly does not require quantified cost-benefit analysis in the technical sense. As for the interpretation of organic statutes and of arbitrariness review under the APA, there is no plausible basis for a requirement of quantified cost-benefit analysis, not even a presumptive requirement.

Conceptual Problems. At the conceptual level, there is a slippage in this literature between a tautology, on the one hand, and a highly sectarian decision-procedure, on the other. The tautology is that a decision-maker should do what is best, all things considered. In that sense, it may always be said, without possibility of contradiction, that the decision-maker should ensure that the "benefits" exceed the "costs." Were a decision-maker to say that "the benefits are X; the costs are Y; we find that Y > X; nonetheless we choose to do X," one would either doubt the decision-maker's rationality or assume some misunderstanding or miscommunication.[45] (As we will see, however, this sort of example assumes certainty, or at least well-formed probability assessments, as to the costs and benefits. Under conditions of genuine uncertainty, perhaps arising from high costs of information, rationality even permits decision-procedures that do not attempt to figure out, in a first-order way, whether benefits exceed costs.)

Thus an informal and nonquantified sense of cost-benefit analysis—thinking about the "pros" and "cons"[46]—is ubiquitous, both in law and in life. Charles Darwin famously drew up a list of pros and cons in deciding whether to marry.[47] But this informal sense of cost-benefit analysis is not what is at stake in the legal debates. In *Business Roundtable*, the SEC offered a detailed qualitative discussion of the pros and cons of its rule.[48] The court nonetheless objected that the agency's "cost-benefit analysis" was inadequate because the agency had not tried hard enough to quantify some of the relevant factors.[49]

As *Business Roundtable* illustrates, proponents urge a particular, highly structured decision-procedure—quantified CBA. That procedure is technical, but it is also highly controversial, even polarizing, especially in its purest form, which is not only quantified but also monetized. Proponents praise it as a mechanism for welfare-maximization, for promoting democratic transparency in agency decision-making, or for securing presidential control of agencies.[50] Opponents criticize it for reducing incommensurables to a common denominator, for smuggling in controversial value judgments and hidden margins of discretion, and for crowding out nonquantifiable considerations.[51]

The problems and promise of quantified CBA have been rehashed many times. The essential point here is that quantified CBA is a specialized, sectarian decision-procedure, not a requirement of rational decision-making. Many demonstrably rational economists, philosophers, lawyers, and other students of decision-making do not believe that rationality requires quantified CBA. Some believe, on the contrary, that best practices of decision-making actually *forbid* resort to quantified CBA, because it has no moral relevance whatsoever and sometimes misleads.[52] More temperately, one might believe that quantified CBA is sometimes useful, sometimes not, but reject the idea that it is inscribed in the very nature of rationality. Quantified CBA is both disputable and widely disputed. To impose it on agencies in the name of rationality would be to squelch reasonable disagreement by sheer force.

Legal Problems. The legal issue is whether judges may require agencies to use quantified CBA, at least presumptively, either as a matter of arbitrariness review under the APA, or else by interpretation of agencies' organic statutes. The best view is that judges have no warrant for so requiring, under current law rightly interpreted in its best light. The Court has emphatically banned judges from imposing decision-procedures on agencies as a matter of federal common law, and there is no source of positive law that might be read to impose a global, judicially enforceable mandate of quantified CBA on agencies, even presumptively.

Quantified CBA is a particular decision-procedure—emphasis on procedure. Under *Vermont Yankee v. NRDC*[53] and *Perez v. Mortgage Bankers Association*,[54] agencies have discretion whether to adopt such procedures, and courts have no power to force them to do so beyond the procedures prescribed by the APA itself. Suppose that an agency is charged with deciding whether to regulate mercury emissions from electric utilities,[55] and suppose also that the court tells the agency that—even after the agency has considered the relevant statutory factors—the agency must if possible quantify and monetize the various factors. What the court has done is to prescribe *how*, by what procedures, the agency is to exercise its discretion. That is the very thing the Court has "time and again . . . reiterated" that lower courts are forbidden to do.[56]

The only way around the *Vermont Yankee* problem is to locate the mandate for cost-benefit analysis either in organic statutes or in Section 706 itself, but neither approach succeeds. Where agency organic statutes are silent or ambiguous, it is wildly implausible that Congress intends (or could be deemed fictionally to intend) a global default rule requiring cost-benefit analysis. Across the broad landscape of federal regulatory statutes, Congress sometimes mandates quantified CBA, sometimes refers vaguely to considerations of "cost," sometimes leaves matters ambiguous, sometimes contents itself with Delphic silence, sometimes explicitly *forbids* consideration of cost, and sometimes mandates other decision-procedures altogether, such as "feasibility" analysis.[57] There is no legal basis to elevate one of these approaches to global default-rule status, apart from a sectarian preference for one approach or the other. The regulatory system writ large, like the Administrative Procedure Act, is a series of "compromises" that allows "opposing social and political forces" to "come to rest."[58] There is irreducible reasonable disagreement about the best regulatory decision-procedure, including the very plausible view that there is no single best decision-procedure, independent of context. This irreducible reasonable disagreement about regulatory strategy implies a single correct legal answer: judges have no warrant to impose a single view on agencies.

The same statutory landscape militates strongly against reading a (presumptive) requirement of quantified CBA into the "arbitrary and capricious" language of Section 706(2)(A). To do so implies that Congress itself acts irrationally whenever it mandates feasibility analysis, or forbids cost considerations, as it sometimes does. Are the proponents prepared to invalidate as irrational all statutes that mandate feasibility, or forbid considerations of cost, perhaps under the Due Process Clause? Invalidate the Occupational Safety and Health Act, perhaps?[59] (It is no answer to say that the standard of rationality review is more deferential for Congress, although that is true.[60] The view at issue is that not doing quantified CBA, when that is possible, is no more rational than using a Ouija board—unconstitutional under any standard.) Whatever the answer to those questions, such provisions show that many presumptively reasonable legislators, at various times, have not thought it irrational to mandate decision-procedures other than quantified CBA. The proponents' reading of Section 706(2)(A) would thus produce an immediate and severe incoherence in the federal regulatory system overall.

Current Law. So there is no basis for either a global default rule requiring quantified CBA whenever statutes are silent or ambiguous, or else for reading an obligation to perform quantified CBA into the arbitrariness standard of Section 706(2)(A). Fortunately, current law emphatically rejects both ideas in any event. The Supreme Court has consistently held that quantified CBA is discretionary for agencies.[61] A brace of recent cases has clarified the terrain.

In *Entergy Corp. v. Riverkeeper*,[62] the Court upheld the EPA's use of cost-benefit analysis in the face of statutory silence with respect to standards in Section 316(b) of the Clean Water Act. The Second Circuit had held that the EPA was not permitted to use cost-benefit analysis in determining the content of regulations under Section 316(b). At issue in the case were EPA regulations concerning the technology required for operators of large power plants that utilize "cooling water intake structures," drawing water in from water sources to cool the plant and in the process killing aquatic life. The Clean Water Act requires that "[a]ny standard . . . applicable to a point source shall require that the location, design, construction, and capacity of cooling water intake structures reflect the *best technology available* for minimizing adverse environmental impact."[63] So-called "closed-cycle" cooling systems re-circulate the water used to cool the facility and therefore extract less water from the local water source and generate less risk of harm to aquatic life. EPA's rule required new sources to use technology approximating the performance of closed-cycle cooling system. For certain classes of existing sources, however, EPA required reductions in the harm to aquatic organisms, but nowhere near the reduction that would be accomplished if EPA mandated performance at the closed-cycle cooling system level.[64] While the closed-cycle cooling system performance would reduce impingement and entrainment mortality by up to 98 percent, the costs of compliance for these existing sources would be nine times greater ($3.4 billion) than reducing aquatic damage by 80 to 95 percent using the alternative performance standards. Put informally, EPA concluded that the marginal costs of achieving the best possible reduction in aquatic harm drastically outweighed the corresponding marginal benefit.

Writing for the majority, Justice Scalia explained that EPA could permissibly read "best" to simply mean "most advantageous." One possible interpretation of "best" is the technology that achieves the greatest reduction in adverse environmental impact.[65] Another, however, is the technology that "most efficiently produces some good."[66] The Court quickly dispensed with the notion that statutory silence necessarily precludes or mandates cost-benefit analysis. On the contrary, discussing several cases in which statutory silence was read to preclude cost-benefit analysis,[67] or at least to not require it,[68] the Court explained that "under *Chevron*, that an agency is not *required* to do [cost-benefit analysis] does not mean that the agency is not *permitted* to do so."[69] Even though other standards in the Clean Water Act might preclude cost-benefit analysis in express terms, EPA was free to adopt a reasonable interpretation of the statutory standard above as allowing cost-benefit analysis. Far from announcing a default rule in favor of cost-benefit analysis, the Court made clear that statutory ambiguity will generally be read to give agencies discretion with respect to whether or not to utilize it.

Environmental Protection Agency v. EME Homer City[70] is similar. The case involved a challenge to EPA's interstate air pollution rules governing the conduct of upwind states that contribute significantly to air pollution in downstream states. The Clean Air Act requires states to eliminate "amounts" of pollution that "contribute significantly to nonattainment" in downwind states.[71] But because multiple states may affect conditions in a downstream state, the statute requires EPA to apportion reductions. The D.C. Circuit had held that the statute required EPA to allocate responsibility for reducing emissions proportionally to each state's physical contribution.[72] EPA's method of determining cost-reduction obligations balanced the magnitude of the state's pollution to downstream air conditions and the costs associated with reducing them.[73] The challengers argued that EPA was forbidden to consider costs, but as in *Entergy* the majority again clarified that unless the statute clearly mandates otherwise, EPA is free to consider costs. "The Agency has chosen, sensibly in our view, to reduce the amount easier, *i.e.*, less costly, to eradicate, and nothing in the text of the Good Neighbor Provision precludes that choice."[74] In short, in the face of statutory silence, the agency is free to use cost-benefit analysis or not, as it sees fit.

In *Utility Air Regulatory Group v. EPA*[75] *(UARG)* the Court considered a challenge to EPA's interpretation of the Clean Air Act as it pertains to greenhouse gases (GHGs). In *Massachusetts v. EPA*,[76] the Court had held that GHG emissions were "pollutants" for at least some purposes of the Clean Air Act. After *Massachusetts v. EPA*, the agency issued greenhouse-gas emission standards for new motor vehicles.[77] Stationary sources are governed by two separate provisions of the Clean Air Act (as relevant here)—the Prevention of Significant Deterioration (PSD) provisions[78] and the Title V permitting program.[79] Those provisions set numerical triggers for what sort of entity is regulated (100 or 250 tons per year of a pollutant).[80] Because GHGs, unlike other air pollutants, are emitted in vastly greater amounts, those numerical thresholds would have brought thousands of new small entities under the rubric of the EPA permitting process.[81] Accordingly, EPA sought to cover initially only those entities emitting more than 100,000 tons of GHGs per year.[82] In short, the Court in *Massachusetts v. EPA* prodded the agency to adopt an ambitious reading of the statute, which then threatened to render part of the existing regulatory framework unworkable.

Without delving too deeply into the technical details of the Clean Air Act, there were essentially two types of sources at issue in the EPA rule challenged in *UARG*. The first group would not have been subject to the PSD or Title V permitting process at all, but for their GHG emissions. The Court held that EPA's interpretation, which brought these thousands of sources into the Act's coverage, was unlawful.[83] The second group of sources was subject to the permitting process for the emission of other air pollutants anyway. For this group of sources, there was a subsequent interpretive question about whether EPA's decision to require Best Available Control Technology (BACT) for GHGs was a permissible interpretation of the statute. The Court held that it was.[84] The challengers essentially argued that BACT does not work for GHGs. The Court's discretion-preserving language is striking: "applying BACT to greenhouse gases is not so disastrously unworkable, and need not result in such a dramatic expansion of agency authority, as to convince us that EPA's interpretation is unreasonable."[85]

Because *UARG* strikes down an EPA interpretation, it might at first glance be read as an aggressive form of judicial review, in tension with *Entergy* and *EME Homer*. In reality, however, it is precisely the opposite. EPA had advanced a view that the agency was required to adopt the same definition of "air pollutant" throughout the Clean Air Act, and therefore GHGs needed to be treated as criteria pollutants. As Justice Scalia explained, however, "the presumption of consistent usage readily yields to context, and a statutory term—even one defined in the statute—may take on distinct characters from association with distinct statutory objects calling for different implementation strategies."[86] Because EPA's rigid interpretation would render the statutory scheme unworkable, it was not a permissible interpretation of the statute. But where the interpretation would not render the scheme unworkable (for "anyway" sources), EPA was free to adopt either interpretation. Indeed, this latter part of the opinion is striking for just how far removed from mandatory cost-benefit analysis it is. The agency was not required to pick a rule that was even close to cost-benefit justified so long as it was "not so disastrously unworkable."[87]

Finally, there is the recent decision in *Michigan v. EPA*,[88] in which the Court invalidated an EPA rule under the Clean Air Act relating to hazardous emissions from power plants. The relevant statutory text authorized regulation only if "appropriate and necessary."[89] As framed by the litigation, the question was whether EPA could defer consideration of costs at the stage of deciding *whether* to regulate, and later take costs into account at the stage of deciding *how much* to regulate—how stringent regulation should be. In an opinion by Justice Scalia, the Court held that under the statutory text, cost was a "relevant factor," and EPA's decision to ignore cost at the first decisional stage was unreasonable.[90] The decision is most easily and naturally read as a *Chevron* decision, on a straightforward statutory issue under the particular scheme of the relevant Clean Air Act provisions.

Proponents of quantified cost-benefit analysis point to seemingly broad language in the opinion,[91] as when the majority opined that "[o]ne would not say that it is even rational, never mind 'appropriate,' to impose billions of dollars in economic costs in return for a few dollars in health or environmental benefits."[92] On the broadest possible reading, this could mean that it is arbitrary and capricious for agencies not to conduct quantified and monetized cost-benefit analysis where possible. Yet this is an interpretation the Court took pains to disavow later in the opinion. Justice Scalia went out of his way to emphasize that while rationality may require "paying attention to the advantages and the disadvantages of agency decisions,"[93] that is not the same as requiring *quantification* of the advantages and disadvantages: "The Agency must consider cost—including, most importantly, cost of compliance— before deciding whether regulation is appropriate and necessary. We need not and do not hold that the law unambiguously required the Agency, when making this preliminary estimate, to conduct a formal cost-benefit analysis in which each advantage and disadvantage is assigned a monetary value. It will be up to the Agency to decide (as always, within the limits of reasonable interpretation) how to account for cost."[94] Decisions about quantification, in other words, are a matter for reasonable agency discretion, contrary to *Business Roundtable*. *Michigan v. EPA* is clearly alert to the distinction between the colloquial, informal sense of "costs and benefits," on the one hand, and formalized quantified and monetized cost-benefit analysis, on the other. The decision is principally an interpretive holding, about the meaning of the phrase "appropriate and necessary" in a particular section of the Clean Air Act. But insofar as it addresses issues of rationality review in passing, it stands only for the unobjectionable proposition that rationality requires consideration of both "the advantages *and* the disadvantages of agency decisions."[95]

This is not to say, of course, that *Michigan v. EPA* is correct. The Court slipped from an unexceptional premise, that agencies should consider both the advantages and disadvantages of their decisions, to the very different and indefensible conclusion that agencies must consider those things all *together*, at every stage of regulatory proceedings. On the contrary, the background presumption of administrative law is that agencies may parcel out the consideration of relevant factors into different stages of proceedings or even different proceedings.[96] Although the presumption may of course be overcome by clear statutory instructions to the contrary, the statutory phrase "appropriate and necessary" should have been deemed insufficient to do so.

Connecting Facts and Choices: Uncertainty, Rationality, and Arbitrariness

In a frequently quoted passage, *State Farm* announced that an agency must "examine the relevant data and articulate a satisfactory explanation for its action including a 'rational connection between the facts found and the choice made.'"[97] This has become a basic principle of rationality review: agencies must explain their choices, in light of the facts. Yet there is much less to this requirement than meets the eye— both as a matter of the theory of rational decision-making, and under current law. The obligation to explain choices, given the facts, is far less demanding than lower courts sometimes assume, although the Court itself has usually understood the problem and followed the correct approach.

The critical problem is that facts sometimes underdetermine agency choices. It is not necessarily the case, and perhaps not even usually the case, that given some state of the world, the agency will always have (let alone be able to give) reasons for choosing one policy over all competitors, or over any given alternative. Rather, it can be the case, and may often be the case, that agencies will face a situation in which (1) the agency is obligated to choose; (2) there exists more than one policy that can be justified, given the best evidence about the state of the world; and yet (3) there is no decisive reason to choose one policy over another.

This is just the uncertainty problem from Chapter 4, in which a rationally arbitrary decision may be inevitable or desirable. In cases of this sort, agencies may validly select policies without a *direct* connection between the "facts found" and the "choices made." Because the facts, the state of the world, underdetermine choices, agencies cannot reasonably be asked to show, based on the facts, that the choice they make is superior to the alternatives. This is not to say that there is no "rational connection" between facts and choices. It is to say that the nature of the rational connection is different than in standard cases. The rational connection lies at the second order, not the first; it arises because the agency has good reason to decide, even if it lacks good reason for the decision. In this sense, the *State Farm* test of "rational connection" is more capacious, more forgiving, and less demanding than is conventionally understood.

Satisficing and Information-Gathering

As we also saw in Chapter 4, uncertainty has another critical dimension, involving the rationality of information-gathering by agencies. Rational agencies will invest resources in acquiring information, which may resolve Knightian uncertainty, transforming it into risk or even certainty. Yet in some cases the value of further investments in information-gathering will itself be genuinely uncertain. If so, the problem of rational arbitrariness will replicate itself at this higher level as well. In a genuinely uncertain choice environment, the decision-maker must stop the search for the best policy sooner or later, somewhere or other, or else fall into an infinite regress—deciding whether to acquire information about the costs of acquiring further information.

We have seen that although *State Farm* and successor cases explicitly repudiate the idea that agencies must consider all feasible policy alternatives, judges sometimes act as though there is such an obligation, often without quite saying so. The underlying impulse here is the tempting thought that *comparative* policy evaluation is a necessary element of rational decision-making, for agencies or indeed for any institution or actor. Surely, the intuition runs, rationality requires choosing the *best* option, relative to the chooser's preferences, within the feasible set of choices. Suppose there is an agency charged with reducing air pollution, at acceptable cost; and suppose the agency were to say that "policy P is cheaper than policy Q, and P yields more reduction in air pollution. But Q is not bad at all; we think it is good enough. We choose Q." Is that not irrational?

Judges who reason this way have an entirely legitimate intuition, but they fail to realize that the intuition does not always hold, and that the conditions under which it fails to hold are especially likely to arise in the administrative setting. The underlying issue is the validity of "satisficing"—of picking something on the ground that it is "good enough." Satisficing is intrinsically non-comparative. The satisficer picks a feasible option whose quality exceeds some predefined aspiration level, regardless of whether there might be an even better option somewhere in the feasible set.[98] In real life, people constantly satisfice; indeed, people who relentlessly seek the best possible option have a mad air about them. The ubiquity of satisficing should alert judges that comparative policy evaluation is an approach that makes sense only under particular conditions.

What are those conditions, and what are the conditions under which satisficing is sensible? Satisficing becomes sensible in the presence of substantial costs of information and search—in a word, under uncertainty.[99] In the earlier example, the agency's choice of Q over P was irrational only because the context of choice was entirely static and transparent; the options were known, as were their full costs and benefits. In static contexts, absent uncertainty, satisficing is indeed irrational and comparative policy evaluation is indispensable.[100] In more dynamic contexts, however, satisficing comes into its own. The satisficing decision-maker applies a stopping rule that constrains the open-ended search for the very best policy, in favor of one that meets or exceeds the aspiration level.

In the presence of information costs and search costs, another strategy is constrained optimization. On this approach, decision-makers should invest in gathering information just up to the point at which the (increasing) marginal costs of doing so equal the expected marginal benefits of further information.[101] Whereas the satisficer stops when the choice at hand is good enough, the constrained optimizer stops looking for a better choice when the marginal benefit of finding a better option, discounted by the probability of finding such an option, is equal to or less than the marginal costs of further search. The optimizing approach, however, assumes that the decision-maker always has epistemically well-grounded probability distributions over the marginal costs and benefits of further search—an implausible assumption. In any event, the two strategies are simply different. "An optimizing strategy places limits on how much we are willing to invest in seeking alternatives. A satisficing strategy places limits on how much we insist on finding before we quit that search and turn our attention to other matters."[102] Finally, even if it were true that satisficing is just a form of optimization-under-constraints, the substantive point remains the same. Whether agency decision-making under uncertainty is described as satisficing or as constrained optimization, the substantive point is that *comparative* evaluation of policies is not always required by rationality.

The crucial twist here is that, while satisficing is a rational strategy for agents with limited time and information who are forced to make choices under uncertainty, the selection of an aspiration level is itself inescapably arbitrary. Nothing in the idea of satisficing, or in the choice situation itself, tells the rationally satisficing agent where to locate the aspiration level, higher or lower. In that sense, satisficing is a strategy of rational a-rationality, of rationally arbitrary decision-making, also along the lines of Chapter 4. Satisficing is an approach that seemingly lacks any justification in first-order reason—an observer may well complain, "Why did you stop there, not somewhere else?"—but it is justified as a strategy, over an array of problems, by higher-order considerations.

All this is important because uncertainty pervades regulation and other forms of agency policy-making. In the administrative setting, choices are rarely fully specified, static, and transparent. The chronic condition of agency policy-making is search for sensible policies under uncertainty; at some point, the agency will have to suspend the search and choose something good enough, even if it is abstractly possible that there exists a better policy that is technically feasible. Administrative-law doctrine, at its best, recognizes exactly this point by underscoring that agencies' obligation to consider policy alternatives is limited to *reasonable* alternatives. The adjective represents an implicit recognition that consideration of technically feasible alternatives is often a game not worth the candle. Even in *State Farm*, the Court was careful to specifically deny that agencies have any obligation to "consider all policy alternatives in reaching decision."[103]

That denial has sometimes been forgotten by lower federal courts. At its worst, intrusive judicial review threatens to create an infinite regress, in which agencies have to be able to give reasons for suspending the search for optimal policies, reasons that require the very information whose absence is the reason for stopping in the first place. "The reason agencies do not explore all arguments or consider all alternatives is one of practical limits of time and resources. Yet, to have to explain all this to a reviewing court risks imposing much of the very burden that not considering alternatives aims to escape."[104]

As in other settings, however, the Supreme Court often displays a better understanding of uncertainty and its significance for administrative law than do the lower courts. Thus *Baltimore Gas & Electric* allowed the Nuclear Regulatory Commission (NRC) to adopt a maximally *optimistic* assumption about the environmental effects of spent nuclear fuel in the remote future, an assumption of "zero release." In the terms explained in Chapter 4, *Baltimore Gas* recognized that under uncertainty maximax is just as valid as maximin. On this view, the NRC's assumption of "zero release" of spent nuclear fuels should not be taken too literally. It was not a prediction that not one iota of such fuels would ever be released. Rather it was a policy choice, one that opted for maximax assumptions—highly optimistic assumptions—in the presence of severe uncertainty.

Comparative Policy Evaluation (Over Time)

More importantly still, *FCC v. Fox*[105] squarely held that comparative policy evaluation is *not* a general requirement of rational agency decision-making. Agencies have *no* general legal obligation, as far as the APA is concerned, to show that the chosen policy is the best among the feasible alternatives, relative to the agency's stated goals. As the Court put it, "[T]he agency must show that there are good reasons for the new policy. But it need not demonstrate to a court's satisfaction that the reasons for the new policy are *better* than the reasons for the old one; it suffices that the new policy is permissible under the statute, that there are good reasons for it, and that the agency *believes* it to be better. . . ."[106] The obligation to show that "there are good reasons for the new policy," coupled with the lack of any obligation to show that chosen policy is better than the alternatives, is in effect a satisficing approach, rather than a comparative one.

A wrinkle in *Fox* is that the issue of comparative policy evaluation was set in a time frame. The case involved a change of agency policy; the principal dissent, by Justice Breyer, urged that agencies should have to show the comparative superiority of the new policy—a somewhat puzzling stance, given Breyer's usual sensitivity to the impossible burdens that a requirement of full comparative evaluation would impose.[107] The Court rejected Breyer's view as too demanding. The Court observed—citing *State Farm*, quite correctly—that rationality review requires agencies to take into account data that can "readily be obtained," but does not require "obtaining the unobtainable."[108] To be sure, the Court added critical qualifiers that close some of the distance between majority and dissent; the Court, for example, acknowledged that agencies should explain changes in factual assertions, and should take into account knowable and known costs of transition to the new policy ("reliance interests").[109] But there remains an irreducible difference between majority and dissent: the Court is very clear that comparative policy evaluation, in and of itself, is not a requirement of rationality review.[110]

The *Fox* rule, denying any agency obligation to engage in comparative policy evaluation, fits perfectly with the principle that agencies may proceed one step at a time, enjoying "broad discretion" to parcel out policy questions across different proceedings, present and future.[111] The two principles actually entail one another. Because agencies need not consider all relevant alternatives *now*, they cannot have any obligation to show that the currently chosen action is superior to the relevant alternatives, which may be allocated to a separate proceeding entirely, or simply put off the table for the time being. The point common to both principles is that agencies need only have some adequate reason for what they do now; they need not rank possible actions and show that the one chosen is best.

Whether the issue is comparative evaluation of feasible policy choices at a given time, or over time, the point is the same. Under uncertainty, in the presence of costs of information and search, rationality does not require agencies to show that they have chosen the best of the technically feasible alternatives. Thanks to *Fox*, the prevailing law of rationality review does not require that either.

Accuracy vs. Other Values: Trade-offs and Decision Rules

It is tempting to think that rationality requires agencies to pick the best expected policy, in the first-order sense. After all, if the agency picks something other than the best expected policy, its choice can be improved upon and is therefore irrational—is it not? Actually not. There are many conditions under which rationality is compatible with choosing something other than the best expected policy.

Mean-Variance Trade-offs. A standard problem for agencies (and all decision-makers) involves mean-variance trade-offs. When making predictions about the effects of different policies, agencies must predict the most likely or average effect of a policy. The agency's "best guess" for example, might be that changing the NAAQS for ozone will save 10,000 lives. But that estimate—the average or mean—has a variance as well. The better the information or data the agency has, the lower the variance. The more speculative or uncertain the information, the higher the variance. Just to illustrate, a good estimate might entail a variance of plus or minus 1,000 lives; a lower quality estimate, a variance of plus or minus 8,000 lives.[112] Assuming the agency has already gathered all cost-justified information, it is entirely rational to pick the policy with the *lower* expected number of lives saved, if that policy option also produces a smaller variance. A strong form of rationality review that requires agencies to pick a policy alternative with the highest expected return would be seriously misguided. Mean-variance trade-offs exist in almost any agency decision-making setting, and agencies should not be required to ignore them by a confused formulation of rationality review by courts.

Speed vs. Accuracy. Increasingly, agencies are asked to formulate new rules under significant time pressure. The timelines that Dodd-Frank established for the promulgation of hundreds of new rules regulating the financial industry were astonishingly short, and as a consequence most of the deadlines were missed by the agencies.[113] The Food and Drug Administration was successfully sued because it failed to meet the aggressive time frame established by the Food Safety Modernization Act.[114] Statutory deadlines respond, in part, to long-standing criticism in the commentary that the pace of agency rulemakings is too slow.[115]

Whether agencies, in fact, tend to move too slowly, it is clearly true that agencies are often under pressure to act more quickly. In the case of true emergencies, the "good cause" exception of the APA will allow agencies to avoid notice-and-comment requirements at least for a brief time period.[116] Yet this is only relevant to a particular subset of agency action, involving legislative rulemaking; there are many other cases in which speed is of the essence. Dollars or lives may be lost if agencies move slowly. In such cases, agencies face an inevitable trade-off between speed and accuracy.

The speed-accuracy trade-off is an important special case of the costs of information-gathering. With more careful study, consultation, the design of new experiments, the construction of new models, and so on, agencies could more accurately identify the best policy. Yet rationality will sometimes dictate acting quickly, trading accuracy for speed, because of the costs of waiting. Indeed, a rule that always favors more accurate decision-making and ignores temporal problems would arguably be irrational—not to mention that it would result in virtually no agency action ever. As should be immediately clear, this is a problem for thicker forms of arbitrariness review, which require a strongly rational connection between the facts known and the choice made. It is often rational, indeed optimal, to not spend the time gathering information so that a clear rational connection exists between *particular* facts and the *particular* choice made, because that would require sacrificing the benefits of expedition. This sort of trade-off does not always exist, but it sometimes does exist, and arbitrariness review should be flexible enough to accommodate.

Asymmetric Error Costs. Administrative-law doctrine on arbitrariness review tends to obfuscate the problem of asymmetric error costs. Criminal law has long been focused on what might be termed *the problem of asymmetric error costs.* The Blackstone principle states that it is better to let ten guilty persons go free than to put one innocent person in jail and is a potential justification for many defendant-favoring rules of criminal procedure.[117] This principle is an outgrowth of the problem of asymmetric error costs: it is much worse to err by putting an innocent person in prison than to err by putting a guilty person on the street, or so the argument goes. Irrespective of whether one agrees with this intuition,[118] the problem of asymmetric costs of errors abounds in the law. Decisions about whether to list endangered species have this flavor. Failing to list a species that should have been protected will result in extinction; listing a species that did not need to be protected will result in some financial costs, but this can be corrected at some later point. Failing to regulate a new pollutant that should have been regulated will result in illness and deaths. Regulating a new pollutant unnecessarily will result in financial costs.

The costs of making mistakes in administrative law are often asymmetric, and it is perfectly rational for agencies to take asymmetric error costs into account. Even if the best available evidence suggests the best policy alternative is X, it is rational for an agency to select policy Y because the costs of error are not symmetric. This is one common justification for the "precautionary principle." Even if the agency has failed to pick the best policy in a first-order sense, it has good second-order reasons for not doing so. The agency's *decision rule* is rational, even if its narrow *decision* is not. It is an open question whether (lower) courts would accept this sort of justification, but they should.

Agency Rationality: A Positive Formulation

So far the discussion has been relentlessly negative. To some degree, negativity is inherent in the nature of the principal claim: there is and should be *less* to rationality review than some judges and commentators seem to think. Nonetheless, a positive formulation of agency rationality and rationality review is desirable, as an alternative to the "hard look" approach.

In a simple positive formulation, the best interpretation of Section 706(2)(A), and of rationality review, is just that *agencies must act based on reasons.* In this simple conception, the aim of Section 706(2) (A) is to exclude agency action that rests on no reasons whatsoever, at any order of analysis—the core meaning of "arbitrary and capricious." The key difference between this conception and the "hard look" conception is that the former, unlike the latter, takes account of nonideal constraints on agency decision-making. It recognizes that limits of time, information, and resources may give agencies good second-order reasons to act inaccurately, nonrationally, or arbitrarily, in a first-order sense. In a particularly naive version of rationality review—a version that nonetheless appears with some frequency in judicial opinions, usually in an implicit form—agencies must have fully specified first-order reasons for their choices, reasons that justify their choices relative to all competitors, in light of the statutory policy goals.

This simple conception opens up space for agencies to act based on reasons at a second or higher order. Such reasons may, for example, justify acting when taking some action or other is necessary or desirable, even when no particular action is sufficiently justified (a rationally arbitrary decision); justify a policy under a decision rule that can predictably be expected to misfire, producing arbitrary results, in some sets of cases (the mean-variance trade-off and the speed-accuracy trade-off); or justify a policy that seems acceptable, but might well be worse than other possible policies in the feasible set, for all anyone knows (satisficing). In all these cases, agencies rightly depart from the simplistic benchmark under which rationality requires choosing the best option within the (known) feasible set. By parallel, arbitrariness review must also depart from the simplistic idea that courts should require agencies to explain, in a first-order sense, why their chosen policies represent the best choice from the (known) feasible set.

Reasonableness and Rationality. I have described this approach as a thin theory of agency rationality, because agencies who act in the ways we have described are emphatically acting rationally at the second or higher order. The nonrationality or a-rationality of their behavior, at the first order, is in the service of rational strategies for coping with environments in which ordinary first-order rationality runs out or misfires.

It is worth mentioning, however, a different description of the problem that some find congenial, and that works equally well. On this alternative description, we might distinguish *reasonable* agency action from fully *rational* agency action. When agencies bump up against the limitations of rational choice, as when they (arbitrarily) pick an aspiration level in order to satisfice under uncertainty, they are acting reasonably, even if not rationally. When the canons of rational choice prove indeterminate or ambiguous, and fail to prescribe a unique choice under conditions of uncertainty, the limits of rationality are reached. It does not follow, however, that chaotic or capricious decision-making is the only alternative. Rather it is possible to decide reasonably, even when rationality has exhausted its force. For many large decisions at the individual level—where to go to college, what profession to pursue, whom to marry—rational choice is impotent or inapposite, yet it is still possible to approach the decision more or less reasonably. Many of the decisions that agencies face have exactly this quality: the stakes are high, the consequences of the alternatives are shrouded in uncertainty, and the decision is either a one-time event, or at least will not be frequently repeated, so that no strong process of learning through trial and error is possible.

In this framework, for purposes of interpreting Section 706(2)(A), "arbitrary and capricious" action is best understood as *unreasoned* agency action. Just as an individual may have excellent reasons to make a decision that cannot be fully justified in rational terms, so too an agency may have excellent reasons to adopt a decision-procedure (like satisficing) that is justifiable by reasons, but yields ultimately nonrational choices in particular cases. Judges who appreciate the limits of rationality, and the dilemmas that face reasonable agencies that must act subject to those limits, should interpret the APA's rejection of arbitrary decision-making in ways that take account of these concerns.

Conclusion: The *Baltimore Gas* Era

State Farm and *Chevron* are said to be two of the pillars of administrative law. Conventional wisdom holds that they are in some tension, with *Chevron* ushering in an era of deferential review of agency legal interpretation and *State Farm* ushering in an era of robust judicial review of agency policy-making. The historical reality, however, is actually quite the contrary. *State Farm* did not usher in an era of aggressive "hard look review." In the Supreme Court, agencies virtually never lose so-called "hard look" cases, and while the lower-court practice is more heterogeneous and includes highly intrusive outliers, *State Farm* review in practice is not systematically "hard look." It is time for the academic commentary to update.

It is time to stop discussing *State Farm* whenever arbitrariness review is mentioned. The better reflex—better both theoretically and as more faithful to the caselaw—would be for lawyers to mention *"Baltimore Gas"* review. Recall that in *Baltimore Gas*, decided the same Term as *State Farm*, the Supreme Court upheld the Nuclear Regulatory Commission's determination that for purposes of licensing under the National Environmental Policy Act, the permanent storage of certain nuclear wastes would be assumed to have *no* significant environmental impact (the "zero release" assumption). Per Judge Bazelon, the D.C. Circuit had struck down the agency's judgment on arbitrariness grounds. The Court overturned that decision in emphatic terms. Quoting *Vermont Yankee*, Justice O'Connor wrote that "administrative decisions should be set aside in this context, as in every other, only for substantial procedural or substantive reasons as mandated by statute . . . , not simply because the court is unhappy with the result reached."[119] Moreover, "a reviewing court must remember that the Commission is making predictions, within its area of special expertise, at the frontiers of science. When examining this kind of scientific determination, as opposed to simple findings of fact, a reviewing court must generally be at its most deferential."[120]

Baltimore Gas made clear (1) that it is generally sufficient that an agency states the nature of its uncertainty—not that it resolve it; (2) that agencies are entitled to adopt any rational assumptions to cope with uncertainty, including highly optimistic assumptions, which are just as rational as highly pessimistic ones; and (3) that courts may not demand the impossible by requiring agencies to explain why they have chosen the assumptions they have, as opposed to other assumptions. *Baltimore Gas* review is in fact more consistent with Supreme Court practice in the past three decades than is *State Farm* (at least in its inflated form, as "hard look review"). When lower courts have strayed toward a thick form of rationality review, the Court has been quick to overrule.

Rightly understood, in light of the broad central tendency of the law over the past several generations, arbitrary and capricious review is thin. It does not require agencies to use cost-benefit analysis; it does not require the resolution of scientific uncertainty; and it does not require that agencies pick the optimal policy, or the most accurate policy, or the best feasible policy, or anything of that sort. It simply requires that agencies act based on reasons. The set of admissible reasons includes second-order or higher-order reasons for acting nonrationally or arbitrarily, as opposed to fully specified first-order reasons. Does this mean the end of judicial review of agency decision-making? Not in the slightest. The Administrative Procedure Act says that agency action may not be arbitrary and capricious, and a straightforward interpretation of that provision commands merely reasoned decision-making—an interpretation that is faithful to the Act's text as well as to the Supreme Court's consistent message that courts should extend abnegation to rationality review, crouching into a far more humble posture than the rhetoric of "hard look" would suggest.

Appendix to Chapter 5

Included here are aggregate statistics, comprising a list of all Supreme Court merits decisions involving an "arbitrary and capricious" holding from 1983 to 2014. There are sixty-four cases total in the data, including *State Farm* itself. Four of the cases were technically decided before *State Farm*, but during the same Term (October Term 1982); an example is *Baltimore Gas*. The case list was generated by multiple independent Westlaw searches of "arbitrary and capricious" in the Supreme Court database(s). Any habeas or criminal cases that did not involve an agency action, and any pure constitutional challenges that did not involve an agency action, are excluded.

Coding most of these cases is relatively straightforward. If the agency wins, the action was not arbitrary and capricious. If the agency loses, it was arbitrary and capricious. The agency win-rate, so to speak, is simply the number of wins divided by the total number of cases (wins and losses).

In a very few cases, there is ongoing confusion about the so-called second step of analysis under *Chevron USA, Inc. v. Natural Resources Defense Council;*[121] these decisions fold arbitrariness analysis into *Chevron* Step Two.[122] However, there are not enough debatable cases of either type to make any real difference; even on the most conservative possible estimate (the estimate maximally biased against our thesis), agencies win arbitrariness challenges in the Supreme Court about 87 percent of the time. The overall trend in the data is clear: it is very rare indeed for the Supreme Court to hold an agency action arbitrary and capricious.

Another minor difficulty arises in the handful of cases in which an opinion relies on both statutory and arbitrariness analysis, in the alternative, to rule against the agency. In these cases, there are three methodological options: (1) count the case as arbitrary in the numerator and include it in the denominator; (2) count the case as not arbitrary in the numerator and count it in the denominator; or (3) count the case neither in the numerator nor in the denominator. The first is the most conservative estimate for our analysis; the second, the most forgiving.

These three approaches produce aggregate arbitrariness loss-rates of (1) $8/64=0.125$; (2) $5/64=0.08$; (3) $8/61=0.13$. This choice then produces a range of agency win-rates between 87 percent and 92 percent. The number of debatable coding decisions is so small as to make no difference. However specified, the basic point remains: agencies win the overwhelming majority of arbitrariness challenges in the Supreme Court. When a case clearly involves a mix of statutory and arbitrariness analysis and the agency loses, the case list so notes.

Date	Case name	Citation	Agency	Action, guidelines, or rule	Arbitrary?
1983	Am. Paper Ins. v. Am. Elec. Power Serv. Corp	461 U.S. 402	FERC	Rate-setting by FERC	Not arbitrary
1983	Baltimore Gas & Elec. Co. v. Natural Res. Def. Council, Inc.	462 U.S. 87	NRC	Notice & comment rules governing licensing decisions	Not arbitrary
1983	Burlington N. v. U.S.	459 U.S. 131	ICC	Rate-setting by ICC	Not arbitrary
1983	Heckler v. Campbell	461 U.S. 458	HHS	Benefits denial based on notice & comment established rules	Not arbitrary
1983	Motor Vehicle Mfrs. Ass'n of U.S., Inc. v. State Farm Mut. Auto. Ins. Co.	463 U.S. 29	NHTSA	Rescission of a rule	Arbitrary
1984	Chevron v. Natural Res. Def. Council	467 U.S. 837	EPA	Notice & comment rules	Not arbitrary
1984	Heckler v. Ringer	466 U.S. 602	HHS	Rule	Not arbitrary
1985	Bennett v. Kentucky Dept. of Educ.	470 U.S. 656	Dept. of Education	Administrative order	Not arbitrary
1985	Heckler v. Chaney	470 U.S. 821	FDA	Decision not to undertake enforcement action	Not arbitrary
1986	Atkins v. Rivera	477 U.S. 154	HHS	Notice & comment rules	Not arbitrary
1986	Bowen v. Am. Hospital Ass'n	476 U.S. 610	HHS	Notice & comment rules	Arbitrary

Year	Case	Citation	Agency	Action	Holding
1986	Japan Whaling Ass'n v. Am. Cetacean Soc.	478 U.S. 221	Sec. of Commerce	Certification by Sec. of Commerce	Not arbitrary
1986	Lyng v. Payne	476 U.S. 926	Dept. of Ag.	Loan denial	Not arbitrary
1987	INS v. Cardoza-Fonseca	480 U.S. 421	INS	Deportation proceeding by ALJ	Not arbitrary
1987	Bowen v. Yucker	482 U.S. 137	HHS	Notice & comment rules	Not arbitrary
1988	Bowen v. Georgetown Univ. Hosp.	488 U.S. 204	HHS	Notice & comment rules	Outside statutory power & arbitrary
1988	City of New York v. FCC	486 U.S. 57	FCC	Notice & comment rules	Not arbitrary
1988	EEOC v. Commercial Office Products Co.	486 U.S. 107	EEOC	Enforcement of an administrative subpoena	Statutory & arbitrary
1989	Marsh v. Oregon Natural Res. Council	490 U.S. 360	Sec. of Army	Construction decision of agency	Not arbitrary
1989	Robertson v. Methow Valley Citizens Council	490 U.S. 332	Forest Service	Permit decision	Not arbitrary
1989	Sullivan v. Zebley	493 U.S. 521	HHS	Adjudication	Arbitrary
1990	Pension Ben. Guar. Corp. v. LTV Corp.	496 U.S. 633	PBGC	Enforcement	Not arbitrary
1990	Sullivan v. Everhart	494 U.S. 83	HHS	Notice & comment rules	Not arbitrary
1991	Am. Hospital Ass'n v. NLRB	499 U.S. 606	NLRB	Enforcement of new rule	Not arbitrary
1991	INS v. Doherty	502 U.S. 314	Attorney General/DOJ	Denial of motion to reopen a deportation proceeding	Not arbitrary

(continued)

(*Contd.*)

Date	Case name	Citation	Agency	Action, guidelines, or rule	Arbitrary?
1991	Rust v. Sullivan	500 U.S. 173	HHS	Notice & comment rules	Not arbitrary
1992	Arkansas v. Oklahoma	503 U.S. 91	EPA	Permit decision	Not arbitrary
1992	United States v. Alaska	503 U.S. 569	Sec. of Army	Licensing decision	Not arbitrary
1993	Good Samaritan Hosp. v. Shalala	508 U.S. 402	HHS	Notice & comment rules	Not arbitrary
1993	Reno v. Flores	507 U.S. 292	INS	Consent decree regarding release of minors	Not arbitrary
1994	ABF Freight Sys. v. NLRB	510 U.S. 317	NLRB	Enforcement order	Not arbitrary
1994	Thomas Jefferson Univ. v. Shalala	512 U.S. 504	HHS	Notice & comment rules	Not arbitrary
1995	Shalala v. Guernsey Mem'l Hosp.	514 U.S. 87	HHS	Reimbursement calculation	Not arbitrary
1996	INS v. Yueh-Shaio Yang	519 U.S. 26	BIA	Enforcement order	Not arbitrary
1996	Smiley v. Citibank (S. Dakota), N.A.	517 U.S. 735	Comptroller of Currency	Notice & comment rules	Not arbitrary
1997	Auer v. Robbins	519 U.S. 452	Dept. of Labor	Notice & comment rules & board interpretation of rules	Not arbitrary
1997	Glickman v. Wileman Bros. & Elliott, Inc.	521 U.S. 457	Dept. of Agriculture	Informal rulemaking	Not arbitrary
1997	United States v. O'Hagan	521 U.S. 642	SEC	Notice & comment rules	Not arbitrary
1998	Allentown Mack Sales & Serv., Inc. v. NLRB	522 U.S. 359	NLRB	Enforcement order	Not arbitrary rule, but not properly applied

Year	Case	Citation	Agency	Action	Result
1998	Regions Hosp. v. Shalala	522 U.S. 448	HHS	Notice & comment rules	Not arbitrary
1999	Dickinson v. Zurko	527 U.S. 150	PTO	PTO decision to deny patent application	Not arbitrary
2000	Pub. Lands Council v. Babbitt	529 U.S. 728	Sec. of Interior	Notice & comment rules	Not arbitrary
2001	U.S. Postal Serv. v. Gregory	534 U.S. 1	Merit Systems Protection Board	ALJ adjudication	Not arbitrary
2002	Nat'l Cable & Telecomms. Ass'n, Inc. v. Gulf Power Co.	534 U.S. 327	FCC	Rate-setting by FCC	Not arbitrary
2002	Ragsdale v. Wolverine World Wide, Inc.	535 U.S. 81	Dept. of Labor	Notice & comment rules	Outside statutory power & arbitrary
2002	United States v. Fior D'Italia, Inc.	536 U.S. 238	IRS	Income tax guidelines	Not arbitrary
2002	Verizon Commc'ns, Inc. v. FCC	535 U.S. 467	FCC	Notice & comment rules	Not arbitrary
2004	Alaska Dept. of Envtl. Conservation v. EPA	540 U.S. 461	EPA	Enforcement order	Not arbitrary
2004	DOT v. Pub. Citizen	541 U.S. 752	Dept. of Transportation	Decision not to regulate	Not arbitrary
2004	Household Credit Serv. v. Pfennig	541 U.S. 232	FRB	Notice & comment rules	Not arbitrary
2004	Norton v. S. Utah Wilderness Alliance	542 U.S. 55	Dept. Interior	Decision not to regulate	Not arbitrary
2005	Nat'l Cable & Telecomms. Ass'n v. Brand X Internet Servs.	545 U.S. 967	FCC	Notice & comment rules	Not arbitrary

(continued)

(Contd.)

Date	Case name	Citation	Agency	Action, guidelines, or rule	Arbitrary?
2007	Massachusetts v. EPA	549 U.S. 497	EPA	Decision not to regulate	Arbitrary
2007	Nat'l Ass'n of Home Builders v. Defenders of Wildlife	551 U.S. 644	EPA	Permit decision	Not arbitrary
2008	Morgan Stanley Capital Grp. Inc. v. Pub. Util. Dist. No. 1 of Snohomish Cnty., Wash.	554 U.S. 527	FERC	Decision not to act	Arbitrary
2008	United States v. Eurodif S.A.	555 U.S. 305	Commerce Dept.	Enforcement	Not arbitrary
2009	FCC v. Fox Television Stations, Inc.	556 U.S. 502	FCC	Enforcement action	Not arbitrary
2011	Douglas v. Ind. Living Ctr. of S. Calif., Inc.	132 S. Ct. 1204	CMS	Rate-setting by CMS	Not arbitrary
2011	Judulang v. Holder	132 S. Ct. 476	BIA	Deportation proceeding by BIA	Arbitrary
2011	Mayo Found. for Med. Educ. & Research v. United States	131 S. Ct. 704	Treasury	Notice & comment rules	Not arbitrary
2012	Astrue v. Capato	132 S. Ct. 2021	Social Security Admin.	Notice & comment rules	Not arbitrary
2013	Sebelius v. Auburn Reg'l Med. Ctr.	133 S. Ct. 817	HHS	Notice & comment rules	Not arbitrary
2014	EPA v. EME Homer City Generation	134 S. Ct. 1584	EPA	Notice & comment rules	Not arbitrary

6

How Law Empowers Nonlawyers

THE ABNEGATION OF THE LAW is by no means solely a matter of doctrine, although it is expressed through doctrine. Law's abnegation is ultimately sociological: it is the decision by one profession, lawyers, to shift some of their own powers to nonlawyers. The relevant power may be to interpret statutes, as under *Chevron*; to formulate legal policy; or to choose administrative procedures. Whatever the nature of the issue, the point is the same. Administrative law directly or indirectly determines the relative influence *within* agencies of various types of professionals—lawyers, scientists, civil servants, political appointees, and others. Above all, administrative law changes the relative importance of lawyers and nonlawyers in bureaucratic decision-making. Major doctrines of administrative law, including the principles underlying *Chevron, Chenery,* and other controlling decisions, may be best understood as episodes in, and contributors to, law's abnegation though allocation of power across professions and offices.

It has to be confessed at the outset that the claims I shall offer hover between hypotheses and empirical assertions. There is very little in the way of systematic empirical work about these questions. But it is not as though there is systematic evidence running in the other direction either. There is no neutral state, and no one has the burden of proof as to such claims. One just has to offer best guesses about how the world of administrative law works, based on informal evidence, and I will offer mine here.

I will proceed by examining cases in which administrative law abnegates power to nonlawyers. Cases of this sort may arise as the direct or indirect result of legal doctrines and rules; on a conceptually distinct margin, they may arise because of conscious efforts by agency personnel to reallocate power within an agency, or instead as the unintended by-product of actions taken in pursuit of other aims. For present purposes, however, it is not essential to pin down exactly how these reallocations of authority come about. The main point is that central doctrines and rules of administrative law effectively allocate authority within the agency away from lawyers and toward nonlawyers.

Chenery

In its first decision in *SEC v. Chenery Corp.*,[1] the Supreme Court announced a fundamental principle of administrative law: agency action can be upheld, if at all, only on the rationale the agency itself articulated when taking action. The corollary of *Chenery* is that agencies may not employ "*post hoc* rationalizations" offered during litigation to save an action whose original rationale is untenable.

Despite its intuitive appeal, the foundations of *Chenery* are far from clear. What exactly is bad about *post hoc* rationalization, at least if the new rationale in fact justifies the agency's action? Outside the courtroom, actors often make good decisions for bad reasons, and if they later realize that there was a good reason for the good decision, so much the better. So long as the rationale the agency offers during litigation is sound, it is not obvious why the court should set aside the agency's action.

On one view, the foundation of the *Chenery* principle—requiring agencies to state the legal grounds for their actions when they act— lies in an aspect of the nondelegation doctrine, which constrains the grant of lawmaking power to agencies.[2] This account holds that nondelegation requires not only that legislation state an "intelligible principle" to guide agency decision-making, but also that agencies state the grounds for their exercise of delegated authority. On this account, *Chenery* is best understood as derived from the general values behind the nondelegation doctrine, which attempts to allocate lawmaking power to politically accountable actors and to ensure a reasoned exercise of that power.

This analysis is unsatisfactory on several grounds. For one thing, it is not helpful to say that the *Chenery* principle derives from a constitutional principle requiring agencies to state the legal grounds for their actions when they act. That account constitutionalizes *Chenery* but otherwise leaves the principle unexplained. Second, the account fits poorly with the actual scope and effect of the *Chenery* principle. Conventionally understood, the point of the nondelegation doctrine is to allocate lawmaking authority between the legislature and the executive. The ban on *post hoc* rationalizations, however, does not involve that sort of allocation across institutions. Rather, the primary effect of the *Chenery* principle is to affect the *timing* of reason-giving by the agency itself. Under *Chenery*, the issue is not *which* institution may act; the issue is *when* the agency—whose legal authority is conceded—must state its reasons. The answer *Chenery* gives is that the agency must speak before, rather than during, litigation. The agency's rationales must not be *post hoc*; if they are, they amount to mere "rationalizations." But this rule does not allocate lawmaking power between the legislature and the executive.

So understood, *Chenery*'s crucial effect is to reallocate power horizontally within agencies. Under a rule that allows *post hoc* rationalizations, lawyers have a crucial role, while other policy professionals do not. It is lawyers who formulate *ex post* reasons that are presented to a court, and those reasons need not be tied to the reasons why the agency acted in the first place. *Chenery*, on the other hand, requires that the *ex ante* reasons be the basis for judicial review of the action; it thereby gives authority to the personnel who help formulate policy before the fact. That group may well include lawyers providing counsel in anticipation of litigation, but it will invariably include other types of professionals as well—scientists, engineers and other technical experts, political appointees within agencies, and civil servants. Lawyers will retain a role even under *Chenery* because agencies that will be held to their initial rationales during later litigation will have an incentive to consult lawyers *ex ante*. Yet *Chenery* in effect ensures that nonlawyers will always have an important *ex ante* role in shaping the agency's official position. Further, it prevents lawyers from speaking officially for the agency by advancing new policy rationales during litigation. *Chenery* is thus best understood not through the prism of nondelegation principles but as a doctrine that constrains the role of lawyers in formulating agency policies.

On this account, *Chenery*'s foundations involve a commitment to (nonlegal) technical expertise at least as much as a commitment to political accountability, yet the nondelegation account of *Chenery* focuses on the latter. For my purposes here, however, the foundations of *Chenery* are not the major problem. The key point, rather, is just that the temporal allocation of reason-supplying authority under *Chenery* has powerful allocation effects across professions; this effect fits the doctrine's scope more closely than does a nondelegation account.

Chevron

The most famous doctrine in all of administrative law is, arguably, the *Chevron* doctrine, which requires judges to defer to reasonable agency interpretations of statutes.[3] In recent years, decisions beginning with *United States v. Mead Corp.*[4] have modified the *Chevron* framework in important ways, in part by attempting to cabin the conditions under which *Chevron* applies in the first place. I will turn to *Mead* shortly; first we need to understand the indirect allocation effects of the classic *Chevron* framework itself.

Before *Chevron*, the law bearing on agencies' interpretive authority was unclear, with competing lines of cases. One view suggested that questions of law were, by their nature, for courts to decide. Another view, stemming from *Skidmore v. Swift & Co.*,[5] was more supportive of deference. This second line of cases agreed in principle that legal questions were for courts. But it also emphasized that courts would afford agencies a type of epistemic deference when their pronouncements were highly expert, were based on accumulated experience, or were especially likely to track legislative intentions. In general, an agency was given deference on the basis of "the thoroughness evident in its consideration, the validity of its reasoning, its consistency with earlier and later pronouncements, and all those factors which give it power to persuade, if lacking power to control."[6]

Importantly, under both lines of caselaw, statutory interpretation was conceived as a search for the single best reading of the statute. Courts might defer to agencies epistemically as experts who are especially likely to find the best meaning, just as a patient might defer to a doctor's diagnostic skills. Yet, in principle, the factors relevant under *Skidmore* and its successors were just pointers to the correct interpretation of the statute.

As E. Donald Elliott has emphasized, however, *Chevron*'s major conceptual innovation was to sweep away the classical notion that all statutes, even in hard cases, have a single best interpretation—a "point estimate" of statutory meaning. Rather, he argues, the *Chevron* framework conceives interpretation as typically involving agency choice within a "policy space," defined by the range of the statute's reasonable interpretations.[7] To be sure, even under *Chevron* there will be some cases in which the statute has only one reasonable reading, in which case there will be a single best point estimate of the statute's meaning. Yet *Chevron*, in contrast to the older framework, does not presuppose that all cases are like that. In the hard cases that tend to provoke litigation and reach appellate courts, agencies will usually have some discretion to choose among policies that fall within the range of reasonable interpretations.

Chevron's recasting of agency interpretation as a choice within a policy space may also have important indirect effects on the roles and importance of various professions within the agency. According to Elliot's account, under a point-estimate model of statutory interpretation, lawyers have a dominant voice within the agency. At a minimum, lawyers have broad power, during internal agency deliberations, to veto policy positions that are otherwise desirable, and indeed legally supportable, on the ground that they are legally incorrect. Under the *Chevron* framework, by contrast, the lawyer's role is relatively constrained. Lawyers identify the range of reasonable interpretations, but policy-making officials, including scientists and political appointees, choose within the range. Again, in some cases the range collapses to a point, but not always or even often. As compared to the predecessor regime, a major effect of *Chevron* is to disempower lawyers within agencies.

Mead as a Sociological Toggle

As with *Chevron*, so too with *Mead*. The latter decision, like the former, plausibly has important effects on the allocation of power within agencies. And we will see that *Mead*, in its turn, is shaped and constrained by the recent decision in *City of Arlington*,[8] which returns to an extremely robust version of *Chevron*. The whole sequence underscores that judicial review of legal questions has left Chief Justice Hughes's framework, and arguably the relevant provision of the Administrative Procedure Act—in which judges would decide "all relevant questions of law"—far behind, as discussed in Chapter 1.

In principle, *Mead* lays out legal preconditions for the *Chevron* framework to apply at all and has thus been dubbed "*Chevron* Step Zero."[9] There are many controversies and uncertainties about the details of the *Mead* analysis—and these uncertainties in themselves tend to make lawyers more important than they would be if *Chevron* simply applied to all agency action—but the main outlines of the framework are clear enough. Under *Mead*, *Chevron* applies if and only if Congress has demonstrated an intention to delegate law-interpreting power to the agency. Whether courts will find such an intention to exist depends, in part, upon procedural proxies: if the agency used formal rulemaking or adjudication or notice-and-comment rulemaking, a court is likely to find that the agency holds law-interpreting authority (although some opinions have suggested that procedural formality is neither necessary nor sufficient to find an intent to delegate). Outside these categories of relatively formal procedure, intent to delegate depends upon a totality-of-the-circumstances inquiry based upon a laundry list of factors. One of the main factors, emphasized in *Mead* itself, is whether the agency's decisions were made in a centralized way or instead by branch offices or line officials; I will return to this point later.

If the *Mead* analysis indicates that the *Chevron* framework does not apply, then agencies are remitted to the preexisting *Skidmore* framework, under which the court assumes that there must be a point estimate of statutory meaning, rather than identifying a range of reasonable readings (although agencies' views will be given epistemic deference). *Mead*, then, is the toggle switch, not only between alternate doctrinal frameworks, but also between two different conceptions of statutory interpretation: the classical one that assumes there are best readings ("point estimates") in all cases, and a modern one that accepts irreducible ambiguity ("range estimates").

Most importantly, *Mead* also toggles between a relatively lawyer-centered approach to statutory interpretation, under the classical framework, and an approach that emphasizes the role of nonlawyer professionals, who choose policies based on technocratic and political factors under the *Chevron* framework. If, as Elliott suggests, *Chevron* has important allocation effects across professions within agencies, then the *Mead* analysis is what determines whether and when those effects will occur.

The consequence is that the stakes of judicial debates over *Mead* are higher than, and somewhat different from, what has been recognized to date. When the *Mead* analysis is restrictive, so that agencies' decisions are frequently remitted to *Skidmore*, lawyers will come to the fore in the agencies' internal deliberations. If, on the other hand, the *Mead* analysis is capacious, so that *Chevron* usually applies, then engineers, scientists, and political appointees will have a larger role. The stakes involve which professionals within agencies will do most of the decision-making, most of the time. By promoting or constraining various types of professionals within agencies, *Mead*, no less than *Chevron*, indirectly determines the relative scope and power of law and of lawyers in the administrative state.

Cost-Benefit Default Rules

A final question about statutory interpretation by agencies involves not whether the *Chevron* framework applies, but which canons and principles of interpretation apply within that framework. Here too, interpretive methods in effect allocate power within agencies, and this has the effect of allocating power between and among professions within agencies. Just as *Chevron* itself tends to reallocate power away from lawyers and toward other professionals, so too interpretive principles may have the same effect—and one in particular definitely does have that effect. Under current law, agencies have broad discretion to use cost-benefit analysis unless statutes explicitly bar them from doing so, and this has the effect of empowering technocrats at the expense of lawyers.

As I argued in Chapter 5, Congress has given no general, explicit instruction on these issues. Accordingly, courts usually fall back upon highly contextual, statute-specific interpretive methods. Some statutes naturally lend themselves to cost-benefit readings, some statutes seemingly require agencies to regulate to the point of maximum "feasibility," and some provide a variety of other decision rules.[10] Yet in most of these statutes, there is sufficient open texture to make the choice of default rules a high-stakes issue.

As also explained in Chapter 5, two important recent cases, *Entergy Corp. v. Riverkeeper, Inc.* and *EPA v. EME Homer City* suggest that a majority of the Roberts Court wants agencies to have broad discretion to use cost-benefit analysis under debatable statutory directives. The emerging caselaw suggests that where statutes are silent or ambiguous, courts should presume that agencies have the authority to engage in cost-benefit analysis. That authority is discretionary; it is up to the agency to decide whether to use cost-benefit analysis, or not to do so. (As I also explained in Chapter 5, *Michigan v. EPA* is not an important counter-example to this claim; it rests on a narrow principle that agencies may not do an incomplete, one-sided analysis of benefits without a corresponding analysis of costs. And even then, it requires only consideration of "costs" and "benefits" in the colloquial sense of pros and cons, rather than quantified cost-benefit analysis in the technical sense.)

For present purposes, the significance of *Entergy* and *EME Homer* is that judicial deference to agency discretion to use cost-benefit analysis reinforces the allocation effects of *Chevron*. The choice whether to use cost-benefit analysis expands the range within which economists, scientists, and other nonlegal professionals effectively may participate in the formulation of agency policy. Where feasibility analysis is mandatory, by contrast, lawyers read sweeping statutory instructions and inform other agency personnel that regulation is mandated unless some threshold of economic disaster is met. The difference is between a decision-procedure that puts nonlawyer professionals on center stage, or rather a procedure that makes technocratic analysis a mere side-constraint on the implementation of a legal mandate that, in the usual case, must simply be obeyed. The bare possibility of cost-benefit analysis, subject to agency discretion whether to use it or not to use it, generally shifts power away from lawyers and toward scientists, economists, engineers, and other policy professionals.

"Hard Look Review"

Under "hard look review," discussed at length in Chapters 4 and 5, agencies have an obligation to provide a reasoned policy analysis for their regulatory choices. Chapter 5 argued that the Court, since *State Farm*, has been far more deferential than the legal culture realizes—to the point where it makes more sense to speak of thin rationality review, rather than "hard look review." Here I will elucidate the consequences for the allocation of powers across professions.

In a world of thin rationality review, agency heads, who are usually political appointees, can choose policy within a very broad range. Although such appointees may choose to be advised by scientists, economists, lawyers, or other professionals, they need not rely on these actors. The main constraints on agency action, in this world, arise not from expertise or from law but from politics—from the reactions of congressional committees, the President, and the general public.

By contrast, the result of "hard look review" would be to empower lawyers at the expense of scientists and other policy experts. On this view, hard look review "justifies the [general counsel's office] in taking positions on the substantive merits of proposals and on the technical and economic validity of the support documents."[11] Lawyers are crucial, either to identify what the relevant factors are or to ensure that the agency's conclusions will not strike other lawyers—namely the judges—as wildly implausible.

The most general point is simply that the choice between thin rationality review and "hard look review" involves much more than the allocation of competence between courts and agencies. "Hard look review" has typically been defended on the ground that the prospect of meaningful judicial oversight will improve "the agency's" decision-making and its policy choices. In light of its internal allocation effects, however, we can see that the composition of agency decision-makers is itself at stake in the choice between "hard look review" and thin rationality review. The Court's consistently deferential approach has affected not only what agencies may do but who within agencies may do it. The reigning practice of weak oversight of agency rationality helps to empower nonlawyers within agencies, and thus aids law's sociological abnegation.

The Administrative Law of Emergencies

The extreme case of thin rationality review arises in the administrative law of emergencies, especially emergencies arising from threats to national security. After 9/11, federal courts applied rationality review in highly deferential ways where agencies made a decision with national security implications. In *Jifry v. Federal Aviation Administration*,[12] we have seen, the Court of Appeals for the District of Columbia Circuit considered a challenge to agency rules promulgated on an emergency basis without notice and comment, under which the Federal Aviation Administration (FAA), acting in conjunction with the Transportation Security Agency (TSA), had revoked the commercial piloting licenses of a group of aliens on the ground that they posed an unacceptable risk of terrorism. The court upheld the agencies' action against both procedural challenges and on "hard look review," noting that "[t]he TSA and FAA deemed such regulations necessary in order to minimize security threats and potential security vulnerabilities to the fullest extent possible."[13]

This is, needless to say, hardly the sort of "probing" and "in-depth" scrutiny that the Court imagined in *Overton Park*.[14] Cases like *Jifry* embody what the political theorist David Dyzenhaus describes as a legal "grey hole"[15]—a judicial stance that provides the form, but not the substance, of judicial oversight. The shift toward legal grey holes tends to disempower law and lawyers. In times of perceived emergency, the opportunity costs of agency inaction are especially high, and courts will be reluctant to block agencies from taking action while ponderous legal proceedings go forward. Ossification, a major objection to "hard look review," becomes especially worrisome, however much of a problem it may or may not be in normal times. Lawyers and judges themselves become acutely aware of the limits of their own knowledge and capacities. Courts are inclined to defer to executive officials, especially the President, and afford the barest rational basis scrutiny to administrative and presidential action. The result is a sociology of abnegation to nonlegal professionals.

Reviewability

Attention to the relationship between empowering courts and empowering lawyers within the agency also suggests a new perspective on reviewability doctrine, one of the most contested issues in administrative law. The questions are whether and when courts should refrain from evaluating agency action. Because the statutory standards are open-ended, courts are the primary architects of the doctrine. Although reviewability is a contested corner of administrative law, the debate is not attentive to the consequences identified here.

Debates over decisions like *Heckler v. Chaney*[16]—which created a presumption that agency nonenforcement decisions are immune to judicial review—pit advocates of legal controls on administration against those who are skeptical of such controls because they prefer agency expertise, executive branch accountability, or legislative controls. Pitching the debate that way is too simple because it ignores the internal effects of these decisions within the agency. If there is little threat of judicial review, then lawyers lose their place at the table as the agency deliberates over the action. Disempowering courts, then, does disable legal constraints but does so in a different way than the conventional debate suggests. It mutes the influence of lawyers within agencies; that means other professionals come to the fore.

The Sociology of Abnegation

In the most general terms, indirect allocation determines which professions—or which mix of professions—will have the upper hand within the agency, shaping its culture and inner workings. The ongoing contest over the roles of expertise, legalism, and politics in administrative law can thus be viewed in sociological terms as a contest among different types of professionals, with different types of training and priorities. Legal rules and institutional structures that empower scientists or engineers will conduce to a technocratic agency culture, while rules and structures that empower lawyers will carry in their wake the distinctive culture of lawyers.

These general points have more specific implications. It is sometimes assumed that empowering courts to decide legal questions leaves agencies free to focus on questions of policy and even encourages them to do so. On a view of this sort, one of the main benefits of a sharp division of functions between agencies and courts is a form of institutional specialization. In light of intra-agency allocation effects, however, this view is illusory. The more robust the power of courts to override agency choices on legal grounds, the larger the role within agencies of lawyers, who must attempt to divine which "point estimate" or single best reading of statutes the courts will announce (under *Chevron*) or which factors that the courts will understand statutes to have made relevant (under "hard look review"). Lawyers within agencies may squeeze out politicians and technocrats; this is the flip side of Elliott's observation that *Chevron* empowers the latter professionals at the expense of the former. All normative perspectives would profit from understanding what the internal allocation effects of possible rules might be.

All this is of more than methodological interest, however. The evidence is not systematic, and would never satisfy an empiricist, but there can be little doubt about the direction and the magnitude of the long-term trend. If we take as a benchmark 1932, the year *Crowell v. Benson*[17] was decided, it is patent that lawyers have increasingly disempowered themselves by developing doctrines that transfer decision-making power to other professions. Of these doctrines, the *Chevron* doctrine is only the most obvious example. Less obviously, the *Chenery I* rule, which appears if anything to be a restriction on agency power, actually works to disempower lawyers within agencies. Most striking is the remarkable recent decision in *City of Arlington*, which finds incomprehensible a restriction on agency authority whose *absence* is incomprehensible to the traditional legal mind, and which subordinates the traditional lawyers' central idea of jurisdiction to the nonlegal enterprise of filling in statutory gaps and ambiguities with policy choices. The abnegation of law is also the shrinking of the lawyers' role, and the lawyers' world.

Conclusion

Law on the Margin

I N C L A S S I C A L constitutional theory, law fills the center of the frame. In the administrative state, however, law becomes a marginal phenomenon. This is so in two senses, technical and colloquial. Both senses share a critical feature: they are self-imposed. Law becomes marginal in a process of self-abnegation.

It is critical that law has not simply been beaten down. Law's empire has not crumpled under conquest from without; law has not been "overcome."[1] Rather the triumph of the administrative state paradoxically occurred as a voluntary abnegation of authority by the law, on terms dictated by law itself, based on considerations internal to the law. Judges and lawyers have collectively realized that the very principles and doctrines that law created to check the administrative state, rightly understood and with their logic worked all the way through, themselves indicate that administrative discretion should be extremely broad. The law has ceded power, not lost it.

The Marginal Place of Law: Technical Sense

In the technical sense, law is a marginal phenomenon because judges and lawyers, at a certain point, begin to define the role of law by asking about law's marginal or incremental contribution to an overall

institutional system. Rather than seeing law and courts as central actors, lawyers and judges come to see other institutions and other types
of decision-makers as the principal deciders, on the front lines, and come
to see themselves as reviewing bodies. When the self-understanding
of judges and lawyers comes to this point, law sees itself as making
contributions at the margin, if at all. On this view, the question for
judges and lawyers is not "what is the right decision?" Rather the question becomes: "given the decision other institutions have made, what
can the *addition* of a layer of legal review add?" In economic terms,
the marginal (technical sense) costs and benefits of additional layers
of review have to be considered, and the shape of the resulting curves
will determine exactly how marginal (in the colloquial sense) law will
be in the administrative state.

How marginal will law actually become, in the hands of judges who
are well-intentioned? The answer is clear enough in principle: assuming
that adding further increments of review has diminishing marginal
benefits and increasing marginal costs, a hypothetical institutional designer will supply additional legal review just up to the point at which
the marginal benefits equal the marginal costs. Judges do not enjoy as
much freedom as an institutional designer to arrange matters, but there
is plenty of flexibility in the institutional practices and legal materials
to allow judges and lawyers to adjust the intensity of review at the margins, through rules and doctrines of access to court, case selection,
deference and standards of review, common-law doctrines of absten-
tion and primary jurisdiction, and the principal merits inquiries of
public law: constitutional and statutory interpretation, substantial evidence or other factual adequacy, procedural validity, and the rationality of official policymaking.

In principle, an optimal system of review will take into account a
bewildering variety of factors to determine marginal costs and benefits.[2] Among these are the sheer out-of-pocket costs of setting up and
staffing additional institutions and layers of review and procedure; the
legal fees and transaction costs associated with incremental layers of
litigation; the comparative epistemic competence of the reviewers, vis-
à-vis the front-line agency decision-makers; the epistemic benefits of
increasing the number of heads addressing a common problem; the
"sentinel effect," or the effect of anticipated review in inducing more

effort on the part of the front-line agency decision-makers; and, cutting in exactly the other direction, epistemic moral hazard, or the tendency of anticipated review to induce less effort on the part of front-line agency decision-makers who know that judges will catch some fraction of their errors.

It is impossible to know, in the abstract, how these factors net out. The values of the relevant variables will of course vary across issue-areas and problems, and over time. The problem as stated is too complex and intractable for judges to solve in terms. Rather judges and lawyers implicitly come to use very rough rules of thumb, such as Coke's maxim that "in a doubtful thing, interpretation goes always for the king"[3]—a kind of precursor of the *Chevron* doctrine, although Coke did not mean it that way. While Coke's maxim identifies a baseline tendency that has already existed, the tendency has consistently gathered strength over time. Increasingly, over time, judges and lawyers come to doubt their own epistemic competence, come to doubt the incremental benefits of incremental review of front-line agency decision-making.

Crowell, Chevron, and Marginalism

Most important of all is the question how, and why, this long-term movement occurs. In other work I have identified *external* mechanisms that cause legislatures to delegate ever-greater powers to the bureaucracy; that cause presidential power to grow over time vis-à-vis that of legislatures and courts; and that cause courts to increasingly defer to the administrative state.[4] In the present work, the focus is on the internal point of view of lawyers, on law's voluntary abnegation (or at least partially voluntary abnegation) to the administrative state. Law abnegates because lawyers come increasingly to see that there are good legal arguments for doing so, and because the pressure for rational consistency impels the best lawyers ever-farther down the path of deference, once the first few steps are taken. Let me take up these two points in turn.

In the easiest cases, statutes clearly delegate authority to agencies rather than courts, and the legal logic is straightforward. Even where statutes are unclear, however, judges come to see that given the existence of administrative agencies, the judicial role is not decision-making, but review. The natural questions are then what the roles of agencies and courts should be, whether and how review can improve upon agency decision-making, what review adds. But this is essentially marginalist thinking, as *Crowell* shows.

Chief Justice Hughes's opinion in *Crowell v. Benson*[5] thought in marginalist terms. When it did so, the judges became aware of their own questionable contributions to the overall institutional system. A judicial doubt about the marginal benefits of judicial review arose—the very tendency that, under the pressure of rational consistency, would eventually grow to swallow Hughes's framework altogether. In the first part of *Crowell*, Hughes was explicit that given an administrative determination of fact under minimally adequate procedures, judicial review promises little additional benefit and threatens to impose incremental delay and litigation costs that will make the overall system worse, not better. As we have seen, Hughes assumed throughout that *de novo* judicial review of legal questions is to be an unquestioned feature of the new settlement of the administrative state. But we may understand *Chevron* as merely extending to legal questions the same skeptical, marginalist, institutionalist mindset that Hughes (schizophrenically) deployed only as to questions of fact. In that regard, *Chevron* was not the beginning but rather the culmination of a long-standing development, originating no later than *NLRB v. Hearst* in 1944, which deferred to agency interpretation on a "mixed" question combining law and fact.[6]

On this understanding of *Chevron*, the basic question that animates its deference principle is whether judges will add value, by inducing higher-quality agency interpretations of law in anticipation of judicial review, or will instead subtract value, by displacing reasonable and well-informed agency interpretations of law in favor of the judges' own estimate of the statute's "true" meaning. *Chevron* deference rests ultimately on the worry that such displacement of reasonable agency views by plenary judicial determination will indeed subtract value from the overall institutional system of decision-making in the administrative state, because judges lack any comparative insight into public values (*Chevron*'s "political accountability" rationale) and because judges often do not understand the consequences of interpreting statutes one way or another (*Chevron*'s expertise rationale).

The strength of the internal legal arguments for deference become ever greater as the complexity and scale of the policy problems facing the administrative state grow. The cases featured in so many textbooks on Legislation and Statutory Interpretation—cases like *Riggs v. Palmer*[7] and *Holy Trinity*[8]—are child's play compared to any average EPA case that the Court hears nowadays. As the administrative state takes on more functions, the complexity and stakes of its decisions rise, and judges become increasingly worried about their marginal value added. Their response is then to marginalize themselves in the colloquial sense.

The Instability of Half-Measures

Another feature of the process is the instability of any and all attempted way stations between the classical constitutional order, on the one hand, and the empire of administration, on the other. It is not that, or not just that, large-scale forces of economics and politics have put the classical Constitution out of reach. It is that the internal logic of the arguments that push law as far as the way stations also push law farther still. Under the pressure of rational consistency, there is no stopping halfway down the path.

I do not want to be misunderstood as claiming that logical coherence always prevails in law. Far from it; the *United States Reports* are full of muddled compromises and *ad hoc* invocations of semi-coherent doctrinal notions (like the "major questions" canon). Rational consistency is a standing pressure that may not always prevail, in given cases, but that operates steadily and relentlessly, and thus has a long-run tendency to shape the law. Like the rising graph of the stock market over time, full of dips, retrenchments, and corrections (large or small) but with a distinct long-run path, the law works itself steadily pure— meaning more deferential—over time, once the first steps have been taken.

Crowell v. Benson itself, and its subsequent fate, illustrate the tendency of law's internal logic to resist half-measures, to take law farther down the path of deference. The marginalist logic of *Crowell* essentially tried to draw a line between ordinary fact-finding, on the one hand, and on the other hand both (1) extra-ordinary facts (jurisdictional and constitutional) and (2) questions of law. The former category was to be entrusted to agencies (subject to deferential review for clear error) on the basis of comparative institutional competence—the marginalist logic that adding *de novo* judicial review of ordinary facts would create additional costs of litigation and uncertainty greater than the marginal accuracy benefits, or indeed with no marginal benefits whatsoever, if specialized agencies were better positioned than generalist courts to find facts. The latter two categories were to be entrusted solely to courts, charged with policing the legal boundaries within which agencies would be allowed to move.

What made Hughes's synthesis seem schizophrenic was its implicit attempt to cabin the institutional logic to one class of questions judges might be called upon to decide. The genie of marginalism is not so easy to confine, however. If the marginalist calculus suggests that courts' value added is questionable or limited on questions of jurisdictional fact, constitutional fact, or even law, then the logic will spill over into those domains and imply deference there as well. Hughes doubtless assumed that courts were naturally superior to agencies on questions of law. But by the time of the *Hearst* case in 1944, and certainly by the time of *Chevron*, fifty-two years later, it had become clear that it was impossible to disentangle legal questions from policy-making decisions, at least as to the complex regulatory statutes that predominate in the modern state. It then became clear in turn that agencies, at least as compared to courts, were better positioned both to make ultimate value choices relevant to regulatory questions (such as the precise rate of trade-off between burdens on regulated firms and protection of public health) and also to determine facts, causation, and the likely consequences of alternative interpretations.

Once the tide of marginalist logic spilled over the levee between ordinary factual questions and other questions, it could no longer be resisted. The line between agency "jurisdiction" and other questions agencies would decide, for example, could no longer be defended. If agencies have a comparative advantage on that question as well, why should courts intervene? So thoroughly were the legalist premises of

Crowell undermined, by the logic that *Crowell* itself legitimated, that the line between jurisdictional and nonjurisdictional questions came to seem not merely senseless but indeed illusory and incomprehensible to all the Justices in *City of Arlington*, even the dissenters.

Defending the Indefensible

After the marginalist logic of *Crowell* (or at least the first half of *Crowell*) spills over from factual to legal questions, including jurisdictional questions, what is left? The final question is what, exactly, judicial review adds, and whether the costs of additional review would exceed the benefits. The law's answer, in substance if not in terms, is that courts have a residual, backstop role in policing indefensible decision-making. So long as agencies can offer a colorable defense of their legal views and policy choices, law's self-chastening implies that judges have no further warrant to intervene.

Obviously what counts as "colorable" will do much of the work. Here a crucial twist, detailed in various ways in Chapters 3, 4, and 5, is that under uncertainty, agencies may even defend the indefensible on systemic or second-order grounds. Agencies, that is, may have good reasons to enter an area, settle an issue, or decide one way or another, even when they can give no adequate reason to decide any one way in particular. The law increasingly recognizes—in cases from *Baltimore Gas & Electric*,[9] to *Methow Valley*,[10] to *FCC v. Fox*[11]—that agencies may have good second-order reasons to act, even when in the nature of things, given genuine uncertainty, they can give no valid first-order reason to justify their particular choices, relative to the alternatives. In particular, the law has—by and large, and increasingly over time— come to recognize that "conservatism" or "precaution" has no theoretical priority in agency decisions under uncertainty. There is no warrant for judges to impose upon agencies some sort of meta-principle for decision-making under uncertainty. Rather agencies have to make decisions whose content is intrinsically unjustifiable, in the sense that rationality does not dictate the decision, nor the opposite. In that sense, agencies must make decisions that are arbitrary. It does not follow, however, that the decisions are "arbitrary and capricious" in a legal sense. So long as agencies can offer a valid reason for engaging in arbitrary decision-making, law now allows them even to defend the indefensible on systemic grounds—the ultimate abnegation of law's mandate to police agency rationality.

The Marginal Place of Law: Colloquial Sense

It is easy to get mired in the details. A page of history being worth a volume of logic, it is important to step back and to appreciate that the arc of the administrative state bends toward deference. The difficult details are in a sense marginal themselves; they are strictly about the question *how much more* deference agencies receive today. From the baseline set by *Crowell*'s attempted synthesis, the long-run direction of movement has invariably been the same, toward greater and greater deference—despite occasional countercurrents and short-term corrections. The magnitude of the change is certainly substantial, and it can reasonably be debated where exactly the new margin lies. But the direction of the change cannot reasonably be debated. On *every* margin identified by Hughes, as to *every* doctrinal category he erected, courts have ceded ground to administrative agencies. Deference on questions of law is now the norm; agencies get deference on the scope of their own jurisdiction and the interpretation of their own regulations, something that drives separation-of-powers traditionalists mad; and the doctrines of jurisdictional fact and constitutional fact are for the most part dead letters.

The direction of change is relentless when viewed at a macro-level, in the aggregate—toward an increasingly marginal place for law. What tends to obscure the trend is a kind of salience or availability bias on the part of lawyers, emphatically including academic lawyers who ought to know better. These lawyers tend to cite the latest Supreme Court case if, in the rare instance, it overturned administrative action, as the Court did in *UARG* from 2014.[12] Otherwise they will cite the Court of Appeals for the District of Columbia Circuit, which overturns agencies with slightly greater frequency.

Salience and availability can be interpreted as a form of neglect of the base rate[13]—here, neglect of the overall population of agency actions that are either unchallenged by law or sustained against legal challenge. Lost in all the administrative-law discourse, focusing

obsessively on *State Farm* and a handful of other cases that declare
agency decision-making inadequately reasoned, is the base rate—the
raw fact that of the myriad of agency actions taken daily, only a min-
iscule fraction are ever challenged in court to begin with, and of those
only a further fraction are ever resolved against the agency. The sheer
scale of the administrative state, with its millions of employees, hundreds of agencies, and countless orders, directives, decisions, policies,
and programs, dwarf the resources and capacities of the legal system to
control. Law's former empire is, increasingly, an outpost on the margins of the administrative imperium.

Self-Defeating Elegies for Law's Empire

But perhaps all this merely shows that the arc of the administrative
state has been bending toward deference for a long time. Can its trajectory be reversed? In Chapters 1 and 2, I considered views offered by
Lawson, Hamburger, and Waldron that are in various ways elegiac—
wistful laments for a lost era of the classical separation of powers and
classical legalism, in which courts purportedly decided all relevant
questions of law without deference to the administrative state. I have
no stake in the question whether there ever was such an era, in fact,
although I am deeply skeptical that there was; we have seen that Jerry
Mashaw's latest comprehensive treatment of the development of
the U.S. administrative state pushes it farther back than many could
have imagined possible,[14] and we have also seen that the picture of heroic common-law judges standing against the encroachments of royal
prerogative is entirely misleading.[15]

In any event, I mean to pursue a different point here: the internal
legal imperatives that have contributed to the shrinking of law's empire also block any attempt to revive and reconstitute it. Running
throughout the debates over the administrative state and the separation of powers is one fact frequently overlooked: the administrative
state was itself brought into being by the operation of the classical institutions, functioning in constitutionally legitimate ways. It is very
odd for theorists to complain about combinations of functions in agencies, and to urge a return to separated functions, when the combination of functions was itself an arrangement created by the operation of

classical institutions with separated powers. Whatever arguments support the separation of powers necessarily support the institutions that
the separated powers, after due deliberation, decided to create. If, for
example, one believes that the classical separation of powers produces
beneficial deliberation by institutions bringing to bear functionally differentiated capacities, then agencies wielding combined functions
will be created only when this sort of excellent deliberation suggests
that such agencies are needed.

The Eternal Recurrence of the Administrative State?

The implication is that the same forces—both external causes and, as
I have argued here, internal reasons—that brought about the administrative state in the first place, from within the classical constitutional
order, would still be operative even if the administrative state were
rolled back. Let us imagine a Lawsonian fantasy: magically, tomorrow,
we awake into a world with none of the administrative agencies that
Lawson finds objectionable. No independent agencies, no agencies exercising powers under unconstitutional delegations, and no agencies
exercising powers under a pre-1937 conception of congressional
lawmaking power. The Lawsonian fantasy would be short-lived. The
classical institutions would, almost certainly, recreate a great deal of the
administrative state's infrastructure, and for essentially the same reasons it was created in the first place. From the standpoint of the originalist critics, one might imagine a kind of nightmare—the eternal
recurrence of the administrative state.

In the epigram that heads the book, when Valéry Giscard
d'Estaing was elected President of France in 1975, he observed that
"[t]here is no question of returning to the pre-1968 situation, if only
for the reason that the pre-1968 situation included the conditions
that led to 1968."[16] On the same grounds, an attempt to "return to
the classical Constitution," with no massive administrative state
and no "headless fourth branch" of administrative power, is incoherent. Those very institutions, operating in a system of mutual in-
teraction, are what produced the administrative state itself. At a
minimum, law's empire and the classical constitutional order are
gone beyond all hope of revival.

Dworkin's Silence

I conclude as I began, with the puzzle of Ronald Dworkin's near-total silence about the administrative state and administrative law. Perhaps Dworkin was simply oblivious, but I have speculated on another explanation. Even those who reject Dworkin's claims to greatness grant him the laurel crown of a master sophist and advocate; and a rule of thumb with the greatest sophists and advocates is that the weak points of their case will be found precisely in the areas of their silence. Dworkin's silence about the administrative state implicitly speaks a book of legal theory—this book.

The history and logic of U.S. administrative law suggest that, in our system anyway, law's empire—in Dworkin's sense that makes courts the heartland of law—cannot coexist with the administrative state. Again, this is not to say that law-enforced-by-courts and the administrative state cannot coexist at all, just that both cannot simultaneously be paramount. Only one can be master; and law has decided to give way. Law's reasons, understood through fit and justification, have pointed the way toward law's abnegation in the face of the administrative state.

Notes

INTRODUCTION

1. Henry Monahan, "*Marbury* and the Administrative State," 83 *Colum. L. Rev.* 1 (1983).
2. David Dyzenhaus, "The Rule of Law as the Rule of Liberal Principle," *in Ronald Dworkin* 56, 60 (Arthur Ripstein ed., 2007).
3. See Jerry L. Mashaw, *Creating the Administrative Constitution* (2012) (for the U.S. case); Paul Craig, *Administrative Law* (7th ed. 2012) (for the U.K. case).
4. David Dyzenhaus acutely suggests that this may have been Dworkin's implicit view of administrative agencies. See Dyzenhaus, "The Rule of Law as the Rule of Liberal Principle," 69–72.
5. Ronald Dworkin, *Law's Empire* 407 (1986).
6. Ibid., 225ff.; Ronald Dworkin, "Hard Cases," 88 *Harv. L. Rev.* 1057 (1975).
7. Dworkin, "Hard Cases," 1083–1109.
8. Dyzenhaus, "The Rule of Law as the Rule of Liberal Principle," 71.
9. Margaret Allars, "On Deference to Tribunals, Deference to Dworkin," 20 *Queen's L.J.* 163 (1994).
10. See, e.g., Paul Craig, *Administrative Law* §§ 19-001–19-016, 21-001–21-008 (7th ed. 2012) (describing evolution of *Wednesbury* unreasonableness test in the United Kingdom); Canadian Union of Pub. Emps., Local 963 v. New Brunswick Liquor Corp., [1979] 2 S.C.R. 227 [C.U.P.E.] (establishing patent unreasonableness test in Canada); Dunsmuir v. New Brunswick, [2008] 1 S.C.R. 190 (replacing patent unreasonableness test with reasonableness test in Canada); see generally Paul Daly, *A Theory of Deference in Administrative Law* (2012); Michael Taggart, "The Tub of Public Law," *in The Unity of Public Law* 455, 472–475 (David Dyzenhaus ed., 2004).
11. Allars, "On Deference to Tribunals, Deference to Dworkin," 183–184.
12. Richard A. Posner, *Overcoming Law* (1995).

13. Francis Bacon, Essay LVI, "Of Judicature," *in Essays* 140 (1995) ("Let judges also remember, that Solomon's throne was supported by lions on both sides: let them be lions, but yet lions under the throne; being circumspect that they do not check or oppose any points of sovereignty."). For an excellent analysis of the history of English public law through the lens of Bacon's problematic, see Stephen N. Sedley, *Under the Throne: Essays on the History of English Public Law* (2015).

14. See Dworkin, *Law's Empire*, 407.

15. Martin M. Shapiro, *Who Guards the Guardians? Judicial Control of Administration* 173 (1988).

16. See Eric A. Posner & Adrian Vermeule, *The Executive Unbound* 10, 85–88 (2010).

17. See Jack Goldsmith, *Power and Constraint* 95–108 (2012).

18. Dworkin, *Law's Empire*, 407.

19. See Frederick Schauer, "Foreword: The Court's Agenda—and the Nation's," 120 *Harv. L. Rev. 4* (2006).

20. See, e.g., Horne v. Department of Agriculture, U.S. (June 22, 2015) (finding a regulatory taking); but see, e.g., Kelo v. City of New London, 545 U.S. 469 (2005) (expansive conception of public use).

21. 285 U.S. 22 (1932).

22. 133 S. Ct. 1863 (2013).

23. Chevron USA, Inc. v. Natural Res. Def. Council, Inc., 467 U.S. 837 (1984).

24. For an argument (albeit from a different perspective) that overruling *Chevron* might make less difference than expected, see Jeffrey A. Pojanowski, "After Deference" (forthcoming *Mo. L. Rev.*).

25. See, e.g., Goldberg v. Kelly, 397 U.S. 254 (1970).

26. See, e.g., Hettinga v. United States, 677 F.3d 471 (D.C. Cir. 2012); Business Roundtable v. SEC, 647 F.3d 1144 (D.C. Cir. 2011).

27. See Am. Radio Relay League, Inc. v. FCC, 524 F.3d 227, 245–247 (D.C. Cir. 2008) (Kavanaugh, J., concurring in part, concurring in the judgment in part, and dissenting in part).

28. United States v. Texas, 579 U.S. (2016).

29. Karl Marx, Preface to the First German Edition of *Capital* (1867).

30. Wendy E. Wagner, "The Science Charade in Toxic Risk Regulation," 95 *Colum. L. Rev.* 1613 (1995).

31. See Daniel R. Ernst, *Tocqueville's Nightmare: The Administrative State Emerges in America, 1900–1940* 137–146 (2014); Adrian Vermeule, "Portrait of an Equilibrium," *The New Rambler* (2015), http://newramblerreview.com/book-reviews/law/tocqueville-s-nightmare (reviewing Daniel R. Ernst, *Tocqueville's Nightmare*). Another review of Ernst seems to acknowledge this point as well. See Jeremy Kessler, "The Struggle for Administrative Legitimacy," 129 *Harv. L. Rev.* 718, 723 (2016).

32. 435 U.S. 519 (1978).

33. 463 U.S. 29 (1983).

34. SEC v. Chenery Corp., 318 U.S. 80 (1943) ("Chenery I").

35. John Rawls, Lecture VI, "The Idea of Public Reason," *in Political Liberalism* 212 (2005).

CHAPTER 1   The Legality of Administrative Law

1. 285 U.S. 22 (1932).
2. *Matthew* 6:24.
3. Daniel R. Ernst, *Tocqueville's Nightmare: The Administrative State Emerges in America, 1900–1940* 51–77 (2014).
4. On Mark Tushnet's reading of *Crowell*, Hughes meant to limit this subcategory to only those jurisdictional facts that were otherwise "fundamental," essentially assimilating the category of jurisdictional facts to the subcategory of constitutional facts (discussed in text following). See Mark Tushnet, "The Story of *Crowell*: Grounding the Administrative State," *in Federal Courts Stories* (Vicki Jackson & Judith Resnik eds., 2010). Although Tushnet's reading is plausible, *Crowell* seems ambiguous on the point. In any event, nothing in my discussion stands or falls on the question.
5. Administrative Procedure Act of 1946, Pub. L. No. 79-404 § 10(e), 60 Stat. 237, 243 (codified at 5 U.S.C. § 706 (2012)).
6. Ibid., § 10(e), 60 Stat. at 244 (codified at 5 U.S.C. § 706(2)(E)).
7. 295 U.S. 495 (1935).
8. NLRB v. Jones & Laughlin Steel Corp., 301 U.S. 1 (1937).
9. 321 U.S. 414 (1944).
10. Charles P. Curtis, Jr., *Lions under the Throne* 164 (1947).
11. See David P. Currie, *The Constitution in the Supreme Court: The Second Century, 1888–1986* 215 (explaining that in the second half of the opinion, "Hughes neatly refuted his own argument.").
12. *Crowell*, 285 U.S. at 57.
13. Chevron USA, Inc. v. Natural Res. Def. Council, Inc., 467 U.S. 837 (1984).
14. See Crowell v. Benson, 285 U.S. 22, 46–54 (1932).
15. See *Chevron*, 467 U.S. at 865–866 (expertise and political accountability); Peter L. Strauss, "One Hundred Fifty Cases per Year: Some Implications of the Supreme Court's Limited Resources for Judicial Review of Agency Action," 87 *Colum. L. Rev.* 1093, 1121–1122 (1987) ("By removing the responsibility for precision from the courts of appeals, the *Chevron* [decision] . . . enhances the probability of uniform national administration of the laws.").
16. See, e.g., United States v. Mead Corp., 533 U.S. 218 (2001).
17. See Henry Monahan, "*Marbury* and the Administrative State," 81 *Colum. L. Rev.* 1 (1983).
18. See, e.g., King v. Burwell, 135 S. Ct. 2480, 2488–2489 (2015); FDA v. Brown & Williamson Tobacco Corp., 529 U.S. 120, 159–161 (2000).
19. See, e.g., Abbe R. Gluck, "The Supreme Court, 2014 Term—Comment: Imperfect Statutes, Imperfect Courts: Understanding Congress's Plan in the Era of Unorthodox Lawmaking," 129 *Harv. L. Rev.* 62, 93–96 (2015) (arguing that "*King* chooses *Marbury* over *Chevron* and, in the process, may have announced a more limited deference doctrine for complex statutes," ibid., 93); Abigail R. Moncrieff, "*King, Chevron*, and the Age of Textualism," 95 *B.U. L. Rev. Annex* 1 (2015) (calling *King v. Burwell* "an unfortunate outcome for *Chevron*—and potentially for the rule of law"); see King v. Burwell.

20. 135 S. Ct. 2480 (2015).
21. For Justice Scalia, Perez v. Mortgage Bankers Ass'n, 135 S. Ct. 1199, 1212 (2015) (Scalia, J., concurring in the judgment). For Justice Thomas, see Michigan v. EPA, 135 S. Ct. 2699, 2712–2714 (2015) (Thomas, J., concurring); Tex. Dep't of Hous. & Cmty. Affairs v. Inclusive Cmtys. Project, Inc., 135 S. Ct. 2507, 2529 (2015) (Thomas, J., dissenting); Wellness Int'l Network, Ltd. v. Sharif, 135 S. Ct. 1932, 1961 (2015) (Thomas, J., dissenting); Dep't of Transp. v. Ass'n of Am. R.Rs., 135 S. Ct. 1225, 1240–1245 (2015) (Thomas, J., concurring in the judgment); *Perez*, 135 S. Ct. at 1217 (Thomas, J., concurring in the judgment). For Justice Alito, whose gestures toward *Chevron* deference are more oblique, see *Perez*, 135 S. Ct. at 1210.
22. See Cass R. Sunstein & Adrian Vermeule, "The New Coke: On the Plural Aims of Administrative Law," 2016 *Sup. Ct. Rev.* (forthcoming).
23. See, e.g., Skidmore v. Swift & Co., 323 U.S. 134 (1944); NLRB v. Hearst Publ'ns, 322 U.S. 111 (1944); Gray v. Powell, 314 U.S. 402, 411 (1941); Rochester Tel. Corp. v. United States, 307 U.S. 125, 146 (1939).
24. See note 9, Introduction.
25. See Commodity Futures Trading Comm'n v. Schor, 478 U.S. 833 (1986); Thomas v. Union Carbide Agric. Prods. Co., 473 U.S. 568 (1985).
26. 133 S. Ct. 1863 (2013).
27. See FPC v. Texaco, Inc., 377 U.S. 33 (1964); United States v. Storer Broad. Co., 351 U.S. 192 (1956).
28. Vermont Yankee Nuclear Power Corp. v. Natural Res. Def. Council, Inc., 435 U.S. 519 (1978).
29. See the debate over this point in Paul R. Verkuil, "Judicial Review of Informal Rulemaking: Waiting for *Vermont Yankee II*," 55 *Tulane L. Rev.* 418 (1981); Richard J. Pierce, Jr., "Waiting for *Vermont Yankee II*," 57 *Admin. L. Rev.* 669 (2005); and Jack M. Beermann & Gary Lawson, "Reprocessing *Vermont Yankee*," 75 *Geo. Wash. L. Rev.* 856 (2007).
30. 463 U.S. 29 (1983).
31. 462 U.S. 87 (1983).
32. 496 U.S. 633 (1990).
33. 498 U.S. 211 (1991).
34. 556 U.S. 502 (2009).
35. See, e.g., Miss. Power & Light Co. v. Mississippi, 487 U.S. 354, 380–382 (1988) (Scalia, J., concurring in the judgment).
36. Crowell, 285 U.S. at 57.
37. See City of Arlington v. FCC, 133 S. Ct. at 1877–1186 (Roberts, C. J., with whom Kennedy, J., and Alito, J., join, dissenting).
38. Paul Craig, "The Legitimacy of U.S. Administrative Law and the Foundations of U.K. Administrative Law: Setting the Record Straight, http://papers .ssrn.com/sol3/papers.cfm?abstract_id=2802784."
39. Cass R. Sunstein, "The Man Who Made Libertarians Wrong about the Constitution," *The New Republic* (May 18, 2014), http://www.newrepublic.com /article/117619/classical-liberal-constitution-richard-epstein-reviewed (reviewing Richard A. Epstein, *The Classical Liberal Constitution* (2014)).

40. See Gary Lawson, "The Rise and Rise of the Administrative State," 107 *Harv. L. Rev.* 1231 (1994).
41. See Bruce Ackerman, *We the People: Transformations* 279–382 (1998).
42. Cass R. Sunstein, "Participation, Public Law, and Venue Reform," 49 *U. Chi. L. Rev.* 976, 987 (1982).
43. James M. Landis, *The Administrative Process* 46 (1938).
44. See generally Jerry L. Mashaw, *Creating the Administrative Constitution: The Lost One Hundred Years of American Administrative Law* (2012).
45. See ibid.
46. Yakus v. United States, 321 U.S. 414 (1944).
47. See James R. Conde & Michael S. Greve, "*Yakus* and the Administrative State," http://papers.ssrn.com/sol3/papers.cfm?abstract_id=2698833.
48. *Yakus,* 321 U.S. at 425–426.
49. Caleb Nelson, "Stare Decisis and Demonstrably Erroneous Precedents," 87 *Va. L. Rev.* 1, 21–46 (2001).
50. See Gary Lawson, "The *Constitutional* Case against *Precedent*," 17 *Harv. J.L. & Pub. Pol'y.* 23 (1994); Gary Lawson, "*Mostly Unconstitutional*: The Case against *Precedent Revisited*," *Ave Maria L. Rev.* 5 (2007): 1.
51. Philip Hamburger, *Is Administrative Law Unlawful?* (2014). The material in this subsection is adapted from my review of Hamburger's book. See Adrian Vermeule, "No," 93 *Tex. L. Rev.* 1547 (2015). Hamburger has since written a rebuttal to the book review (a rare beast indeed). See Philip Hamburger, "Vermeule Unbound," *Tex. L. Rev.* (forthcoming), http://papers.ssrn.com/sol3/papers.cfm?abstract_id=2691181. Hamburger's main complaint is that I mischaracterize his thesis, which Hamburger now says is based on the U.S. Constitution after all (at least in some purposive, extended sense, attending to the central evils the Constitution was intended to prevent). See ibid. (manuscript at 1, 7–14). Yet my characterization is exactly the same as Gary Lawson's understanding—and Lawson is sympathetic to Hamburger. Despite his sympathies, Lawson too thinks that Hamburger's thesis is deeply unclear. See Gary Lawson, "The Return of the King: The Unsavory Origins of Administrative Law," 93 *Tex. L. Rev.* 1521, 1526 (2015) ("[T]he book's biggest defect is its failure to define precisely what it means by the term 'unlawful.' "); ibid., 1532 ("[W]hat underlying conception of lawfulness drives his analysis? I honestly do not know. . . ."). And Lawson, too, believes that Hamburger— reconstructed as best one can—mainly speaks as though "unlawfulness" is defined according to putative deep and ancient principles of English or Anglo-American constitutionalism, rather than according to the U.S. Constitution itself. See ibid., 1530 ("[Hamburger] often seems to use the term 'constitutionalism' to describe a very broad set of principles that are part of the Anglo-American legal and political tradition rather than simply adherence to concrete norms in the United States Constitution."). Readers with particularly low opportunity costs might compare my review and Lawson's to both Hamburger's original and to his latest effort. In my view, Hamburger's reply either changes his claim outright, while denying that he is doing so, or so muddies the waters that it is now no longer worth the effort to fish in them.

52. See Hamburger, supra note, at 316–319.
53. Ibid., at 491.
54. Again, Hamburger now denies this, but—along with Gary Lawson—I believe it is the best reconstruction of his argument. See supra note 51.
55. Ibid., at 492.
56. As Gary Lawson also concludes. See supra note 51.
57. Hamburger's recent reply, which attempts to rehabilitate his claim as an argument about lawfulness under the U.S. Constitution, is at best hard to square with such emphatic disavowals. See supra note 51.
58. See Hamburger, supra note, at 15; see also ibid., at 493 ("The danger of prerogative or administrative power . . . arises not simply from its unconstitutionality, but more generally from its revival of absolute power.").
59. 517 U.S. 748, 758 (1996).
60. *City of Arlington*, 133 S. Ct. at 1873 n.4.
61. See Whitman v. Am. Trucking Ass'ns, 531 U.S. 457, 488–490 and n.1 (2001) (Stevens, J., concurring).
62. 133 S. Ct. 1863, 1873 n.4 (2013).
63. 143 U.S. 649 (1892).
64. 220 U.S. 506 (1911).
65. 276 U.S. 394 (1928).
66. Youngstown Sheet & Tube Co. v. Sawyer, 343 U.S. 579 (1952).

CHAPTER 2   Separation of Powers without Idolatry

1. 332 U.S. 194 (1947).
2. 339 U.S. 33, 40 (1950).
3. See Leonid Hurwicz, "Nobel Prize Lecture: But Who Will Guard the Guardians?" (Dec. 8, 2007), http://www.nobelprize.org/nobel_prizes/economic -sciences/laureates/2007/hurwicz_lecture.pdf [http://perma.cc/S352-D7YG].
4. James M. Landis, *The Administrative Process* 46 (1938).
5. Ibid., 36.
6. Ibid., 10.
7. See Federal Trade Commission Act, 15 U.S.C. §§ 41–58 (2012).
8. 421 U.S. 35 (1975).
9. U.S. Const. Amend. XIV.
10. *Withrow*, 421 U.S. at 52.
11. 333 U.S. 683 (1948).
12. Ibid., 701.
13. Ibid.
14. Wong Yang Sung v. McGrath, 339 U.S. 33, 40–41 (1950).
15. See Perez v. Mortgage Bankers Ass'n, 135 S. Ct. 1199, 1208–1209 & n.4 (2015); Auer v. Robbins, 519 U.S. 452 (1997).
16. See William E. Scheuerman, *Liberal Democracy and the Social Acceleration of Time* 1–9 (2004).
17. See Yakus v. United States, 321 U.S. 414, 424 (1944) (Stone, C. J.) ("The Constitution as a continuously operative charter of government does not demand the impossible or the impracticable [and] does not require that Congress find for

itself every fact upon which it desires to base legislative action or that it make for itself detailed determinations which it has declared to be prerequisite to the application of the legislative policy to particular facts and circumstances impossible for Congress itself properly to investigate."); Carl Schmitt, *The Crisis of Parliamentary Democracy* 48–50 (Ellen Kennedy trans., 1985) (1923).

18. William E. Scheuerman, "The Economic State of Emergency," 21 *Cardozo L. Rev.* 1869, 1887 (2000).

19. See Panama Refining Co. v. Ryan, 293 U.S. 388 (1935); A.L.A. Schechter Poultry Corp. v. United States, 295 U.S. 495, 537–538 (1935); Yakus v. United States, 321 U.S. 414, 424 (1944).

20. United States v. Mead Corp., 533 U.S. 218, 227–230 (2001).

21. Philippe Aghion et al., "Endogenous Political Institutions," 119 *Q.J. Econ.* 565, 570 (2004).

22. Jeremy Waldron, "Separation of Powers in Thought and Practice?," 54 *B.C. L. Rev.* 433 (2013).

23. See John F. Manning, "Separation of Powers as Ordinary Interpretation," 124 *Harv. L. Rev.* 1939, 1944–1945 (2011).

24. Waldron, "Separation of Powers in Thought and Practice?," 466.

25. Ibid., 467 (emphasis added).

26. Ibid., 459.

27. Ibid., 460.

28. Ibid., 459.

29. 332 U.S. 194 (1947).

30. Ibid., 202–203 (emphasis added).

31. Bowles v. Seminole Rock & Sand Co., 65 S. Ct. 1215 (1945); Auer v. Robbins, 519 U.S. 452 (1997); Perez v. Mortgage Bankers Ass'n, 135 S. Ct. 1199, 1208–1209 & n.4 (2015).

32. See Ron Levin, Testimony before the United States Senate Committee on Homeland Security and Governmental Affairs, Subcommittee on Regulatory Affairs and Federal Management (April 28, 2015) ("the strongest justifications [for *Auer*] run parallel to the justifications for *Chevron*").

33. Cf. Henry Monahan, "*Marbury* and the Administrative State," 83 *Colum. L. Rev.* 1 (1983) (making a parallel argument in the Chevron setting).

34. 546 U.S. 243 (2006).

35. 131 S. Ct. 2254, 2266 (2011) (Scalia, J., concurring).

36. 133 S. Ct. 1326, 1341 (2013) (Scalia, J., concurring in part and dissenting in part).

37. Ibid., 1341.

38. Ibid., 1342.

39. Perez v. Mortgage Bankers Ass'n, 135 S. Ct. 1199, 1212–1213 (2015) (Scalia, J., concurring in the judgment).

40. Ibid., 1208 n.4 (majority opinion).

41. See United Student Aid Funds v. Bible, No. 15-861, cert. denied, May 16, 2016.

42. See ibid. (Thomas, J., dissenting from denial of certiorari).

43. Cass R. Sunstein & Adrian Vermeule, "The New Coke: On the Plural Aims of Administrative Law," 2016 *Sup. Ct. Rev.* (forthcoming) (manuscript, 18–27).

44. See Chapter 1, note 62 and accompanying text.

45. 131 S. Ct. 2254, 2266 (2011).

46. 133 S. Ct. 1863, 1873 n.4 (2013).
47. See Jack L. Goldsmith & John F. Manning, "The President's Completion Power," 115 *Yale L.J.* 2280 (2006).
48. See Article, Section 8 (Necessary and Proper Clause).
49. J. W. Hampton Jr. & Co. v. United States, 276 U.S. 394, 409 (1928).
50. The argument here is incorporated into Cass R. Sunstein & Adrian Vermeule, "The Unbearable Rightness of *Auer*," http://papers.ssrn.com/sol3/papers.cfm?abstract_id=2716737.
51. See David Zaring, "Reasonable Agencies," 96 *Va. L. Rev.* 135 (2010).
52. Cass R. Sunstein & Adrian Vermeule, "The Unbearable Rightness of Auer," http://papers.ssrn.com/sol3/papers.cfm?abstract_id=2716737, at 9.
53. 133 S. Ct. at 1874–1875.
54. For valuable discussion, see Aaron L. Nielson, "Beyond Seminole Rock," 105 *Geo. L.J.* (2017) (forthcoming).
55. For discussion of the close connection between *Auer* and agency choice and between rulemaking and adjudication, see Levin, supra note, at 16–17.
56. See M. Elizabeth Magill, "Agency Choice of Policymaking Form," 71 *U. Chi. L. Rev.* 1383 (2004).
57. SEC v. Chenery Corp., 332 U.S. 194, 202–203 (1947).
58. Decker v. Nw. Envtl. Def. Ctr., 133 S. Ct. 1326, 1329 (2013).
59. Skidmore v. Swift & Co., 323 U.S. 134, 140 (1944).
60. See Bowles v. Seminole Rock & Sand Co., 325 U.S. 410 (1945) (deferring to agency interpretation of regulations).
61. *Perez*, at—, slip op. at 13; FCC v. Fox Television, 129 S. Ct. 1800, 1811 (2009).
62. See *Perez*, 575 U.S. at—n.4 (collecting qualifications). The same note also alludes to the possibility that *Auer* deference might not apply "when there is reason to suspect that the agency's interpretation does not reflect the agency's fair and considered judgment" (ibid). This last point is a well-established qualification to the Court's periodic practice of affording *Auer* deference even to agency interpretations contained in briefs and other litigation-related documents. See, e.g., Talk America, Inc. v. Michigan Bell Telephone Co., 131 S. Ct. 2254, 2261 (2011) ("we defer to an agency's interpretation of its regulations, even in a legal brief" unless there is some "reason to suspect that the interpretation does not reflect the agency's fair and considered judgment on the matter in question.") (internal quotations and citations omitted).

CHAPTER 3   Deference and Due Process

1. Which probably had a different original meaning altogether. See generally Nathan S. Chapman & Michael W. McConnell, "Due Process as Separation of Powers," 121 *Yale L.J.* 1672 (2012).
2. See, e.g., Stephen G. Breyer, Richard B. Stewart, Cass R. Sunstein, Adrian Vermeule, & Michael Herz, *Administrative Law and Regulatory Policy* 675 (7th ed. 2011) ("[W]hile legislatures are free to define the substantive content of property entitlements, the due process clause gives the judiciary an independent and final say on the adequacy of the procedures for determining and vindicating those entitlements."); Ronald A. Cass, Colin S. Diver, Jack M.

Beermann, & Jody Freeman, *Administrative Law* 616 (6th ed. 2011) (describing administrative due process cases as two-step inquiries for courts); see generally Richard J. Pierce, Jr., Sidney A. Shapiro, & Paul R. Verkuil, *Administrative Law and Process* 237–247 (6th ed. 2014).

3. 424 U.S. 319 (1976).
4. 470 U.S. 532, 541 (1985) ("The right to due process is conferred, not by legislative grace, but by constitutional guarantee.").
5. 435 U.S. 519 (1978).
6. 135 S. Ct. 1199 (2015).
7. I refer only to the Due Process Clause of the Fifth Amendment, and will address only due process claims against federal agencies. Although a few of the relevant cases have involved state agencies, see, e.g., Goldberg v. Kelly, 397 U.S. 254 (1970), the central lines of precedent I will address have all arisen in a federal setting, and state agencies present distinctive problems that I bracket here.
8. Environmental Protection Agency, Amendments to Streamline the National Pollutant Discharge Elimination System Program Regulations: Round Two, 65 Fed. Reg. 30886, 30898 (2000), appeal dismissed, Dominion Energy Bracton Point LLC v. Johnson, 443 F.3d 12 (2006).
9. Informal Hearing Procedures for Nuclear Reactor Operator Licensing Adjudications, 55 Fed. Reg. 36801–01, 36802–03 (Sept. 7, 1990) (codified at 10 C.F.R. pt. 2); see also Changes to Adjudicatory Process, 69 Fed. Reg. 2182–01 (Jan. 14, 2004) (codified at 10 C.F.R. pt. 2) (explaining that informal hearing procedures are consistent with constitutional due process).
10. Procedures for the Issuance, Denial, and Revocation of Certificates of Label Approval, Certificates of Exemption from Label Approval, and Distinctive Liquor Bottle Approvals (93F-029P), 64 Fed. Reg. 2122–01, 2124–25 (Jan. 13, 1999).
11. Surety Companies Doing Business with the United States, 79 Fed. Reg. 61992–01, 61996–97 (Oct. 16, 2014) (codified at 31 C.F.R. § 223.20).
12. Control of Communicable Diseases, 70 Fed. Reg. 71892–01, 71895–96 (Nov. 30, 2005).
13. Regulations Implementing the Federal Coal Mine Health and Safety Act of 1969, as Amended, 64 Fed. Reg. 54966–01, 54994–95 (proposed Oct. 8, 1999) (codified at 20 C.F.R. § 725.414).
14. Board of Immigration Appeals: Procedural Reforms to Improve Case Management, 67 Fed. Reg. 54878–01, 54881–82 (Aug. 26, 2002) (codified at 8 C.F.R. pt. 3); Executive Office for Immigration Review; Board of Immigration Appeals: Streamlining, 64 Fed. Reg. 56135–01, 56137–39 (Oct. 18, 1999) (codified at 8 C.F.R. pt. 3); Administrative Deportation Procedures for Aliens Convicted of Aggravated Felonies Who Are Not Lawful Permanent Residents, 60 Fed. Reg. 43954–01, 43955–57 (Aug. 24, 1995) (codified at 8 C.F.R. § 242).
15. Representation—Case Procedures, 79 Fed. Reg. 74308–01, 74371–73 (Dec. 15, 2014) (codified at 29 C.F.R. § 102.63).
16. Administrative Fines, 65 Fed. Reg. 31787–01, 31787–88 (May 19, 2000) (codified at 11 C.F.R. pts. 104, 111).
17. Single Family Mortgage Insurance; Appraiser Roster Removal Procedures, 65 Fed. Reg. 17974–01, 17974–75 (Apr. 5, 2000) (codified at 24 C.F.R. pt. 200).

18. Kerry v. Din, 135 S. Ct. 2128, 2140 (2015) (Kennedy, J., concurring in the judgment) (quoting Kleindienst v. Mandel, 408 U.S. 753, 770 (1972)).

19. Vermont Yankee Nuclear Power Corp. v. Natural Res. Def. Council, Inc., 435 U.S. 519, 544 (1978).

20. 135 S. Ct. 1199 (2015).

21. Chevron, U.S.A., Inc. v. Natural Res. Def. Council, Inc., 467 U.S. 837 (1984).

22. Mathews v. Eldridge, 424 U.S. 319, 349 (1976).

23. See, e.g., Bd. of Regents v. Roth, 408 U.S. 564 (1972); Perry v. Sindermann, 408 U.S. 593 (1972); Goldberg v. Kelly, 397 U.S. 254 (1970); Wisconsin v. Constantineau, 400 U.S. 433 (1971); Paul v. Davis, 474 U.S. 693 (1976). See also Peter L. Strauss et al., *Gellhorn & Byse's Administrative Law* 812 (10th ed. 2003).

24. Arnett v. Kennedy, 416 U.S. 134, 154 (1974) (plurality opinion).

25. See, e.g., Daniels v. Williams, 474 U.S. 327 (1986).

26. See Minnesota State Bd. for Community Colleges v. Knight, 465 U.S. 271 (1984); Bi-Metallic Investment Co. v. State Bd. of Equalization, 239 U.S. 441 (1915). The APA definition of a rule focuses on the "future effect" of a rule rather than on its generality. See 5 U.S.C. § 551(4) (2012) (defining "rule" as "an agency statement of general or particular applicability and future effect").

27. Henry J. Friendly, "Some Kind of Hearing," 123 *U. Pa. L. Rev.* 1267 (1975).

28. North American Cold Storage Co. v. Chicago, 211 U.S. 306 (1908).

29. Tumey v. State of Ohio, 273 U.S. 510 (1927). There is a class of indirect pecuniary interests shared by professional groups that is also disqualifying. See Gibson v. Berryhill, 411 U.S. 564 (1973) (independent optometrists regulating competitor chain-store optometrists). But compare Friedman v. Rogers, 440 U.S. 1, 18–19 (1979).

30. Withrow v. Larkin, 421 U.S. 35 (1975).

31. 397 U.S. 254 (1970).

32. See United States v. Carroll Towing Co., 159 F.2d 169, 173 (2d Cir. 1947) ("[T]he owner's duty . . . to provide against resulting injuries is a function of three variables: (1) The probability [of injury]; (2) the gravity of the resulting injury . . . ; (3) the burden of adequate precautions. Possibly it serves to bring this notion into relief to state it in algebraic terms: if the probability be called P; the injury, L; and the burden, B; liability depends upon whether B is less than L multiplied by P: i.e., whether B < PL.").

33. 341 U.S. 494, 510 (1951) ("In each case [courts] must ask whether the gravity of the 'evil,' discounted by its improbability, justifies such invasion of free speech as is necessary to avoid the danger.") (quoting United States v. Dennis, 183 F.2d 201, 212 (2d Cir. 1950), aff'd, 341 U.S. 494 (1951)) (internal quotation marks omitted).

34. Mathews v. Eldridge, 424 U.S. 319, 335 (1976).

35. Ibid., 339–345.

36. See, e.g., Jerry L. Mashaw, *Due Process in the Administrative State* (1985).

37. See, e.g., Zivotofsky v. Clinton, 132 S. Ct. 1421 (2012).

38. See 5 U.S.C. § 706(2)(A) (instructing reviewing courts to set aside agency "action, findings, and conclusions" that are "arbitrary, capricious, [or] an abuse

of discretion"); Motor Vehicle Mfrs. Ass'n of U.S., Inc. v. State Farm Mut. Auto. Ins. Co., 463 U.S. 29, 43 (1983) ("The scope of review under the 'arbitrary and capricious' standard is narrow and a court is not to substitute its judgment for that of the agency. Nevertheless, the agency must examine the relevant data and articulate a satisfactory explanation for its action including a 'rational connection between the facts found and the choice made'" (quoting Burlington Truck Lines v. United States, 371 U.S. 156, 168 (1962))). In the conventional formulation, agencies must also avoid "clear error[s] of judgment." See ibid. If this is meant to imply a substantive review for clear error, as opposed to procedural review, then it is applied so rarely as to be something of a dead letter. At the Supreme Court level, perhaps the only example is Part V.B of State Farm. See ibid., 51–57.

39. See, e.g., Pac. States Box & Basket Co. v. White, 296 U.S. 176, 180–182 (1935).
40. Citizens to Preserve Overton Park, Inc. v. Volpe, 401 U.S. 402, 416 (1971).
41. Skidmore v. Swift & Co., 323 U.S. 134, 140 (1944).
42. Mathews v. Eldridge, 424 U.S. 319, 349 (1976).
43. Ibid., 344.
44. Medina v. California, 505 U.S. 437, 446 (1992).
45. 456 U.S. 188 (1982).
46. Ibid., 200 (emphasis added) (citations omitted).
47. See 5 U.S.C. § 553(a)(2) (exempting from rulemaking requirements "a matter relating to agency management or personnel or to public property, loans, grants, benefits, or contracts."); Breyer et al., *Administrative Law and Regulatory Policy*, 520.
48. Walters v. Nat'l Ass'n of Radiation Survivors, 473 U.S. 305 (1985).
49. Ibid., 307.
50. See ibid., 309–311, 315.
51. Ibid., 308.
52. Ibid., 319–320 (citing *Schweiker*, 456 U.S. 188, and *Mathews*, 424 U.S. at 349).
53. Ibid., 321 (quoting *Mathews*, 424 U.S. at 344).
54. See sources cited supra note 114.
55. 902 F.2d 1580 (9th Cir. 1990) (unpublished opinion).
56. Ibid.
57. See, e.g., Anderson v. White, 888 F.2d 985, 994–995 (3d Cir. 1989) (deferring to agency choice of administrative review procedures in Tax Refund Intercept Program and expressing belief that "the precise choice of hearing procedures is better left to the persons administering TRIP under the flexible balancing test the Supreme Court has prescribed [in Mathews]," ibid., 944); Gibbs v. SEC, 25 F.3d 1056 (10th Cir. 1994) (unpublished opinion) (deferring to SEC's good-faith judgment that a hearing and cross-examination by telephone afforded defendant "all the process due," ibid., *3); see also, e.g., Old Republic Ins. Co. v. Fed. Crop Ins. Corp., 947 F.2d 269, 282 (7th Cir. 1991) (applying the *Mathews* test independently but seemingly deferentially, while quoting the "substantial weight to good faith judgments" passage, to uphold the constitutionality of the FCIC's administrative procedures); Turnage v. United States, 639 F. Supp. 228 (E.D.N.C. 1986) (same, to uphold the constitutionality of the Food and Nutrition Service's denial of an evidentiary

hearing prior to disqualifying a retailer from participating in the federal food stamp program).

58. 505 U.S. 437 (1992).
59. See ibid., 442–446. Another example is Weiss v. United States, 510 U.S. 163 (1994), which declined to apply the *Mathews* framework to the military justice system, on the ground that judicial deference is "at its apogee" in that context. Ibid., 177 (quoting Rostker v. Goldberg, 453 U.S. 57, 70 (1981)) (internal quotation marks omitted).
60. See *Medina*, 505 U.S. at 444.
61. 432 U.S. 197 (1977). The actual test under *Patterson* is whether the state procedure "offends some principle of justice so rooted in the traditions and conscience of our people as to be ranked as fundamental." Ibid., 202 (internal quotation marks omitted).
62. *Medina*, 505 U.S. at 445–446.
63. See Ake v. Oklahoma, 470 U.S. 68 (1985); United States v. Raddatz, 447 U.S. 667 (1980).
64. See *Medina*, 505 U.S. at 444 (distinguishing *Raddatz* and *Ake*).
65. See, e.g., Rachel E. Barkow, "Institutional Design and the Policing of Prosecutors: Lessons from Administrative Law," 61 *Stan. L. Rev.* 869 (2009); Rachel E. Barkow, "Administering Crime," 52 *UCLA L. Rev.* 717 (2005).
66. 416 U.S. 134 (1974).
67. *Arnett*, 416 U.S. at 151–154 (emphasis added).
68. See, e.g., Frank H. Easterbrook, "Substance and Due Process," 1982 *Sup. Ct. Rev.* 85 (1983).
69. *Arnett*, 416 U.S. at 166–167 (Powell, J., concurring in part and concurring in the result in part).
70. See, e.g., Ingraham v. Wright, 430 U.S. 651 (1977); Bishop v. Wood, 426 U.S. 341 (1976).
71. 470 U.S. 532 (1985).
72. *Loudermill*, 470 U.S. at 541 (quoting *Arnett*, 416 U.S. at 167 (Powell, J., concurring in part and concurring in result in part)).
73. See, e.g., Pierce et al., *Administrative Law and Process*, 244 ("If the judiciary defers to legislative or executive value judgments, as a plurality of the Court argued it should in Arnett, the result would be total emasculation of the Due Process Clause.").
74. *Arnett*, 416 U.S. at 154.
75. Vermont Yankee Nuclear Power Corp. v. Natural Res. Def. Council, Inc., 435 U.S. 519, 544 (1978).
76. See generally Antonin Scalia, "*Vermont Yankee:* The APA, the D.C. Circuit, and the Supreme Court," 1978 *Sup. Ct. Rev.* 345.
77. See *Vermont Yankee*, 435 U.S. at 543.
78. See Bi-Metallic Inv. Co. v. State Bd. of Equalization, 239 U.S. 441, 445 (1915). To be sure, *Vermont Yankee* was extended to informal adjudication in *Pension Benefit v. LTV*. See Pension Ben. Guar. Corp. v. LTV Corp., 496 U.S. 633, 653–655 (1990). In any event I am simplifying a bit here for clarity. In fact the procedures at issue in *Vermont Yankee* lay at the boundary between rulemaking and adjudication, because the agency was developing general policy

assumptions that would be used in subsequent licensing proceedings, which are adjudicative.

79. *Vermont Yankee*, 435 U.S. at 525.

80. Ibid., 525 (emphasis added) (quoting FCC v. Schreiber, 381 U.S. 279, 290 (1965)) (internal quotation marks omitted).

81. For an overview of resource allocation in administrative law, see Eric Biber, "The Importance of Resource Allocation in Administrative Law," 60 *Admin. L. Rev.* 1 (2008); for the relationship between resource allocation and the timing of agency action and inaction, see Cass R. Sunstein & Adrian Vermeule, "The Law of 'Not Now': When Agencies Defer Decisions," 103 *Geo. L.J.* 157 (2014).

82. This is not to suggest that resource allocation first appears as a central theme in *Vermont Yankee*. On the contrary, it is among the most venerable arguments for lodging procedural discretion in agencies. See, e.g., Moog Indus. v. FTC, 355 U.S. 411 (1958) (holding that an agency may proceed against only one out of several similarly situated competitors, because "the Commission alone is empowered to develop that enforcement policy best calculated to achieve the ends contemplated by Congress and to allocate its available funds and personnel in such a way as to execute its policy efficiently and economically," ibid., 413).

83. 470 U.S. 821 (1985).

84. See ibid., 832 (grounding *Vermont Yankee* in agency authority to allocate resources through procedural choices).

85. See, e.g., Paul R. Verkuil, "Judicial Review of Informal Rulemaking: Waiting for *Vermont Yankee II*," 55 *Tulane L. Rev.* 418 (1981); Richard J. Pierce Jr., "Waiting for *Vermont Yankee II*," 57 *Admin L. Rev.* 669 (2005); Paul R. Verkuil, "The Wait Is Over: *Chevron* as the Stealth *Vermont Yankee II*," 75 *Geo. Wash. L. Rev.* 921 (2007); Jack M. Beermann & Gary Lawson, "Reprocessing *Vermont Yankee*," 75 *Geo. Wash. L. Rev.* 856 (2007).

86. Perez v. Mortgage Bankers Ass'n, 135 S. Ct. 1199 (2015) (quoting FCC v. Fox Television Stations, Inc., 556 U.S. 502, 513 (2009)); *Vermont Yankee*, 435 U.S. at 549, 544 (internal citations omitted).

87. See Alaska Professional Hunters Ass'n v. FAA, 177 F.3d 1030 (D.C. Cir. 1999); Paralyzed Veterans of America v. D.C. Arena L.P., 117 F.3d 579 (D.C. Cir. 1997).

88. *Perez*, 135 S. Ct. at 1207 (quoting FCC v. Fox Television Stations, Inc., 556 U.S. 502, 513 (2009)); *Vermont Yankee*, 435 U.S. at 549, 544) (internal citations omitted).

89. See, e.g., Chem. Waste Mgmt., Inc. v. EPA, 873 F.2d 1477 (D.C. Cir. 1989); City of W. Chicago v. U.S. Nuclear Regulatory Comm'n, 701 F.2d 632 (7th Cir. 1983). The Ninth Circuit seems internally conflicted. Compare United Farmworkers of America v. EPA, 592 F.3d 1080 (9th Cir. 2010) (statutory reference to "public hearing" does not trigger formality), with Marathon Oil v. EPA, 564 F.2d 1253 (9th Cir. 1977) (formal proceedings triggered even absent "on the record" language in statute).

90. 443 F.3d 12 (1st Cir. 2006).

91. *Dominion Energy*, 443 F.3d at 17–18.

92. Ibid., 18. To be clear, *Dominion Energy* reviewed EPA's *Mathews* analysis only in the course of determining whether the agency's statutory position was reasonable, not as part of a direct due process challenge, for the simple reason that no such challenge was brought or considered. The leading cases in other circuits, however, have clearly considered both statutory and due process arguments in turn. See *Chemical Waste Management*, 873 F.2d at 1480–1485; *City of West Chicago*, 701 F.2d at 642–647.

93. 5 U.S.C. § 706(2)(A) (2012).

94. See, e.g., Judulang v. Holder, 132 S. Ct. 476, 483 n.7 (2011).

95. See City of Arlington v. FCC, 133 S. Ct. 1863 (2013).

96. Crowell v. Benson, 285 U.S. 22, 57 (1932).

97. See Mississippi Power & Light Co. v. Mississippi ex rel. Moore, 487 U.S. 354, 386–387 (1988) (Brennan, J., dissenting).

98. See *City of Arlington*, 133 S. Ct. at 1868–1874.

99. Melissa M. Berry, "Beyond Chevron's Domain: Agency Interpretations of Statutory Procedural Provisions," 30 *Seattle U. L. Rev.* 541, 589 (2007). Berry's important critique argues that "agency expertise is a weak rationale for deference to agency interpretations of procedural provisions" because substantive and procedural requirements are distinguishable and "courts have more expertise in interpreting procedural requirements." Ibid.

100. Mathews v. Eldridge, 424 U.S. 319, 344 (1976) ("[P]rocedural due process rules are shaped by the risk of error inherent in the truthfinding process as applied to the generality of cases, not the rare exceptions.").

101. See, e.g., Walters v. Nat'l Ass'n of Radiation Survivors, 473 U.S. 305, 321 (1985) ("In applying [the Mathews] test we must keep in mind, in addition to the deference owed to Congress, the fact that the very nature of the due process inquiry indicates that the fundamental fairness of a particular procedure does not turn on the result obtained in any individual case; rather, 'procedural due process rules are shaped by the risk of error inherent in the truth-finding process as applied to the generality of cases, not the rare exceptions.'" (quoting *Mathews*, 424 U.S. at 344)).

102. *Mathews*, 424 U.S. at 349.

103. See John Hart Ely, *Democracy and Distrust* (1980).

104. Ibid., 105–179.

105. See Elizabeth Magill, "Agency Self-Regulation," 77 *Geo. Wash. L. Rev.* 859, 868 (2009).

106. See Pierce et al., *Administrative Law and Process*, 361.

107. See ibid., 367; see also Paul Verkuil, "A Study of Informal Adjudication Procedures," 43 *U. Chi. L. Rev.* 739 (1976).

108. See Pension Ben. Guar. Corp. v. LTV Corp., 496 U.S. 633, 653–655 (1990).

109. See Richard J. Pierce, Jr., 2 *Administrative Law Treatise* § 9.1 ("Agencies almost invariably provide procedures greater than those required by the APA when they engage in informal adjudication.").

110. Compare Pierce et al., *Administrative Law and Process*, 236–237 ("An agency often perceives its dominant goal as maximizing the accuracy and fairness of its decision-making process consistent with the resources available to it. In such circumstances, the agency may voluntarily choose

decision-making procedures more demanding than those imposed by Congress or the courts.").

111. See, e.g., Statement of Andrew Cerseney, SEC Director of Enforcement, Nov. 21, 2014, https://www.sec.gov/News/Speech/Detail/Speech/1370543 515297 (explaining that the SEC is vigilant to reverse ALJ decisions that erroneously rule in the agency's favor).

112. See FCC v. Fox Television Stations, Inc., 556 U.S. 502, 523 (2009) ("The independent agencies are sheltered not from politics but from the President, and it has often been observed that their freedom from presidential oversight (and protection) has simply been replaced by increased subservience to congressional direction.").

113. See, e.g., Nina A. Mendelson, "Disclosing 'Political' Oversight of Agency Decision Making," 108 *Mich. L. Rev.* 1127 (2010); Kathryn A. Watts, "Proposing a Place for Politics in Arbitrary and Capricious Review," 119 *Yale L.J.* 2 (2009).

114. See *Attorney General's Manual on the Administrative Procedure Act* 40 (1947).

115. See generally Vermeule, "Contra *Nemo Iudex in Sua Causa*," 122 *Yale L.J.* 384 (2012).

116. Jeremy Waldron, "The Core of the Case against Judicial Review," 115 *Yale L.J.* 1346, 1400 (2006).

117. Nixon v. United States, 506 U.S. 224, 234–236 (1993).

118. *City of Arlington*, 133 S. Ct. at 1874.

CHAPTER 4   Rationally Arbitrary Decisions

1. See Frank Knight, *Risk, Uncertainty and Profit* (1921).

2. Bayesians believe, very roughly speaking, that meaningful subjective probabilities can always be attached to possible outcomes, even for events that happen only once. Nabil Al-Najjar suggests that there is a Bayesian translation for the points I wish to make here. See Nabil I. Al-Najjar, "A Bayesian Framework for the Precautionary Principle," 44 *J. Legal Stud.* S2, S337–S365 (2016). Although I happen to believe that the Bayesian approach in general rests on arbitrary foundations, in that there exists a large domain of regulatory and political questions as to which Bayesian "prior probabilities" have no epistemic foundation or warrant whatsoever, the legal claims I make here do not depend on that belief, and I have neither any need nor any qualifications to take a controversial stand within decision theory. I therefore have no quarrel with anyone who wishes to understand my claims in Bayesian terms.

3. 462 U.S. 87 (1983).

4. 556 U.S. 502 (2009).

5. 134 S. Ct. 1584 (2014).

6. 5 U.S.C. § 706(2)(A) (2012).

7. White Stallion Energy Ctr. LLC v. EPA, 748 F.3d 1222, 1233 (D.C. Cir. 2014) (quoting Natural Res. Def. Council v. EPA, 194 F.3d 130, 136 (D.C. Cir. 1999)).

8. See Pac. States Box & Basket Co. v. White, 296 U.S. 176 (1935).

9. 401 U.S. 402 (1971).

10. 463 U.S. 29, 43 n.9 (1983) ("We do not view as equivalent the presumption of constitutionality afforded legislation drafted by Congress and the presumption of regularity afforded an agency in fulfilling its statutory mandate.").

11. See Louis J. Virelli III, "Deconstructing Arbitrary and Capricious Review," 92 *N.C. L. Rev.* 721 (2014).

12. 467 U.S. 837 (1984).

13. 533 U.S. 218 (2001).

14. New York v. Nuclear Regulatory Comm'n, 681 F.3d at 482.

15. 681 F.3d 471, 482, 474 (D.C. Cir. 2012).

16. *Baltimore Gas & Electric*, 462 U.S. at 103.

17. Marsh v. Oregon Nat. Res. Council, 490 U.S. 360 (1989); Lands Council v. Mc-Nair, 537 F.3d 981 (9th Cir. 2008).

18. 490 U.S. 332, 352 (1989).

19. 42 U.S.C. § 4321 *et seq.*

20. Foundation on Economic Trends v. Weinberger, 610 F. Supp. 829, 837–838 (D.C. Cir. 1985).

21. See Jon Elster, "Excessive Ambitions," 4 *Capitalism & Society* 1 (2009).

22. Tucson Herpetological Society v. Salazar, 566 F.3d 870, 873 (9th Cir. 2009) (quoting 58 Fed. Reg. 62,624, 62,625 (Nov. 29, 1993)).

23. Ibid., 879.

24. Ibid., 877.

25. Ibid., 883 (Noonan, J., dissenting).

26. See Joseph Y. Halpern, *Reasoning about Uncertainty* (2005).

27. See 5 U.S.C. §§ 556(d), 706(2)(E) (2012).

28. See Drew Fudenberg & Eric Maskin, "The Folk Theorem in Repeated Games with Discounting or with Incomplete Information," 54 *Econometrica* 533 (1986).

29. Tri-Valley CAREs v. U.S. Dep't of Energy, 671 F.3d 1113 (9th Cir. 2012).

30. Tri-Valley CAREs, 671 F.3d at 1119.

31. Martin L. Weitzman, "On Modeling and Interpreting the Economics of Catastrophic Climate Change," 91 *Rev. Ec. & Stat.* 1 (2009).

32. Gary Yohe & Richard S. J. Tol, "Precaution and a Dismal Theorem: Implications for Climate Policy and Climate Research" (Wesleyan University, Working Paper FNU-145, 2007).

33. Cass R. Sunstein, *Worst-Case Scenarios* (2007); Cass R. Sunstein, *Risk and Reason: Safety, Law, and the Environment* (2002).

34. Kenneth J. Arrow & Leonid Hurwicz, "An Optimality Criterion for Decision-Making under Ignorance," *in Uncertainty and Expectations in Economics: Essays in Honour of G. L. S. Shackle* (C. F. Carter & J. L. Ford eds., 1972).

35. Richard T. Woodward & Richard C. Bishop, "How to Decide When Experts Disagree: Uncertainty-Based Choice Rules in Environmental Policy," 73 *Land Ec.* 492 (1997).

36. David Kelsey & John Quiggin, "Theories of Choice under Ignorance and Uncertainty," 6 *J. Ec. Surveys* 133, 136–137 (1992).

37. See Council on Environmental Quality, Implementation of Procedural Provisions, 43 Fed. Reg. 55,978, 55,984 (Nov. 29, 1978).

38. See Carla Mattix & Kathleen Becker, "Scientific Uncertainty under the National Environmental Policy Act," 54 *Admin. L. Rev.* 1125 (2002).

39. Ibid., 1133.

40. 490 U.S. 332, 356 (1989).

41. Greater Yellowstone Coalition, Inc. v. Servheen, 665 F.3d 1015 (9th Cir. 2011).

42. Ibid., 1028 (quoting 72 Fed. Reg. 14,866, 14,929 (Mar. 29, 2007)).

43. Ibid., 1030 (citing *Tucson Herpetological Society*, 566 F.3d at 879).

44. 462 U.S. 87 (1983).

45. Ibid., 105.

46. See George J. Stigler, "The Economics of Information," 61 *J. Polit. Econ.* 213 (1961).

47. See Avinash K. Dixit & Robert S. Pyndyck, *Investment under Uncertainty* (1994).

48. See Elster, "Excessive Ambitions."

49. See Hans O. Melberg, "A Critical Discussion of Jon Elster's Arguments about Rational Choice, Infinite Regress and the Collection of Information" (unpublished thesis, 1999).

50. Sidney Winter, "Economic 'Natural Selection' and the Theory of the Firm," 4 *Yale Econ. Essays* 225 (1964).

51. See Cass R. Sunstein & Edna Ullmann-Margalit, "Second-Order Decisions," 110 *Ethics* 5 (1999).

52. Jonathan Baert Wiener, "Managing the Iatrogenic Risks of Risk Management," 9 *Risk: Health, Safety & Env't* 39 (1998).

53. Leif Johansen, *Lectures*, 144, quoted in Jon Elster, "Bad Timing," *in The Thief of Time* (Chrisoula Andreou & Mark D. White eds., 2010).

54. R. B. McKenzie, "On the Methodological Boundaries of Economic Analysis," 12 *J. Econ. Issues* 627 (1978).

55. *Greater Yellowstone Coalition*, 665 F.3d at 1028.

56. 241 F.3d 722 (9th Cir. 2001).

57. Ibid., 732.

58. See ibid., 732–733.

59. 5 U.S.C. § 706(2)(A) (2012).

60. Wendy E. Wagner, "The Science Charade in Toxic Risk Regulation," 95 *Colum. L. Rev.* 1613 (1995).

61. See Yehonatan Givati & Matthew C. Stephenson, "Judicial Deference to Inconsistent Agency Statutory Interpretations," 40 *J. Legal Stud.* 85 (2011).

62. See Massachusetts v. EPA, 549 U.S. 497 (2007).

63. See Tri-Valley CAREs v. U.S. Dep't of Energy, 671 F.3d 1113 (9th Cir. 2012); Jifry v. FAA, 370 F.3d 1174 (D.C. Cir. 2004).

64. See Tucson Herpetological Society v. Salazar, 566 F.3d 870 (9th Cir. 2009).

65. See Bus. Roundtable v. SEC, 647 F.3d 1144 (D.C. Cir. 2011).

66. David Stradling & Richard Stradling, "Perceptions of the Burning River: Deindustrialization and Cleveland's Cuyahoga River," 13 *Envt'l Hist.* 515 (2008).

CHAPTER 5   Thin Rationality Review

1. See, e.g., Judulang v. Holder, 132 S. Ct. 476 (2011) (declaring an immigration rule arbitrary and capricious).
2. See appendix infra.
3. 462 U.S. 87 (1983).
4. 566 U.S. 502 (2009).
5. 134 S. Ct. 1584 (2014).
6. 132 S. Ct. 476 (2011).
7. State Farm, 463 U.S. at 51.
8. 549 U.S. 497 (2007).
9. 554 U.S. 527 (2008).
10. Massachusetts v. EPA, 549 U.S. at 534.
11. For an overview of the law bearing on review of agency "inaction," see Cass R. Sunstein & Adrian Vermeule, "The Law of 'Not Now': When Agencies Defer Decisions," 103 *Geo. L.J.* 157 (2014). Very roughly speaking, the Court says that (1) agency non-enforcement decisions are presumptively unreviewable, Heckler v. Chaney, 470 U.S. 821 (1985); (2) agency refusals to engage in rulemaking are reviewable, although that review is "extremely limited" and "highly deferential," Massachusetts v. EPA, 549 U.S. at 527–528.
12. There is an exception to the presumption against nonreviewability of agency enforcement decisions, for cases in which the agency has entirely abdicated its enforcement responsibility. See Heckler v. Chaney, 470 U.S. at 833 n.4; Sunstein & Vermeule, "The Law of 'Not Now.' "
13. E.g., Judulang v. Holder, 132 S. Ct. 476 (2011) (holding that an agency's immigration decision rested on irrelevant factors and "turn[ed] deportation decisions into a 'sport of chance,' " ibid., 478 (quoting Di Pasquale v. Karnuth, 158 F.2d 878, 879 (2d Cir. 1947))).
14. Thomas J. Miles & Cass R. Sunstein, "The Real World of Arbitrariness Review," 75 *U. Chi. L. Rev.* 761, 765 (2008).
15. See Richard J. Pierce, Jr., "What Do the Studies of Judicial Review of Agency Actions Mean?," 63 *Admin. L. Rev.* 77, 84 (2011).
16. Miles & Sunstein, "The Real World of Arbitrariness Review," 766.
17. A total of 653 cases were reviewed, with 554 from the NLRB and the remainder from the EPA. See ibid., 774.
18. See ibid., 777.
19. See ibid., 779 (figure 1).
20. 647 F.3d 1144 (D.C. Cir. 2011).
21. Ibid., 1150 (internal quotation marks and citations omitted).
22. See, e.g., James D. Cox & Benjamin J. C. Baucom, "The Emperor Has No Clothes: Confronting the D.C. Circuit's Usurpation of Sec Rulemaking Authority," 90 *Tex. L. Rev.* 1811 (2012); Jill E. Fisch, "The Long Road Back: *Business Roundtable* and the Future of SEC Rulemaking," 36 *Seattle U. L. Rev.* 695 (2013); Grant M. Hayden & Matthew T. Bodie, "The Bizarre Law and Economics of *Business Roundtable v. SEC*," 38 *J. Corp. L.* 101, 102 (2012); Bruce Kraus & Connor Raso, "Rational Boundaries for SEC Cost-Benefit

Analysis," 30 *Yale J. Reg.* 289, 293 (2013); Cass R. Sunstein & Adrian Vermeule, "Libertarian Administrative Law," 82 *U. Chi. L. Rev.* 393, 437–448
(2015); John C. Coates IV, "Cost-Benefit Analysis of Financial Regulation:
Case Studies and Implications," 124 *Yale L.J.* 882, 917 (2015).

23. For discussion and references, see Sunstein & Vermeule, "Libertarian Ad-
    ministrative Law."
24. For the details, see ibid.
25. 435 U.S. 519 (1978).
26. 462 U.S. 87 (1983).
27. 135 S. Ct. 1199 (2015).
28. David Zaring, "Reasonable Agencies," 96 *Va. L. Rev.* 135 (2010).
29. See Stephen M. Johnson, "Ossification's Demise? An Empirical Analysis of
    EPA Rulemaking from 2001–2005," 38 *Envtl. L.* 767, 784 (2008).
30. Anne Joseph O'Connell, "Political Cycles of Rulemaking: An Empirical Por-
    trait of the Modern Administrative State," 94 *Va. L. Rev.* 889, 932 (2008).
31. Jason Webb Yackee & Susan Webb Yackee, "Administrative Procedures and
    Bureaucratic Performance: Is Federal Rule-Making 'Ossified'?," 20 *J. Pub.
    Admin. Res. & Theory* 261 (2009).
32. *State Farm*, 463 U.S. at 43.
33. Citizens to Preserve Overton Park, Inc. v. Volpe, 401 U.S. 402, 416 (1971).
34. *State Farm*, 463 U.S. at 51 ("Nor do we broadly require an agency to consider
    all policy alternatives in reaching decision. It is true that rulemaking cannot
    be found wanting simply because the agency failed to include every alterna-
    tive device and thought conceivable by the mind of man . . . regardless of how
    uncommon or unknown that alternative may have been. . . . But the airbag
    is more than a policy alternative to the passive restraint standard; it is a tech-
    nological alternative within the ambit of the existing standard.") (internal
    quote omitted).
35. See Pension Ben. Guar. Corp. v. LTV Corp., 496 U.S. 633, 646 (1990) ("If agency
    action may be disturbed whenever a reviewing court is able to point to
    an arguably relevant statutory policy that was not explicitly considered,
    then a very large number of agency decisions might be open to judicial
    invalidation.").
36. See *Pension Benefit*, 496 U.S. at 646–652.
37. See City of Arlington v. FCC, 133 S. Ct. 1863 (2013).
38. See Mobil Oil Exploration & Producing Southeast Inc. v. United Distrib. Cos.,
    498 U.S. 211, 230–231 (1991) ("An agency enjoys broad discretion in deter-
    mining how best to handle related, yet discrete, issues in terms of proce-
    dures and priorities. . . . [A]n agency need not solve every problem before it
    in the same proceeding. This applies even where the initial solution to one
    problem had adverse consequences for another area that the agency was ad-
    dressing.") (internal citations omitted).
39. See Moog Indus. v. FTC, 355 U.S. 411 (1958) (allowing the FTC to cull one
    firm from the herd); ibid., 413 ("[W]hether all firms in the industry should be
    dealt with in a single proceeding or should receive individualized treatment
    are questions that call for discretionary determination by the administra-
    tive agency.").

40. See Thomas W. Merrill & Kristin E. Hickman, "*Chevron*'s Domain," 89 *Geo. L.J.* 833 (2001); Cass R. Sunstein, "*Chevron* Step Zero," 92 *Va. L. Rev.* 187 (2006).

41. FDA v. Brown & Williamson and King v. Burwell both say that *Chevron* deference does not apply to questions of great "economic and political significance." See King v. Burwell, 135 S. Ct. 2480, 2488–2489 (2015); FDA v. Brown & Williamson Tobacco Corp., 529 U.S. 120, 159–160 (2000).

42. See generally Cass R. Sunstein, *Risk and Reason* 6, 99–132; Cass R. Sunstein, "Cognition and Cost-Benefit Analysis," 29 *J. Legal Stud.* 1059 (2000) (advocating cost-benefit analysis as a corrective to cognitive problems and judgment errors). Compare Richard A. Posner, *Catastrophe: Risk and Response* 139 (2005); Sidney A. Shapiro & Christopher H. Schroeder, "Beyond Cost-Benefit Analysis: A Pragmatic Reorientation," 32 *Harv. Envt'l L. Rev.* 441, 446–450 (2008) (describing adoption of CBA as part of a "'comprehensive rationality' that rational choice theorists consider essential to rational decisionmaking"); Amartya Sen, "The Discipline of Cost-Benefit Analysis," 29 *J. Legal Stud.* 931, 935 (2000) ("At the risk of oversimplification, explicit valuation is a part of the insistence on a rationalist approach, which demands full explication of the reasons for taking a decision, rather than relying on an unreasoned conviction or on an implicitly derived conclusion.").

43. Cass R. Sunstein, "Cost-Benefit Default Principles," 99 *Mich. L. Rev.* 1561 (2001); Cass R. Sunstein, *The Cost-Benefit State* 59–60 (2002).

44. See Sunstein's separate section in "Libertarian Administrative Law," 441 (with which Vermeule emphatically disagrees, see ibid., 443–446), in which Sunstein seemingly endorses the following propositions: "To the extent that available evidence permits quantification, it would be arbitrary not to quantify. . . . To the extent that Business Roundtable stands for this general principle, it is on firm ground. . . . Indeed, it would generally seem arbitrary for an agency to issue a rule that has net costs (or no net benefits), at least unless a statute requires it to do so."

    See also Justice Scalia's statement at oral argument in Michigan v. EPA: "I'm not even sure I agree with the premise that when—Congress says nothing about cost, the agency is entitled to disregard cost. I would think it's classic arbitrary and capricious agency action for an agency to command something that is outrageously expensive and in which the expense vastly exceeds whatever public benefit can be achieved. I would think that's—that's a violation of the Administrative Procedure Act." Transcript of Oral Argument at 14, Michigan v. EPA, 135 S. Ct. 2699 (2015) (No. 14–46). The actual decision in Michigan v. EPA did not go nearly that far, however, as discussed later.

45. Sen, "The Discipline of Cost-Benefit Analysis," 934.

46. Ibid. (describing a "general social choice" approach to cost-benefit analysis). For a clear-minded treatment of the distinctions among intuitive judgment, unquantified CBA, and quantified CBA, see John C. Coates IV, "Cost-Benefit Analysis of Financial Regulations: Case Studies and Implications," 124 *Yale L.J.* 882, 892–893 (2015).

47. 2 *The Correspondence of Charles Darwin 1837–1843* 444 (Frederick Burkhardt & Sydney Smith eds., 1986). Cases like Darwin's list actually suggest that some decisions ought not to be made even on the basis of *informal* cost-benefit analysis, although we need not establish that proposition here.

48. See Facilitating Shareholder Director Nominations, 75 Fed. Reg. 56,668, 56,753–71 (Sept. 16, 2010).

49. See Bus. Roundtable v. SEC, 647 F.3d 1144, 1149–1151 (D.C. Cir. 2011).

50. See, e.g., Matthew D. Adler & Eric A. Posner, *New Foundations of Cost-Benefit Analysis* 100 (2006); Richard L. Revesz & Michael A. Livermore, *Retaking Rationality: How Cost-Benefit Analysis Can Better Protect the Environment and Our Health* 12–13 (2008); Cass R. Sunstein, *The Cost-Benefit State* 6–10 (2002).

51. See, e.g., Coates, "Cost-Benefit Analysis of Financial Regulations: Case Studies and Implications"; Frank Ackerman & Lisa Heinzerling, *Priceless* 7–12 (2004); Thomas O. McGarity, *Reinventing Rationality* 142–159 (1991); David M. Driesen, Douglas A. Kysar, & Amy Sinden, "Cost-Benefit Analysis: New Foundations on Shifting Sand," 3 *Reg. & Governance* 48, 55–56 (2009).

52. See Adler & Posner, "Rethinking Cost-Benefit Analysis," 172 (discussing objections).

53. 435 U.S. 519 (1978).

54. 135 S. Ct. 1199 (2015).

55. See Michigan v. EPA, 135 S. Ct. 2699 (2015).

56. *Perez*, 135 S. Ct. at 1207 (2015). Michigan v. EPA clearly declined to impose any such requirement. See infra notes 92–95 and accompanying text.

57. See Jonathan S. Masur & Eric A. Posner, "Against Feasibility Analysis," 77 *U. Chi. L. Rev.* 657, 658 (2010) (collecting examples). Masur and Posner criticize feasibility but do not claim that Congress should be taken to intend to require that agencies perform quantified CBA whenever statutes are silent or ambiguous.

58. Wong Yang Sung v. McGrath, 339 U.S. 33, 40 (1950).

59. Compare Cass R. Sunstein, "Is OSHA Unconstitutional?," 94 *Va. L. Rev.* 1407 (2008). Sunstein criticizes OSHA on nondelegation grounds but is also sharply critical of feasibility analysis. The logic of his view is that the Act is patently irrational and therefore vulnerable to a Due Process challenge.

60. See *State Farm*, 463 U.S. at 43 n.9 (1983) ("We do not view as equivalent the presumption of constitutionality afforded legislation drafted by Congress and the presumption of regularity afforded an agency in fulfilling its statutory mandate.").

61. See Amy Sinden, "Cass Sunstein's Cost-Benefit Lite: Economics for Liberals," 29 *Colum. J. Envt'l L.* 191, 240 (2004); Thomas O. McGarity, "Professor Sunstein's Fuzzy Math," 90 *Geo. L.J.* 2341, 2343 (2002).

62. 129 S. Ct. 1498 (2009).

63. 33 U.S.C. § 1326(b) (2012) (emphasis added).

64. 556 U.S. 208, 215–216 (2009); National Pollutant Discharge Elimination System—Final Regulations to Establish Requirements for Cooling Water Intake Structures at Phase II Existing Facilities, 69 Fed.Reg. 41,576 (July 9, 2004) (codified at 40 C.F.R. pts. 9, 122–125).

65. *Entergy,* 556 U.S. at 218.
66. Ibid.
67. Ibid., 223 (discussing Whitman v. American Trucking Assns., Inc., 531 U.S. 457 (2001)).
68. Ibid. (discussing American Textile Mfrs. Institute, Inc. v. Donovan, 452 U.S. 490 (1981)).
69. Ibid. (emphasis in original).
70. 134 S. Ct. 1584 (2014).
71. 42 U.S.C. § 7410(a)(2)(D)(i) (2012).
72. EME Homer City Generation, L.P. v. EPA, 696 F.3d 7, 21 (D.C. Cir. 2012).
73. See Federal Implementation Plans: Interstate Transport of Fine Particulate Matter and Ozone and Correction of SIP Approvals, 76 Fed. Reg. 48,208, 48,254 (Aug. 8, 2011); see also *EME Homer,* 134 S. Ct. at 1597.
74. *EME Homer,* 134 S. Ct. at 1607.
75. 134 S. Ct. 2427 (2014).
76. 549 U.S. 497 (2007).
77. See UARG, 134 S. Ct. at 2436–2437.
78. 42 U.S.C. § 7470 *et seq.* (2012).
79. 42 U.S.C. § 7661 (2012).
80. See 42 U.S.C. §§ 7479(1), 7661(2)(B), 7602(j) (2012).
81. See Regulating Greenhouse Gas Emissions under the Clean Air Act, 73 Fed. Reg. 44,420, 44,498–44,999 (proposed July 30, 2008); *UARG,* 134 S. Ct. at 2436.
82. See Prevention of Significant Deterioration and Title V Greenhouse Gas Tailoring Rule, 75 Fed. Reg. 31,514, 31,523–524 (June 3, 2010).
83. See *UARG,* 134 S. Ct. at 2443–2446.
84. See ibid., 2448–2449.
85. Ibid., 2448.
86. Ibid., 2441 (quoting Envtl. Defense v. Duke Energy Corp., 549 U.S. 561, 574 (2007)) (internal quotation marks omitted).
87. Ibid., 2448.
88. 135 S. Ct. 2699.
89. 42 U.S.C. § 7412 (2012).
90. Michigan v. EPA, 135 S. Ct. at 2711–2712.
91. Cass R. Sunstein, "Thanks, Justice Scalia, for the Cost-Benefit State," *Bloomberg View* (July 7, 2015), http://www.bloombergview.com/articles/2015-07-07/thanks-justice-scalia-for-the-cost-benefit-state (calling the opinion in Michigan v. EPA a "ringing endorsement of cost-benefit analysis by government agencies").
92. Michigan v. EPA, 135 S. Ct. at 2707.
93. Ibid. (emphasis removed).
94. Ibid., 2711; accord ibid., 2717 (Kagan, J., dissenting) ("As the Court notes, [accounting for costs] does not require an agency to conduct a formal cost-benefit analysis of every administrative action.").
95. Ibid., 2707 (emphasis in original).
96. See Mobil Oil Expl. & Producing Se., Inc. v. United Distrib. Cos., 498 U.S. 211, 230–231 (1991) ("An agency enjoys broad discretion in determining how

best to handle related, yet discrete, issues in terms of procedures and priorities. . . . [A]n agency need not solve every problem before it in the same proceeding.").

97. *State Farm*, 463 U.S. at 43 (quoting Burlington Truck Lines v. United States, 371 U.S. 156, 168 (1962)).

98. See Michael Slote, *Beyond Optimizing* (1989).

99. See Herbert A. Simon, *Reason In Human Affairs* 85 (1983); Michael Byron, "Satisficing and Optimality," 109 *Ethics* 67 (1998); Herbert A. Simon, "A Behavioral Model of Rational Choice," 69 *Q.J. Econ.* 99 (1955).

100. Compare David Schmidtz, *Rational Choice and Moral Agency* 28–40 (1995); David Schmidtz, "Satisficing as a Humanly Rational Strategy," *in Satisficing and Maximizing: Moral Theorists on Practical Reason* 31 (Michael Byron ed., 2004).

101. See George J. Stigler, "The Economics of Information," 69 *J. Pol. Econ.* 213 (1961).

102. Schmidtz, *Rational Choice and Moral Agency* 34–35; see also Jonathan Brodie Bendor, Sunil Kumar, & David A. Siegel, "Satisficing: A 'Pretty Good' Heuristic," 9 *B.E. J. Theoretical Econ.* (2009).

103. *State Farm*, 463 U.S. at 51.

104. Stephen Breyer et al., Administrative Law & Regulatory Policy (7th ed., 2014) 393.

105. 556 U.S. 502 (2009).

106. Ibid., 515.

107. See Breyer et al., Administrative Law & Regulatory Policy, at 393.

108. *Fox*, 556 U.S. at 519.

109. Ibid., 515.

110. Ron Levin summarizes *Fox* as follows: "The Court's position on the issue comes down to this: Unless reliance interests or inconsistent readings of a factual record are involved, open acknowledgment of the change and a defense of the new policy on its own terms should ordinarily suffice." Ronald M. Levin, "Hard Look Review, Policy Change, and *Fox Television*," 65 *Miami U. L. Rev.* 555, 573 (2011). The latter clause is what the *Fox* majority and the dissent disagreed about.

111. Mobil Oil Exploration & Producing Southeast Inc. v. United Distrib. Cos., 498 U.S. 211, 230 (1991).

112. We use the plus or minus nomenclature only for expositional purposes. The agency is summarizing a probability distribution and we could explain with the mean-variance problem with greater formality. The point here is a simple one, however.

113. See Jacob E. Gersen, "Administrative Law Goes to Wall Street: The New Administrative Process," 65 *Admin. L. Rev.* 689, 692, 724–725 (2013).

114. Ctr. for Food Safety v. Hamburg, 954 F. Supp. 2d 965 (N.D. Cal. Apr. 22, 2013).

115. See, e.g., Stephen Breyer, *Breaking the Vicious Circle* 57–59 (1993); Thomas O. McGarity, "Some Thoughts on 'Deossifying' the Rulemaking Process," 41 *Duke L.J.* 1385; Richard J. Pierce, Jr., "Seven Ways to Deossify Agency Rulemaking," 47 *Admin. L. Rev.* 59 (1995); Paul R. Verkuil, "Com-

ment: Rulemaking Ossification—A Modest Proposal," 47 *Admin. L. Rev.* 453 (1995).

116. See Jifry v. FAA, 370 F.3d 1174 (D.C. Cir. 2004) (upholding, against arbitrariness challenge, an FAA regulation promulgated without notice and comment under the "good cause" exception); Adrian Vermeule, "Our Schmittian Administrative Law," 122 *Harv. L. Rev.* 1095, 1122–1125 (2009) (examining the "good cause" exception).

117. See Daniel Epps, "The Consequences of Error in Criminal Justice," 128 *Harv. L. Rev.* 1065 (2015) (describing and challenging the Blackstone principle).

118. See ibid., 1094–1124 (offering a "dynamic" critique of the Blackstone principle based on its systemic consequences for the criminal justice system).

119. Baltimore Gas & Elec. Co. v. Natural Res. Def. Council, Inc., 462 U.S. 87, 97 (1983) (internal quotation marks omitted).

120. Ibid., 103.

121. 467 U.S. 837 (1984).

122. See, e.g., Judulang v. Holder, 132 S. Ct. 476, 483 n.7 (2011) (stating that *Chevron* Step Two examines whether the agency interpretation is "arbitrary and capricious in substance") (internal quotation omitted).

CHAPTER 6   How Law Empowers Nonlawyers

1. 318 U.S. 80 (1943).

2. Kevin M. Stack, "The Constitutional Foundations of *Chenery*," 116 *Yale L .J.* 952 (2007).

3. Chevron USA Inc. v. Natural Resources Defense Council, 467 U.S. 837 (1984).

4. 533 U.S. 218 (2001).

5. 323 U.S. 134 (1944).

6. Ibid., 140.

7. E. Donald Elliott, "*Chevron* Matters: How the *Chevron* Doctrine Redefined the Roles of Congress, Courts, and Agencies in Environmental Law," 16 *Vill. J. Evtl. L.* 1, 11–12 (2005).

8. City of Arlington v. FCC, 133 S. Ct. 1863 (2013).

9. Cass R. Sunstein, "*Chevron* Step Zero," 92 *Va. L. Rev.* 187 (2006).

10. For examples, see Jonathan S. Masur & Eric A. Posner, "Against Feasibility Analysis," 77 *U. Chi. L. Rev.* 657 (2010).

11. Thomas O. McGarity, "The Internal Structure of EPA Rulemaking," *Law & Contemp. Probs.* 57, 67 (Autumn 1991).

12. 370 F.3d 1174 (D.C. Cir. 2004).

13. *Jifry,* 370 F.3d at 1179.

14. Citizens to Preserve Overton Park v. Volpe, 401 U.S. 402 (1971).

15. David Dyzenhaus, *The Constitution of Law: Legality in a Time of Emergency* 3 (2006).

16. 470 U.S. 821 (1985).

17. 285 U.S. 22 (1932).

Conclusion

1. Contra Richard A. Posner, *Overcoming Law* (1995).
2. See Adrian Vermeule, "Second Opinions and Institutional Design," 97 *Va. L. Rev.* 1347 (2011).
3. Sir Edward Coke, House of Commons (July 6, 1628). Adam Tomkins, *Our Republican Constitution* 70–71, 74 (2005). For a more recent version of the point, see David Zaring, "Reasonable Agencies," 96 *Va. L. Rev.* 135 (2010). It is irrelevant that the original context of Coke's point was his attempt to constrain the monarch by the Petition of Right. The aphorism may still illuminate our very different circumstances today; his formulation has transcended its time. Compare Hamburger, "Vermeule Unbound," supra note chap. 1, n.51.
4. Adrian Vermeule, *Mechanisms of Democracy* (2007); Eric A. Posner & Adrian Vermeule, *The Executive Unbound* (2010); Adrian Vermeule, "Optimal Abuse of Power," 109 *Nw. U. L. Rev.* 673 (2015).
5. 385 U.S. 22 (1932).
6. See NLRB v. Hearst Publications, 322 U.S. 111 (1944).
7. 115 N.Y. 506 (1889).
8. Church of the Holy Trinity v. United States, 143 U.S. 457 (1892).
9. 462 U.S. 87 (1983).
10. 490 U.S. 332 (1989).
11. 556 U.S. 502 (2009).
12. Utility Air Regulatory Group v. EPA, 134 S. Ct. 2427 (2014).
13. See Daniel Kahneman & Amos Tversky, "Evidential Impact of Base Rates," in *Judgment Under Uncertainty: Heuristics and Biases* (Daniel Kahneman, Paul Slovic, & Amos Tversky eds., 1982).
14. See Jerry L. Mashaw, *Creating the Administrative Constitution* (2012).
15. See Paul Craig, supra note chap. 1, n.38; Adam Tomkins, *Our Republican Constitution* (2005).
16. Jon Elster, *Sour Grapes: Studies in the Subversion of Rationality* 87 n.5 (1983).

Acknowledgments

My family, Yun Soo, Emily, Spencer, Auntie, and O-ma, supported the project at every stage, even though the kids believe that "administrative law" isn't a real thing. Evelyn Blacklock, Harvard Law Class of 2016, provided outstanding and untiring research assistance and incisive comments. Ellen Keng kept the ship on course, with a firm hand at the tiller. If it weren't for her, nothing would get done. Thomas Embree LeBien at Harvard University Press and Debbie Masi provided invaluable suggestions and editing.

The book evolved over the course of several years, through workshops and conversations with many friends and colleagues. Particular thanks for comments at workshops are owed to Amy Coney Barrett, Anthony Bellia, Patricia Bellia, Rev. William Dailey, CSC, Richard Fallon, Nicole Stelle Garnett, Rick Garnett, Jacob Gersen, Jack Goldsmith, Randy Kozel, Ron Levin, Elizabeth Magill, John Manning, Martha Minow, Michael Moreland, John Nagle, Jeff Pojanowski, Cass Sunstein, and Mark Tushnet. Manning and Tushnet each read and commented on the whole manuscript within the space of an Acela trip—above and beyond the call of duty. The Notre Dame public law faculty held a roundtable on the manuscript, which helped sharpen the critical arguments. I am deeply grateful for all this assistance.

Some of these same friends and colleagues, and others as well, commented on a number of the papers that became stepping-stones for the book. The original papers are noted below. Particular thanks are due to several coauthors, Jake Gersen, Liz Magill, and Cass Sunstein, who graciously encouraged me to further explore themes discussed in our joint work. Any errors I have introduced are my own, but whatever is good, true, and honorable is very much a fruit of our collaboration.

"The Unbearable Rightness of *Auer*," forthcoming *University of Chicago Law Review*, http://papers.ssrn.com/sol3/papers.cfm?abstract_id=2716737

"The New Coke: On the Plural Aims of Administrative Law," *Supreme Court Review* 1 (2015) (with Cass R. Sunstein)

"Deference and Due Process," 129 *Harvard Law Review* 1890 (2016)

"What Legitimacy Crisis?" *Cato Unbound* (May 9, 2016), http://www.cato-unbound.org/2016/05/09/adrian-vermeule/what-legitimacy-crisis

"Thin Rationality Review," 114 *Michigan Law Review* 1355 (2016) (with Jacob Gersen)

"Rationally Arbitrary Decisions," *Journal of Legal Studies* (2015) 44:S2, S475-S507

"The Administrative State: Law, Democracy and Knowledge" in *The Oxford Handbook of the U.S. Constitution* (Mark Graber, Sandy Levinson, and Mark Tushnet eds., 2015)

"Optimal Abuse of Power," 109 *Northwestern University Law Review* 673 (2015)

"No," 93 *Texas Law Review* 1547 (Review of Philip Hamburger, *Is Administrative Law Unlawful?*) (2015)

"Allocating Power within Agencies," 120 *Yale Law Journal* 1032 (2011) (with Elizabeth Magill)

Index of Cases

General Index

Abdication, 17, 27, 30, 43–47
Abuse of power, 57–59, 121; optimal, 59–60; prevention, 61; unavoidable by-product, 68
Abuse of power, private, 57–58, 62–65, 122; corporate power, 62, 64
Administrative agencies: "intelligent realism," 62; motivations of, 116–120, 234n110; power to set prices, 27; reasonable or rational action, 188; separation of functions, 72–74, 77; statutory authority, 26, 43, 80, 202. *See also* Combination of powers
Administrative constitutionalism, 88, 124
Administrative law: allocation of power, 197; evidentiary hearings, 92–94, 98; interdependence of substance and procedure, 107–110, 113, 234n99; jurisdiction, statutory limits of, 111; jurisdictional interpretations, 35, 36, 80, 112; lawful or unlawful, 16, 47–50; "political question doctrine," 95; procedural due process in, 90–102, 106, 109, 120, 123; resource allocation, 108, 114, 233n82; retroactivity, 72, 82, 85. See also *Mathews* test
Administrative law judge (ALJ), 65
Administrative Procedure Act of 1946 (APA), 24, 125; "administrative law judge," 65; arbitrary decisions under, 137, 172, 190; comparative policy

evaluation, 183–184, 243n110; constitutional requirements, 92, 107, 202; "good cause" exception, 185; internal understanding, 8; judicial review provisions, 26–27, 39, 112; notice-and-comment process, 39, 40, 74–75; section 553, 33, 74–75; section 555, 117–118; section 706, 19–20, 39–40, 96, 150, 155, 157–158; section 706 action based on reason, 187–188; section 706 and cost-benefit analysis, 173, 241n59; section 706 and rationality standard, 130–131; section 706 and unreasoned action, 188
Affordable Care Act, 31
Alito, Samuel, 31, 44, 76, 162
Allars, Margaret, 5–6
Anglo-American legal culture, 49–50
Arbitrary and capricious, 96–97, 101, 190–191, 228n62, 230n38; agencies favored, 160–161; agency ossification, 40, 165–166, 206; appeals court review, 160–163; asymmetric error costs, 186; cost-benefit analysis, 170–178; minimum rationality standard, 131; second-order reasons for, 19–21, 22, 135–137, 150–151, 157, 215; selection effects, 164–166. *See also* Administrative Procedure Act of 1946 (APA), section 706
Arrow-Hurwicz framework, 142, 145